Criminal Injustice

D1561093

Criminal Injustice

*How Politics and Ideology
Distort American Ideals*

Matthew B. Robinson

CAROLINA ACADEMIC PRESS

Durham, North Carolina

Library of Congress Cataloging-in-Publication Data

Robinson, Matthew B.
  Criminal injustice : how politics and ideology distort American ideals / Matthew B. Robinson.
      pages cm
  Includes bibliographical references and index.
  ISBN 978-1-61163-635-2 (alk. paper)
  1. Criminal justice, Administration of--Political aspects--United States. 2. Criminal justice, Administration of--United States. 3. Crime--Political aspects--United States. I. Title.

  HV9950.R6347 2015
  364.973--dc23

                          2014042070

Carolina Academic Press
700 Kent Street
Durham, North Carolina 27701
Telephone (919) 489-7486
Fax (919) 493-5668
www.cap-press.com

Contents

Preface

"The discrepancy between American ideals and American practice creates a dry rot which eats away at the foundations of our democratic faith."
— Helen Gahagan Douglas

The "criminal justice system" is the term used to describe the inter-connected agencies of the police, courts, and corrections. Its assumed goals are to reduce crime in society while simultaneously protecting the rights of those being processed through the system. We call these goals *crime control* and *due process*, respectively—both ideals held deeply by American citizens. Unfortunately, the criminal justice system sometimes fails to meet these ideals in the real world.

Americans expect to live safely (crime control) as well as to be treated fairly by our government (due process). In fact, a quick examination of the two documents most famously cited as examples of American ideals—the US Declaration of Independence and the US Constitution—shows this to be the case.

This is from the US Declaration of Independence:

> We hold these truths to be self-evident, that all men are created equal, that they are endowed by their Creator with certain unalienable Rights, that among these are Life, Liberty and the pursuit of Happiness.[1]

Some of the key words from this document—which we used to declare our independence from Great Britain—include equal, Rights, Life, Liberty, and the pursuit of Happiness. Each of these terms relates directly to public safety or crime control (such as Life and the pursuit of Happiness, both of which are threatened by crime) and equality or due process (such as Rights and Liberty, which must be protected as a person is processed through the criminal justice system).

And this is from the US Constitution:

> We the People of the United States, in Order to form a more perfect Union, establish Justice, insure domestic Tranquility, provide for the common defence, promote the general Welfare, and secure the Blessings of Liberty to ourselves and our Posterity, do ordain and establish this Constitution for the United States of America.[2]

---

1. National Archives (2012). The charters of freedom. Declaration of Independence. Retrieved December 1, 2012 from: http://www.archives.gov/exhibits/charters/declaration_transcript.html.
2. National Archives (2012). The charters of freedom. US Constitution. Retrieved December 1, 2012 from: http://www.archives.gov/exhibits/charters/constitution_transcript.html.

Some of the key words from this document—which represents the foundation of our government—include Justice, domestic Tranquility, common defence, general Welfare, and Liberty. Each of these terms also relates directly to public safety or crime control (such as domestic Tranquility, common defence, and general Welfare), and equality or due process (such as Justice and Liberty). Tranquility (which means peace) and Welfare (which refers to "being well") are obviously threatened by crime, and crime fighting ideally helps provide for our common defence. Yet, the war on crime must also respect Justice by protecting our Liberty because Americans also value their freedom from unwarranted government interference in their lives. In fact, a review of the Bill of Rights, shown in Table A, illustrates that half of them deal with how government is to deal with people accused of crimes!

Table A. Bill of Rights

Amendment I

Congress shall make no law respecting an establishment of religion, or prohibiting the free exercise thereof; or abridging the freedom of speech, or of the press; or the right of the people peaceably to assemble, and to petition the Government for a redress of grievances.

Amendment II

A well regulated Militia, being necessary to the security of a free State, the right of the people to keep and bear Arms, shall not be infringed.

Amendment III

No Soldier shall, in time of peace be quartered in any house, without the consent of the Owner, nor in time of war, but in a manner to be prescribed by law.

Amendment IV

The right of the people to be secure in their persons, houses, papers, and effects, against unreasonable searches and seizures, shall not be violated, and no Warrants shall issue, but upon probable cause, supported by Oath or affirmation, and particularly describing the place to be searched, and the persons or things to be seized.

Amendment V

No person shall be held to answer for a capital, or otherwise infamous crime, unless on a presentment or indictment of a Grand Jury, except in cases arising in the land or naval forces, or in the Militia, when in actual service in time of War or public danger; nor shall any person be subject for the same offence to be twice put in jeopardy of life or limb; nor shall be compelled in any criminal case to be a witness against himself, nor be deprived of life, liberty, or property, without due process of law; nor shall private property be taken for public use, without just compensation.

Amendment VI

In all criminal prosecutions, the accused shall enjoy the right to a speedy and public trial, by an impartial jury of the State and district wherein the crime shall have been committed, which district shall have been previously ascertained by law, and to be informed of the nature and cause of the accusation; to be confronted with the witnesses against him; to have compulsory process for obtaining witnesses in his favor, and to have the Assistance of Counsel for his defence.

Amendment VII

In Suits at common law, where the value in controversy shall exceed twenty dollars, the right of trial by jury shall be preserved, and no fact tried by a jury, shall be otherwise re-examined in any Court of the United States, than according to the rules of the common law.

Amendment VIII

Excessive bail shall not be required, nor excessive fines imposed, nor cruel and unusual punishments inflicted.

Amendment IX

The enumeration in the Constitution, of certain rights, shall not be construed to deny or disparage others retained by the people.

Amendment X

The powers not delegated to the United States by the Constitution, nor prohibited by it to the States, are reserved to the States respectively, or to the people.

Americans clearly value public safety and justice for these values have been enshrined in our nation's founding documents. To achieve these goals, we created a criminal justice system, a network of agencies that, unfortunately, sometimes falls short of these ideals when it comes to actual practice.

Why does this happen? In this book it is suggested it is because of the influence of politics and ideology on criminal justice practice. *Politics* refers to governing decisions about how to deal with social problems and distribute resources in society, and *ideology* means the beliefs and values that guide political decisions and underlie our societal institutions. Law-making is obviously impacted by politics because lawmaking is a political process (we even call the people who make the law politicians!). And laws largely determine whose ideology becomes the dominant one in society.

Here are some examples. Should we outlaw and prevent gay marriage or tolerate, condone, and even celebrate it? Should we continue with our prohibitive approach towards drugs such as marijuana by arresting, convicting, and punishing people who possess the drug or should we legalize drugs and regulate them for safety? Should women be able to control their own reproductive cycles including aborting fetuses or should abortion be illegal? Should we sentence murderers to death and execute them or is there a better alternative? Should we criminalize killings by corporations (e.g., deaths by defective products) or should we ignore them? Answers to such questions determine whose beliefs and values (i.e., whose ideology) dominate in America. It is politicians who make these determinations for us, and they do this by creating criminal laws at the state and federal level of government.

Because all criminal justice activity stems from the criminal law, it is a fact that criminal justice practice is also impacted by politics and ideology. As will be shown in this book, politics and ideology often distort America's ideal goals of crime control and due process, oftentimes resulting in ineffective and unfair criminal justice policies. That is, politics and ideology distort the ideals of Americans found in the Declaration of Independence and the US Constitution.

This book will demonstrate how this is true and argues that the main problem with criminal justice practice is that it does not target the most harmful acts in America; instead it focuses heavily only on a handful of harmful acts committed by certain groups of people under certain circumstances. This occurs because of who makes the law and who pays for it; these people create laws and policies that benefit them and their financial backers rather than "the people" more generally. Further, media coverage of crime and criminal justice reinforces myths of crime (including who is dangerous and who is not) which helps maintain the focus of criminal justice agencies on street crime rather than on other forms of harmful behavior that actually cause far more damage to society.

Innocent Bias

The most important concept in this book is the term *innocent bias*. Innocent bias is unfairness in criminal justice that exists because of unfair criminal laws. It is called "innocent" because it does not emerge from intentional discrimination on the part of individual police officers, prosecutors, or other agents of criminal justice. Instead, innocent bias occurs when criminal justice agents innocently enforce biased criminal laws.

The main bias of the criminal law is this: Only some harmful or dangerous acts are defined as *crimes*—behaviors that violate the criminal law. An even smaller number are legislated as *serious crimes*—supposedly the most harmful and common of these crimes (e.g., murder). A much larger number of harmful or dangerous acts are perfectly legal, and still others are illegal but not vigorously pursued by criminal justice agencies. This is unfair or biased because it means that only some criminals are held accountable for the harms they inflict on other people.

It also turns out that those people we hold accountable for their harmful behaviors are very different than the ones we do not hold accountable for the harmful behaviors they commit. Specifically, the people we arrest, prosecute, convict, and punish for crimes and serious crimes tend to be young, poor, minority males, while the people that are rarely processed through the criminal justice system are older, wealthier, white males (the very same people who create the law and own the mainstream media).

This does not occur because individual police officers, prosecutors, and other criminal justice officials are biased against people based on their race, ethnicity, social class, age, or sex; instead it occurs because in the United States, we define harmful acts of some groups as crimes more than others—these are the acts focused on by the criminal justice system.

Further, some forms of harmful behavior are featured in the mainstream media while others are generally ignored, which keeps out attention focused squarely on only certain kinds of harms. If you think of the criminal law and media coverage of crime as spotlights—beams of light that direct our attention to some harmful behaviors—both are shining directly on only a small fraction of harmful behaviors; the rest continue in the darkness. One goal of this book is to bring light onto these behaviors so that those people who commit them will be held accountable for them, in the interests of justice and fairness.

Chapter by Chapter

The book offers six chapters. In Chapter 1, the main argument of the book is introduced and summarized. The *criminal justice system* is defined and its ideal goals of reducing crime and doing justice are discussed. Then, the arguments of scholars who are more critical of criminal justice and believe it is designed to do very different things are examined; these scholars assert that the criminal justice system is aimed at oppressing people of color, poor people, and/or women. The argument of this book is that oppression based on class, race, and gender can occur without being intended just because of the political and ideology nature of the criminal law and criminal justice policy.

In Chapter 2, the terms politics and ideology are defined and two conflicting political ideologies in the United States—conservatism and liberalism—are examined. This chapter shows that the conservative ideology has had the most impact on thinking about crime and especially the criminal law and criminal justice policy since the 1980s; for this reason, we've strayed from the ideals of the Declaration of Independence and the US Constitution. Specifically, it is conservatives who have created laws and criminal justice policies that do not provide for public safety or crime reduction while simultaneously eroding liberty and resulting in unequal criminal justice outcomes for poor people and people of color. Since this conservative ideology is embraced today by both Republicans and Democrats, it is not the fault of one political party or another.

Chapter 3 focuses on the two institutions that are most responsible for creating actual policy as well as shaping public opinion about crime and criminal justice—the law and the media. You'll see that lawmakers are not representative of the US population; most people do not vote and those that do are not representative of the US population; and money plays a huge role in determining who runs for, wins, and maintains office. This raises the possibility that the law does not serve the interests of the people. Further, the people who own the media are also not representative of the US population and the mainstream media are owned and operated by corporations whose main interest is generating profit. This means it is possible that our conceptions of crime created in the law and reinforced in the media are not accurate, since the law only defines some harmful acts as crimes and because media coverage of crime tends to focus on violent street crimes committed by certain people under certain circumstances while ignoring white-collar and corporate crimes.

In Chapters 4 and 5, the criminal law is examined in detail, and street crime is compared and contrasted with white-collar and corporate crime. The data in these chapters clearly show that acts of elite deviance (e.g., white-collar and corporate crime) cause far more property loss as well as death and destruction than all street crimes combined, even those identified in the criminal law as the most serious. Specifically, acts such as fraud and false advertising cause more property loss than crimes such as theft, burglary, and robbery, yet we focus on the latter while generally ignoring the former. Also, I illustrate that defective products and hazardous working conditions kill and injure more people every year than murder and assault, yet we arrest, convict, and punish people for the latter while people who commit the former are rarely held accountable for their actions. This amounts to a serious bias implicit in criminal justice—innocent bias—one that will be found as one moves through the entire criminal justice system.

Finally, in Chapter 6, the process of innocent bias in criminal justice is examined. Each branch of criminal justice is examined, from police, to courts, to corrections, to demonstrate serious disparities in arrests, convictions, and being subjected to serious punishments. An explanation for why poor people and people of color—and especially young, poor men of color—are so disproportionately subjected to the most severe criminal punishments in America.

To the Reader

Most introductory criminal justice texts start with the perspective that the American criminal justice meets its ideal goals. They introduce and discuss main concepts and terms without offering critical assessments. I want you, the reader, to learn not only about the ideals of criminal justice in America, but also about the realities. Whereas other texts emphasize the way things are supposed to operate, *Criminal Injustice* places greater emphasis on the way agencies of American criminal justice system really operate.

This book focuses on injustice in criminal justice, an important topic for students and citizens alike to understand. Of course, people who study criminal justice and who work within agencies of American criminal justice need to gain an understanding of basic, introductory-level concepts and issues in order to become more knowledgeable and to become better employees. Many fine texts are on the market to meet this need. But this book takes a different approach: it begins with injustice as a problem.

As you read this book, I challenge you to keep an open mind. Do not allow your deeply entrenched beliefs about crime, criminal justice, or politics to interfere with your understanding of the main argument of the book. If this reading has been assigned to you, remember that you do not have to agree with the argument I put forth in this book, but you do need to understand it. In fact, I challenge you to read the book from a critical perspective, not automatically believing everything you read. Read the book from a perspective that will allow you to discover your own truth. Your own truth, after all, is the only truth that will matter to you. We live in an era where fact-checking is pretty easy to do. So, if something in the books sounds unbelievable, fact-check it and see what you learn.

Major Features

To make the book more useful for readers, several features are included. First, key terms are identified in bold at the end of each chapter. Second, discussion questions are included that can be used by instructors using the book in college classrooms to generate discussion on the most important topics discussed in the book. Third, several activities are included in each chapter to generate activities for active learning. Some of these are designed to be conducted in class whereas others are meant for students to use out of class in order to learn more. These activities should be used to make class more relevant for the real world and to increase student interest in the material.

Criminal Injustice

Chapter 1

Criminal Justice: Ideals and Realities

"There is no greater tyranny than that which is perpetrated under the shield of the law and in the name of justice."

—Montesquieu, *The Spirit of the Laws*

Main Argument of the Book

Although criminal justice practice is ideally aimed at reducing crime (crime control) and assuring fairness for all those that are processed through the criminal justice system (due process), the criminal justice system is oftentimes ineffective and unfair. This book shows both how and why this occurs.

Although criminal justice practice is not intended to be ineffective at reducing crime or discriminatory against any group in society, the criminal justice system fails to meaningfully reduce crime (especially those acts that pose the greatest threat to Americans) and it often operates in very discriminatory ways. That is, in the real world, American criminal justice sometimes conflicts with its ideal goals.

The primary way the criminal justice system fails to reduce crime is by failing to even target or go after the most harmful acts in America, instead focusing heavily only on a handful of harmful acts committed by certain groups of people under certain circumstances. The main reason this occurs is the lawmaking process; the law does not represent the interests of all Americans equally. An examination of who makes the law, who votes for it, and who pays for it will demonstrate this reality.

The primary way the criminal justice system is discriminatory is by focusing mostly on certain groups of people in society—people who are perceived to be disproportionately committing certain types of crimes—even though data clearly show that these people are not the most dangerous people in society. The main reason this occurs is because of myths about dangerousness that are created through the lawmaking process and reinforced in mainstream media accounts of crime and criminal justice. Media coverage of crime and criminal justice reinforces myths of crime (including who is dangerous and who is not), which helps maintain the focus of criminal justice agencies on street crime rather than on other forms of harmful behavior that actually cause far more damage to society. In sum, biases in criminal justice have been institutionalized, meaning they stem from institutions in society—in particular the law and the media—and do not thus stem from individual (bad) actors.

The Problem Is the Law (and the Media)

There are dozens of texts and literally hundreds of studies on the (in)efficacy and (un)fairness of criminal justice practice. But criminal justice scholars tend to focus far more attention on the enforcement agencies of criminal justice rather than the bodies that create the law, including the criminal law. So, when they examine whether criminal justice agencies are fair or unfair based on factors such as race, class, and gender, they tend to focus exclusively on the police, courts, and corrections (e.g., see Alexander, 2012; Walker, Spohn, & DeLone, 2012). This is problematic for one major reason: The law itself creates biases in criminal justice practice; if one ignores the lawmaking process, these biases are obviously missed.

Here is a quick example: Imagine conducting a study to see if American policing is biased against any group in American society. If you ignore the criminal law, you might examine whether police use factors such as race, class, or gender to *profile* some groups more than others, thereby increasing their odds of being stopped, questioned, searched, and arrested by the police (Withrow, 2010).

Indeed, many studies find evidence consistent with **racial profiling** by the police. For example, one recent study of a large, Midwestern municipal jurisdiction over an eight-month period found that young, Black males were most likely to be searched by the police for discretionary reasons—i.e., in cases where a search was not required (Tillyer, Charles, & Robin, 2012). Yet, does this mean that police officers are racially biased? Or could it be that they are simply enforcing racially biased laws? It is the law, after all, that is being enforced by the police, which is why they are often referred to as *law enforcement* officers; it is the law that determines which harmful behaviors police pursue and which they ignore.

If the law is biased, then so too will be policing. The main argument of this book is that the criminal law is biased in one very important way, and that is that only some harmful or dangerous acts are defined as *crimes* and *serious crimes*. There are dozens of harmful or dangerous acts that are perfectly legal, and still others are illegal but not vigorously pursued by agencies like the police. This creates bias because only some criminals are held accountable for the harms they inflict on other people, and those people tend to be younger, poor, male, and of color (Shelden, 2007).

One example illustrates how this can impact policing. If the law defines crack cocaine as more serious than powder cocaine because of perceptions that it is more dangerous or more linked to violent crime, then logically the police will pursue crack cocaine more vigorously than powder cocaine. Even assuming there is absolutely no racial bias in individual police officers, a greater focus on crack cocaine will still result in racial disparities in arrests because African Americans are more likely to be involved in dealing crack cocaine than powder cocaine (Beckett, Nyrop, & Pfingst, 2006; Beckett, Nyrop, Pfingst, & Bowen, 2005). This would be true even though African Americans are less involved than whites in dealing all other drugs (Tonry, 2012).

Guess what explains the greater focus on crack cocaine than powder cocaine by the police? The answer is the criminal law, which since the 1980s has treated crack cocaine more seriously than powder cocaine. Specifically, laws enacted in 1986 and 1988 made penalties for crack cocaine 100 times greater than penalties for powder cocaine, even though the two drugs are so similar that crack cocaine is actually made from powder cocaine (Robinson & Scherlen, 2013). Analyses of criminal justice that ignore the criminal law miss this important form of bias, introduced in the preface of this book as **innocent bias**. The process of innocent bias will be more fully explained later in the book.

Finally, it needs to be reiterated that the media also have significant responsibility here. With regard to the case of crack cocaine, for example, it was the mainstream news media that focused the nation's attention on crack cocaine rather than powder cocaine in the 1980s. National newspapers and major television news stations focused unprecedented attention on violence associated with crack cocaine, working together with politicians to focus the nation on the drug. The result was tough new laws that would ultimately be enforced by the police and courts, leading to a massive increase in imprisonment as well as enormous racial disparities in drug arrests (Reinarman & Levine, 1997). Yet the problem is not policing or even prisons per se, but rather is the whole criminal justice system, and especially the law.

Out-of-Class Activity:
Read the article "Race and Class Differences in Print Media Portrayals of Crack Cocaine and Methamphetamine" by Jennifer Cobbina: http://www.albany.edu/scj/jcjpc/vol15is2/Cobbina.pdf.
Then answer these questions:

1) How did race impact media coverage of crack cocaine use in the 1980s?
2) How is media coverage of the supposed current methamphetamine problem different than coverage of crack cocaine?
3) Does media coverage of drugs increase the odds that states will arrest and incarcerate more drug users and dealers? If so, how might this impact different races within the country?

What Is the Criminal Justice System?

The criminal justice process begins with lawmaking. Criminal laws define some behaviors as crimes (while ignoring others) and specify punishments for violations of the law (Samaha, 2013). Yet, strangely, the lawmaking process is not considered to be part of the criminal justice system. This is because the criminal justice system is an enforcement mechanism, meaning police, courts and corrections all enforce or carry out the law, making each set of agencies part of the executive branch of government. Lawmakers obviously make the law and thus are part of the legislative branch of government.

The **criminal justice system** is the term used to describe three interdependent components that enforce the criminal law — the police, courts, and correctional facilities within the federal government, as well as the agencies of criminal justice of each of the fifty states. Sam Walker (2011) thus claims that the United States actually has 51 criminal justice systems. Additionally, each state has scores of municipalities, each with its own law enforcement agencies and, in some cases, its own forms of courts and correctional facilities, as does the District of Columbia.

You can think of the criminal justice system as a whole, made up of these three interdependent components across all these government jurisdictions, something like a pie with three pieces. Although each of these components has its own functions and personnel, they are expected to work together as a unified whole, in balance, to serve some common purposes in an organized and harmonious manner. This is why scholars refer to the process of arresting, convicting, and punishing criminals as the processes of the criminal justice "system."

The primary responsibilities of each component of criminal justice include the following:

- **Police:** Investigating alleged criminal offenses, apprehending suspected criminal offenders, assisting the prosecution with obtaining criminal convictions at trial, keeping the peace in the community, preventing crime, providing social services, upholding Constitutional protections of suspects;
- **Courts:** Determining guilt or innocence of suspected offenders at trial (adjudication), sentencing the legally guilty to some form(s) of punishment, interpreting laws made by legislative bodies, setting legal precedents, upholding Constitutional protections of the accused; and
- **Corrections:** Carrying out the sentences of the courts by administering punishment, providing care and custody for accused and convicted criminals, upholding Constitutional protections of clients.

Although each of these agencies of criminal justice has its own goals, ideally they will also share some larger goals. These are discussed next.

Why Do We Have a Criminal Justice System? The Ideal View

Although there is no "official" source one can consult in order to find out what the US criminal justice system is intended to do, criminal justice scholars assert that the criminal justice system has two related goals:

1) Reducing crime; and
2) Doing justice.

Note that these two goals are related to the terms introduced in the preface—*crime control* (reducing crime) and *due process* (doing justice).

Reducing Crime

Police, courts, and corrections are obviously aimed at reducing crime, or "crime-fighting" as some like to call it. This can be achieved through reactive means (after the crime occurs) or proactive means (before the crime occurs). The former type of crime fighting is generally called **crime control**, whereas the latter is often referred to as **crime prevention** (Lab, 2004).

In the United States, crime reduction is mostly reactive in nature. For example, American policing has historically been aimed at reacting to calls for service from crime victims (after the crimes occur). Our agencies of criminal justice try to apprehend, prosecute, convict, and punish offenders after a crime is discovered by or reported to the police. Crime prevention includes any means to eliminate the causes of crime so that crime does not occur and does not need to be dealt with by criminal justice agencies (Robinson, 2013). Although some American criminal justice activity is aimed at crime prevention, the great bulk of it can be described as crime control.

As I show in this book, crime prevention is not as popular as crime control largely due to politics (Beckett, 1997; Beckett & Sasson, 2000; Gest, 2001; Simon, 2007). In a nutshell, crime prevention is viewed as "too liberal" or "too soft" an idea to be popular in the current state of conservative, get-tough-on-crime approaches to crime control (Gest, 2001). Liberal and conservative ideologies about crime are discussed in Chapter 2.

Doing Justice

Another goal of the criminal justice system is **doing justice**. Although there are conflicting conceptions of justice (Sandel, 2010), the one that is probably most valued by Americans based on the values stated in the Declaration of Independence and the US Constitution is the one concerned with ensuring that the criminal justice process is fair and impartial, a view of justice based on equality.

Doing justice assumes that persons will be treated equally in the eyes of the law— that justice will be blind. Justice thus would not be present when any group is somehow left out or singled out for differential treatment by the law. This conception of justice is represented by the figure of "a blindfolded woman with a scale in one hand and a sword in the other" called *Lady Justitia*, shown in Figure 1.1. It is also what is meant by "With liberty and justice for all" in the pledge of allegiance—that the government will treat its citizens with "fairness, equity" and in a manner that is right (Kappeler & Potter, 2004).

This conception of justice pertains to due process. Americans like to think of themselves as a free people, granted at birth with certain liberties (Sandel, 2010). Thus, if a government official suspects a person has committed a crime, the Constitutional rights of that person must be protected as he or she is processed through the criminal justice system. This explains the fact that five of the ten "Bill of Rights" deal with rights enjoyed by people accused of crimes by their government (as noted in the Preface).

Due Process versus Crime Control

These two goals of criminal justice—reducing crime and ensuring fairness and impartiality—often conflict. Sometimes, ensuring that all individuals' rights are protected means that guilty people will go free. Alternatively, getting all the "bad guys" means that some "good guys" may get caught up in criminal justice processes, too. It is difficult to do one well without being somewhat of a failure at the other.

Figure 1.1. Lady Justitia

Gorosi/Shutterstock.com

Consider this real-life example: In America's wars on crime, drugs, and now terrorism, criminal justice agencies strive to protect Americans from being hurt by these harmful behaviors. Yet, with all the civil liberties protections afforded to American citizens, it can at times be difficult to sustain convictions at trial for even the most serious of criminal behaviors. We could likely be more effective in our fights against crime, drugs, and terrorism if police were not constrained by the US Constitution as they are now. If we allowed police to spy on citizens by monitoring their phone calls, texts, emails, and Internet activities—without warrants—they'd likely more easily discover and be able to disrupt criminal behavior, as well as gather enough quality evidence to assure criminal convictions. But freeing the police in such cases means sacrificing liberty, a price many Americans are not willing to pay (and of course, many are, including Presidents George W. Bush and Barack Obama, both of whom authorized widespread spying programs as part of the "war on terror").

So the government will ideally strive to achieve a balance between fighting crime (to do justice for its victims) and being fair and impartial (to do justice for the accused). Thus, throughout our history, the priorities of American justice have shifted back and forth, much like a pendulum or a set of scales being continually rebalanced. During some periods, emphasis has been placed on apprehending and punishing criminals over ensuring fairness in the criminal justice process. At other times, crime fighting has taken a back seat to ensuring that the criminal justice system operates impartially.

Out-of-Class Activity:
Examine the website "Timeline of NSA Domestic Spying" by the Electronic Frontier Foundation:
https://www.eff.org/nsa-spying/timeline
Then answer these questions:

1) When did domestic spying on Americans begin?
2) What kinds of spying have occurred?
3) Do such programs help us achieve our crime control goals but diminish our due process rights? Explain.

Due Process versus Crime Control: Two Fictional Models

There has always been tension between those who want a *due process model* of criminal justice and those who would prefer a *crime control model* of criminal justice. These terms represent two fictional models of justice put forth by Herbert Packer (1968), in his book, *The Limits of the Criminal Sanction*. Although neither of the two models actually exists or ever can in reality, Packer attempted to describe two polar extremes—one model most concerned with preserving individual liberties and the other with maintaining order in the community and fighting crime. As citizens, we have a choice as to which model we like best and which one we want our real criminal justice system to be most like; we vote for politicians who either stand for values consistent with the due process model or crime control model.

Table 1.1 depicts these models at opposite ends of a continuum. The **due process model** is aimed at ensuring that individual liberties are protected at all costs, even if guilty people sometimes go free. In other words, the due process model values individual freedom, and the way to protect individual freedom is to uphold Constitutional protections. It places a high value on the adversarial nature of justice, whereby a prosecutor and defense attorney battle it out in court to find the truth and make sure that justice is achieved. *Reliability* is the most important value of the due process model, for it is imperative that the right person be convicted of the crime of which he or she is accused. Packer's metaphor for this model was an "obstacle course" because, in order to ensure that no innocent persons were wrongfully convicted, the prosecution would have to overcome numerous obstacles in order to convict anyone.

Table 1.1. Due Process versus Crime Control

	Crime Control Model	Due Process Model
Most important goal	Reduce crime	Protect rights
Cherished value	Efficiency	Reliability
Metaphor	Assembly line	Obstacle course
In practice	Increase powers of police, prosecutor	Decrease power of police, prosecutor

The **crime control model** is aimed at protecting the community by lowering crime rates, even if, on occasion, innocent persons are mistakenly convicted. The crime control model also values individual freedom but suggests that the way to protect individual freedom is to protect people from criminals. It places a high value on informal processes such as *plea bargaining* (when a prosecutor and defense attorney agree out of court to an appropriate sentence for an accused criminal) to expedite criminal justice operations. In this model, very few criminal trials would be held, because they are expensive and unnecessary for establishing legal guilt. *Efficiency* is the most important value of the crime control model, for it is imperative that the criminal justice system operates as quickly as possible in order to keep up with the large numbers of criminal cases that enter it each day. Packer's metaphor for this model was an "assembly line" because individual defendants would be quickly processed through the criminal justice system outside of the courtroom through plea bargaining rather than criminal trials.

Note that justice is an important value in both models. Yet, proponents of each model view justice differently. For example, people who want the American criminal justice system to resemble the fictional due process model find most appealing the following terms from the US Declaration of Independence and US Constitution: "equal"; "Rights"; and "Liberty." To them, justice is mostly concerned with protecting our equal freedoms. Proponents of making America's criminal justice system more like the fictional crime control model would be more concerned with these terms from of the US Declaration of Independence and US Constitution: "Life"; "pursuit of Happiness"; "domestic Tranquility"; and "common defence." To them, justice is mostly concerned with assuring public safety. Proponents of both models would emphasize welfare, or well-being, but they might define the term differently: to crime control proponents, welfare means safety whereas to supporters of due process, welfare means freedom.

Each of these conceptions of justice is important to Americans, but criminal justice activity over the past several decades reflects an emphasis on **retributive justice** at the expense of **procedural justice**. In other words, US politicians are more concerned with holding the guilty accountable for their crimes to achieve justice for victims than with ensuring fairness and equality in criminal justice practice to achieve justice for defendants, even in the face of overwhelming evidence that innocent people are often convicted of crimes they did not commit (Acker & Redlich, 2011). As I'll show in this book, American criminal justice began moving away from due process values toward crime control values in the 1960s, and became fully entrenched in a system that most resembles a crime control model in the 1980s. This resulted from actions of lawmakers at the state and federal level of government who sought to achieve objectives related to their ideological views of society and government. This issue is addressed more fully in Chapter 2.

There is little doubt that our criminal justice system most resembles a crime control model today, and a quick examination of how we spend our money in criminal justice illustrates the point. A criminal justice system that places a higher value on crime fighting than on due process will allocate a larger percentage of its resources to police, because they are responsible for making arrests of suspected offenders, and/or to corrections, because its agencies have sole authority over punishing offenders. A criminal justice system that places a greater value on due process would allocate a larger share of resources to courts, because the judicial process determines the guilt or innocence of criminal justice clients. The primary protection innocent persons have from government overzealousness is high-quality defense attorneys and neutral, objective judges. If we value due process, these actors ought to be well equipped to do their jobs.

Data from the Bureau of Justice Statistics (2012) show that, in 2006, federal, state, and local governments spent almost $215 billion for civil and criminal justice. The largest share of justice spending went to law enforcement ($99 billon). This is followed by spending on corrections, including jails, prisons, probation, and parole ($69 billion). The smallest share of resources was spent on courts ($47 billion). This means 46% of spending went to policing, 32% went to corrections, and only 22% went to courts. These figures are more consistent with a crime control model than a due process model of criminal justice.

In American criminal justice, government agencies allocate much more funding for police to apprehend suspected criminals and for correctional facilities to punish convicted criminals. Overburdened courts receive relatively little funding, despite the fact that it is the role of the courts to ensure that justice or due process is served—that is, that the innocent are not wrongfully convicted and that the guilty do not go free. In American criminal justice, the reality is that almost no one gets a criminal trial and instead defendants are herded like cattle into the courts where they will nearly all plead guilty as a reward for not taking up the court's limited resources. Because of plea bargaining, guilty criminals receive less punishment than they deserve and defendants who are innocent but end up pleading guilty anyway in the coercive environment of the American court system get more punishment than they deserve (Walker, 2011). Implications for justice in the United States are troubling because it appears that we are less concerned with spending resources to determine that we get the "right" people who commit crimes than we are with just getting *any* people and punishing them. This may be an alarming realization for Americans who believe in procedural justice.

The disparity in spending in favor of crime control functions results from America's "war on crime," now encompassing a "war on drugs" and "war on terror." The war on crime started to take hold of the nation in the 1960s, the war on drugs in the 1970s, and the war on terror in the 1990s. These wars have not made Americans safer and have eroded due process over time thereby distorting American ideals. This issue is addressed in Chapter 2.

Why Do We Have a Criminal Justice System? A More Pessimistic View

But maybe this is all irrelevant. Several serious scholars assert that criminal justice is not at all aimed at reducing crime or doing justice in the first place, but instead at goals far more sinister—serving limited interests, controlling some segments of the population, and maintaining the status quo in society. Some of their research concludes that the criminal justice system is biased against people of color, especially African Americans (Alexander, 2012). According to this work, criminal justice is a tool to maintain the status quo of racial stratification in the United States. Other research suggests the criminal justice system targets and most harms poor people (Reiman & Leighton, 2013; Shelden, 2007). According to this work, criminal justice is a mechanism used to serve the wealthy by controlling the poor and thus it can be seen as a social class maintenance system. Still other research concludes that, given the very close relationships between race and social class in the US, that it is difficult to determine if criminal justice practice is biased against people of color *or* poor people, and that criminal justice is at least sometimes biased against people of color *and* the poor (Walker, Spohn & DeLone, 2012). Finally, additional research explores relationships between gender and criminal justice, suggesting gender bias in the United States (Chesney-Lind, 2006). Below, examples of each of these arguments are reviewed, some suggesting racial bias, others social class bias, still others demonstrating race *and* class bias in criminal justice, and the final demonstrating gender bias.

Criminal Justice as a Racial Caste System

Michelle Alexander (2012) argues that criminal justice is a mechanism intended to control African Americans. Specifically, she sees mass imprisonment of especially African American males as an intentional **racial caste system**, which she says denotes "a stigmatized racial group locked into an inferior position by law and custom" (p. 12). Her argument is based on the fact that America has always had racial caste systems—from slavery to the current day—and she says such systems do not end, they are just redesigned or change forms over time.

Alexander examines US history and suggests that when slavery was abolished, a new form of racial caste system eventually emerged called **Jim Crow**, a system named after a minstrel show character. At the heart of the Jim Crow system was the notion of "separate but equal," where blacks would supposedly have equal access to societal institutions, but this access must remain separate from that of whites. So there were separate entrances to buildings, separate water fountains, segregated schools, and even separate seating arrangements on city buses, in movie theaters, restaurants, and so much more. Alexander also discusses the intense domestic terrorism blacks faced at the hands of groups such as the Ku Klux Klan, not to mention the police, in order to maintain this racial caste system.

After the Jim Crow system was finally defeated legally as a result of the Civil Rights Movement—meaning the nation's institutions would finally have to be desegregated so that, among other things, blacks could attend the same schools as whites—America's racial caste system would have to change again. This time, according to Alexander, it was the criminal justice system that would step in to take the lead (just as police maintained Jim Crow by enforcing the criminal laws at the time). So today, where it is not legally permissible to discriminate using race in America's "colorblind society," we instead use the "legitimate" or "race neutral" factor of "criminality" to control minorities. To Alexander, black is synonymous with criminal.

How did this happen, according to Alexander? The "law and order" approach to crime control that started in the 1960s was born in response to the Civil Rights Movement, which was depicted by southern politicians as a breakdown in law and order. That is, the acts of civil disobedience engaged in by groups such as the National Association for the Advancement of Colored People (NAACP), Student Nonviolent Coordinating Committee (SNCC), Congress on Racial Equality (CORE), and Martin Luther King, Jr.'s Southern Christian Leadership Conference (SLC) were often depicted by national, state, and local politicians as criminal behaviors in need of criminal justice intervention. As noted by Katherine Beckett & Theodore Sasson (2000: 49):

In an effort to sway public opinion against the civil rights movement, southern governors and law enforcement officials characterized its tactics as 'criminal' and indicative of the breakdown of 'law and order.' Calling for a crackdown on the 'hoodlums,' 'agitators,' 'street mobs,' and 'lawbreakers' who challenged segregation and Black disenfranchisement, these officials made rhetoric about crime a key component of political discourse in race relations.

And of course, participants as well as leaders in the movement were arrested by police, hosed down by firefighters, attacked by police and police dogs, as well as assaulted and murdered (the political context of this time is further examined in Chapter 2).

It did not help that riots in the streets and images of lawlessness were widely depicted in the news and meaningfully connected to civil disobedience and the civil rights movement itself. And even though studies would eventually show that many riots were actually initiated by the police through excessive use of force against innocent and peaceful marchers, politicians were able to frame these events as examples of threats to life, liberty, domestic tranquility, and the general welfare of society—the very values that Americans enshrined in the Declaration of Independence and US Constitution. At the very least, the civil rights movement became seen by many as a serious threat to the status quo of American society and the racial caste system that has always been part of it.

When Jim Crow laws were overturned, something else had to take the place of Jim Crow; Alexander claims it is America's current system of mass imprisonment. So perhaps it is not a coincidence that America's boom in imprisonment began just five years after the murder of the man who stood at the center of the Civil Rights Movement's work for equality, Dr. Martin Luther King, Jr. King was assassinated in April 1968 and increases in imprisonment began in 1973, as shown in Figure 1.2. That is, it took only five years from the death of the nation's most important civil rights leader for the nation to begin its transition to mass imprisonment, a phenomenon that has most severely impacted African Americans.

According to Alexander, such a development does "not require racial hostility or overt bigotry to thrive" (p. 14) only indifference to the suffering of millions of Americans who are seen simply in the eyes of Americans as criminals. As noted by Alexander, "Today, mass incarceration defines the meaning of blackness in America: black people, especially black men, are criminals. That's what it means to be black" (p. 197). So today, to many Americans, "black" and "crime" are synonymous and thus imprisoning people viewed as dangerous appears perfectly normal.

Just how bad is it for African Americans in America today? According to Alexander, there are more black people in prison today in the US than there were in South Africa during Apartheid. And "a black child born today is less likely to be raised by both parents than a black child born during slavery" (p. 180). This is true even though blacks are not actually more dangerous than whites (this issue will be further discussed in Chapters 4 and 5).

Criminal justice bias, according to Alexander, occurs in two stages:

> The first step is to grant law enforcement officials extraordinary discretion regarding whom to stop, search, arrest, and charge for drug offenses, thus assuring that conscious and unconscious racial beliefs and stereotypes will be given free

Figure 1.2. US State and Federal Prison Population, 1925–2012

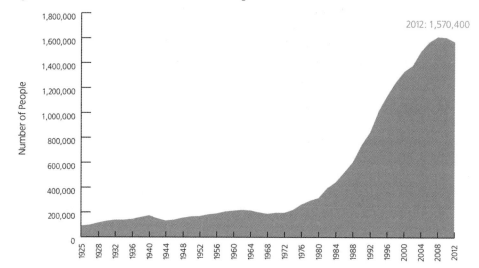

Source: http://www.sentencingproject.org/template/page.cfm?id=107.
Courtesy of The Sentencing Project.

rein. Unbridled discretion inevitably creates huge racial disparities. Then, the damning step: Close the courthouse doors to all claims by defendants and private litigants that the criminal justice system operates in a racially discriminatory fashion. Demand that anyone who wants to challenge racial bias in the system offer, in advance, clear proof that the racial disparities are the product of intentional racial discrimination—i.e., the work of a bigot (p. 103).

Interestingly, even though Alexander points out that lawmakers are wealthy, older, white males, she does not identify this as the primary source of bias in criminal justice; this book argues that it is. And even though she acknowledges that there are "a wide variety of laws" that keep blacks at the bottom of the pecking order of society (p. 184), she puts the real blame on police (where overt biases do in fact exist, at least in some places at some times), and legal decisions reached by the US Supreme Court about what is required to prove racial bias in criminal sentencing. Yet, as Alexander herself points out, it is white men who dominate politics, control the nation's wealth, and write the rules by which we all have to live (p. 255). My argument is that *this* is the primary bias in criminal justice.

Alexander does, however, focus attention on the drug war as the primary culprit that explains mass incarceration of young black men in America. And in her summary of this new racial caste system, she writes that it works like this:

- Phase one—police round up large numbers of young black men as part of the drug war;
- Phase two—courts deny these people meaningful legal representation and coerce them to plead guilty; and

- Phase three—correctional facilities house them, largely invisibly, until their release dates, after which the stigma of conviction follows and harms them for the rest of their lives (pp. 185–186).

The **drug war** is a term that summarizes America's approach to fighting drug producers, growers, manufacturers, sellers, possessors, and users in order to reduce drug use. Why do we fight a drug war? Because of the criminal law, which first determined that certain drugs are illegal and that second called for strict criminal penalties for producing, growing, manufacturing, selling, possessing, and using drugs. So, according to Alexander's argument, the law really is the problem.

In-Class Activity:
Bring up the article, "Race and the Drug War," by the Drug Policy Alliance:
http://www.drugpolicy.org/race-and-drug-war
Flip through "The Basics" and read them aloud.
Then discuss this issue:
Is the drug war racist? If African Americans are no more likely to use drugs, why does it so greatly impact them?

A similar argument is made by Michael Tonry (2012), although he does not use the term "racial caste system." Claiming that few Americans believe in white supremacy and that few politicians make open appeals to racism, nevertheless, Tonry shows the devastating effects of criminal justice punishment on blacks. Not only are they more likely to be arrested, convicted, and incarcerated, they are less able to successfully participate in normal, American life, which has detrimental impacts "on their children, their families, and their communities" (p. ix).

In terms of imprisonment, Tonry demonstrates that: "At any time in the first decade of the twenty-first century one-third of young black men in their twenties were in jail or prison or on probation or parole. Imprisonment rates for black men have for a quarter century been five to seven times higher than those for white men" (p. ix). In fact, he shares evidence showing how many criminal justice policies have their greatest impact on African Americans. Table 1.2 shows the racial breakdown of various punishments in contemporary America. Compare these numbers to the racial and ethnic make-up of larger society, and you see that African Americans and Latinos are vastly overrepresented among correctional populations.

Like Alexander, Tonry points out that America has always had systems in place to discriminate against people of color: "A variety of cultural practices and legal institutions maintained traditional American patterns of racial dominance and hierarchy for more than three centuries, and contemporary drug and crime policies do it today." Prior to the criminal justice system, the way that blacks were kept at the bottom of the social hierarchy was slavery, Jim Crow, and then "the big-city ghettos and employment and housing discrimination kept blacks subordinate. And when industrialization and the flight of jobs to the suburbs left disadvantaged blacks marooned in urban ghettos, the modern wars on drugs and crime took over" (p. 5).

Table 1.2. Race, Ethnicity, and Punishment

	White	Black	Hispanic
Jail inmates (2011)	45%	38%	16%
State prison inmates (2010)	31%	39%	23%
Federal prison inmates (2011)	59%	38%	34%
US Population (2010)	72%	13%	16%

Sources: http://www.albany.edu/sourcebook/pdf/t6172011.pdf; http://www.albany.edu/sourcebook/pdf/t6332010.pdf; http://www.albany.edu/sourcebook/pdf/t600222011.pdf; http://www.census.gov/prod/cen2010/briefs/c2010br-02.pdf.

This might sound like some kind of conspiracy theory because Tonry claims that criminal justice control of blacks "help(s) white Americans maintain social, economic, and political dominance over blacks." Yet he rejects this idea of a conspiracy and instead suggests that policies simply evolve to serve the interests of whites, and that whites merely rationalize the policies because the policies serve their interests (p. 4).

The specific laws and policies identified by Tonry that explain racial disparities in criminal justice outcomes include the war on drugs, police profiling (defined earlier in the book, where police use race to identify people worthy of being stopped and searched), greater police presence in minority areas (especially in open air drug markets where black dealers tend to sell drugs), prosecutorial and judicial bias (where both prosecutors and judges are tougher on blacks than whites for some crimes), disparate sentences for crack cocaine and powder cocaine (discussed earlier), mandatory sentencing laws including **three strikes laws** and **truth-in-sentencing laws.**

These policies were created and voted for mostly by whites, and Tonry claims that, at the least, the racially disparate outcomes of such policies were not unforeseeable. Yet, race or racism were not explicitly used by politicians to justify these policies; instead, race and racism are implicit to them. Tonry concludes:

> Because politicians after 1970 could no longer openly appeal to antiblack sentiments they used code words, one of which was *crime*. The war on drugs and crime rapidly expanded ... Because it was disproportionately black people who went to prison white voters felt comfortable to pay that price, especially since it perpetuated the economic and social tradition of white dominance over a socially disorganized black underclass (p. 134).

This is quite similar to the argument of Alexander who suggests seeing crime and imprisonment as "black things" is normal in our "colorblind" society. In fact, a great deal of evidence exists to suggest that "blackness" and crime are often treated synonymously in the media (Russell-Brown, 2008). This issue is addressed in Chapter 3.

> **In-Class Activity:**
> Pull up the report, "Racial Divide: California's 3 Strikes Law," by the Justice Policy Institute: http://www.justicepolicy.org/research/2022
> Read the main findings aloud.
> Then discuss this issue:
> Why have three strikes laws been disproportionately applied to African Americans and Latinos? Is it discrimination or because they are more involved in serious street crime?

Criminal Justice as a Lower Class Suppression System

Jeffrey Reiman & Paul Leighton (2013) suggest that the criminal justice system is biased against the poor at all stages of the process, from policing, to courts, all the way through corrections. Their argument — titled the **Pyrrhic defeat theory** — is based on the military term, pyrrhic victory, which is a victory that comes with such high costs in lost money and troops that it does not feel like a victory. Riemann & Leighton change the original term to describe American criminal justice, arguing that criminal justice loses in its fight against crime and its efforts to be fair, but this failure amounts to a victory for those who benefit from these failures. So they suggest that criminal justice is really aimed at failing to reduce crime and achieve fairness because these failures produce enough benefits to powerful people that they amount to a success.

Reiman & Leighton suggest that criminal justice processes are actually aimed at **population control** and **serving limited interests**. Their main argument is that interests of those in power are served when we focus almost exclusively on street crimes rather than other types of harmful behaviors, including white-collar crimes, corporate crimes, and even governmental deviance. At the same time, those people whom we fear most (e.g., young, minority males) are routinely rounded up by the police and sent off to some form of government-controlled institution (e.g., jail or prison) or community alternative (e.g., halfway house, boot camp). This amounts to a form of population control, so that the enemies in the war on crime can never win and can never achieve the types of success that can be enjoyed by those with the power to achieve.

Among other things, Reiman & Leighton argue that the label of "crime" (particularly "serious crime") is not used for the most harmful and frequently occurring acts that threaten us. They claim that the criminal law distorts the image of crime so that the most dangerous threats are seen as coming from below us (i.e., from the lower class) when they really come from above us (i.e., from the upper class). They refer to this as a **carnival mirror** (p. 67). Extremely dangerous acts committed by the wealthy and powerful (such as unsafe workplaces, environmental pollution, unnecessary surgery, and unnecessary prescriptions) are either not illegal or are but are not vigorously pursued by criminal justice agencies even though they kill and injure far more people than crime every year (more on this in Chapter 5).

Thus, these authors agree with the argument of this book that the primary source of bias in criminal justice is the law. Reiman & Leighton state this simply when they write, "when crimes are defined in the law, the system concentrates primarily on the

Table 1.3. Race and Economic Outcomes

	White	Black	Hispanic
Unemployment Rate (2010)	8%	13%	11%
People below Poverty (2009)	12%	26%	25%
Children below Poverty (2009)	17%	35%	33%
Median Household Income	$55,412	$32,229	$38,624
Net Worth (2011)	$89,537	$6,314	$7,683

Sources: http://www.census.gov/prod/2012pubs/p60-243.pdf; http://www.census.gov/compendia/statab/2012/tables/12s0712.pdf; http://www.census.gov/people/wealth/files/Wealth_Tables_2011.xlsx; http://www.census.gov/compendia/statab/2012/tables/12s0627.pdf.

predatory acts of the poor and tends to exclude or deemphasize the equally or more dangerous predatory acts of those who are well off" (p. 4). They add that the label of crime "is not used in America to name all or the worst of the actions that cause misery and suffering to Americans. It is reserved primarily for the dangerous actions of the poor" (p. 66).

Reiman & Leighton review studies of white-collar and corporate crime, along with government and non-government estimates of the damages these acts cause. And they demonstrate that behaviors such as occupational disease and injury, unnecessary medical care, misuse of prescription drugs, environmental pollution, and so forth, injure and kill far more Americans than street crime (p. 95). Further, they cause far more property loss than street crime (p. 131). Some of these numbers are identified in Chapters 4 and 5.

Reiman & Leighton argue that the criminal justice system is designed to function in a way that "aims its weapons against the poor, while ignoring or treating gently the rich who prey upon their own fellows"—that it is designed to fail "to protect Americans from predatory business practices and to [not] punish those well-off people who cause widespread harm" (p. xvii). So, rather than being aimed at eliminating crime or achieving justice, Reiman & Leighton entertain the idea that the goal of the criminal justice system is "to project to the American public a credible image of the threat of crime as a threat from the poor." In order to do this, we must be presented "with a sizable population of poor criminals" so the system must "fail in the struggle to eliminate the crimes that poor people commit, or even to reduce their number dramatically" (p. 1).

To these authors, criminal justice is not a system specifically designed to harm African Americans—not a racial caste system—but instead is a system that actually targets the poor. Yes, minorities including blacks are greatly impacted by criminal justice, but that is mostly because they are disproportionately likely to be poor. In America, African Americans have lower incomes than whites, less overall wealth, and are more likely to suffer from unemployment, poverty, child-poverty, and so on (Walker, Spohn & DeLone, 2012). Consider data from the US Census, shown in Table 1.3.

So a system that targets poor crime will undoubtedly catch a large number of African Americans, although these authors also acknowledge that racial discrimination does exist in criminal justice. Reiman & Leighton are more specific and describe the "typical criminal" (or who the system pursues) as male, young, urban, poor, and black: "Poor, young, urban, (disproportionately) black males make up the core of the enemy forces in the crime war" (p. 69).

Reiman & Leighton argue that criminal justice system failure was not set in place by some vast conspiracy of old, rich, white men who wanted to protect their limited interests (although these are the people who wrote the US Constitution and who, today make the laws!). Instead, they argue, criminal justice evolved over time into processes that are unjust and that protect limited interests. They refer to this argument as **historical inertia** (p. 6). Those who benefit from the system obviously have no reason to change the status quo, and those harmed by the inherent biases of the criminal justice system do not have the intellectual or financial means to change it. The authors write:

> [W]e are not maintaining that the rich and powerful intentionally make the system fail to gather the resulting benefits. Our view is rather that that the system has grown up piecemeal over time and usually with the best of intentions. The unplanned and unintended overall result is a system that not only fails to substantially reduce crime, but also does so in a way that serves the interests of the rich and powerful. One consequence ... is that those who could change the system feel no need to do so. And thus it keeps on rolling along (p. 6).

With regard to those "best intentions," Reiman & Leighton suggest policy makers "are sincerely doing what they believe is right" (p. 178) based on a view of crime that dates back to pre-industrial times. This view of crime — which is likely the same view you hold — is built on myths of harmful behaviors created by the law and reinforced by media coverage of crime (more on this in Chapter 3).

A final way criminal justice serves limited interests is by failing to account for structural causes of crime that are widely known to be criminogenic. Reiman & Leighton, for example, discuss **economic inequality** in society and poverty as major sources of crime that are largely ignored by US politicians; this turns out to be a solid predictor of violent crime rates in a society (Robinson & Beaver, 2009). Tonry (2012: ix) concurs, noting that the characteristics of criminals who end up in prison are these: "disadvantaged childhoods, child abuse, unstable home lives, bad educations, lack of employable skills, and drug and alcohol dependence."

Instead of working to reduce these crime-producing influences, the criminal justice system assumes that individual criminals are completely responsible for their behaviors, consistent with the conservative ideology that underlies contemporary criminal justice policy (this issue is discussed further in Chapter 2). By operating on this assumption, it reinforces the idea that society has no hand of responsibility in creating or preventing crime. Further, by effectively presenting lower class criminals as fully responsible for not only their criminality but also their poverty, the criminal justice system "sanctifies the status quo with its disparities of wealth, privilege and opportunity, and thus serves the interests of the rich and powerful in America — the very ones who could change criminal justice policy if they were really unhappy with it" (p. 4).

In fact, according to Reiman & Leighton, lawmakers also pursue policies such as tax cuts, **downsizing**, **outsourcing**, and so forth, which make criminogenic factors like poverty and economic inequality worse. Thus, during the past three decades and more, the wealthy have gotten richer while the poor have gotten poorer, and the middle-class essentially remains stagnant. This increases strains on the poor, which make crime a more likely outcome (Aaltonen, Kivivuori & Martikainen, 2011).

Similarly, Randy Shelden (2007) argues that the criminal justice system is a tool used to control the "dangerous classes," who are poor and minorities, but also young and of-tentimes female. Shelden says he is not claiming "some vast conspiracy among the 'ruling class'... to use the law and the legal system to trample on the rights of ordinary citizens, especially the poor." Nor is he arguing "that every law is a mere reflection of the interest of this class—or any class for that matter." Instead, he points out that if you simply ex-amine

> *the results* of the law in general and the daily operations of the criminal justice system—that is the outcomes of legal decision—the entire system *generally* comes down hardest on those with the least amount of power and influence, and *generally* comes down in the most lenient fashion on those with the most power and influence (p. xiii).

Shelden's critical analysis of the history of criminal justice practice in the United States is thus not a conspiracy theory because he does not argue that discrimination is intentional on the part of criminal justice actors. Yet, he does show widespread disparities in criminal justice outcomes from arrest to conviction to imprisonment, suggesting that one function of criminal justice (whether intended or not) is controlling segments of the population, as suggested by Jeffrey Reiman & Paul Leighton. And Shelden demon-strates that there are biases in criminal justice based not only on social class, but also on race and gender (p. 3).

Similar to Reiman & Leighton, Shelden suggests social class matters in criminal justice, mostly because of the criminal law. He writes that social class helps determine "which behaviors come to be defined as 'criminal' and thus subject to their enforcement" by criminal justice agencies; "*who* is to be defined as 'criminal'"; "how far into the criminal justice system a particular case is processed"; and "the final sentence of a criminal case" (pp. 3–4). Shelden's argument is that lawmakers are more likely to define behaviors of the powerless as crimes, that powerless people are most likely to be depicted as criminals, that criminal justice agencies more vigorously pursue their crimes than the harmful acts of the powerful, and that the criminal justice system tends to come down much harder on the poor than the wealthy. Shelden's argument is thus consistent with the argument of this book.

The main bias that harms the powerless while benefiting the powerful, according to Shelden, is that criminal justice generally ignores the harmful acts of the latter:

> Statistically speaking, the gravest threats to us are not from robbers, burglars, rapists, and the like; rather, they are from those who wear suit and tie to work, or a white medical coat, or who occupy plush offices in corporate headquarters or powerful positions within the government. Their weapons are ballpoint pens, scalpels, computers, or their voices (as when they decide to go to war) (p. 6).

And Shelden provides evidence that corporate crime—things like fraud, hazardous working conditions, defective products, unnecessary medical procedures, and similar behaviors—are far more damaging than the street crimes on which we focus. This issue will be addressed in Chapters 4 and 5.

That the criminal law generally ignores such acts in favor of more dramatic and visible crimes like murder, robbery, carjacking, and similar acts, "reflects the interests of the ruling class" by "deflect(ing) attention from the crimes committed by their own class" (p. 13). In this way, it is the criminal law that is *the* problem in criminal justice. Earlier, Lawrence Friedman (1993: 101) made a similar point:

> Law is a fabric of norms and practices in a particular society; the norms and practices are social judgments made concrete: the living, breathing embodiment of society's attitudes, prejudices, and values. Inevitably, and invariably, these are slanted in favor of the haves; the top-riders, the comfortable, respectable, well-to-do people. After all, articulate, powerful people *make* the laws; and even with the best will in the world, they do not feel moved to give themselves disadvantage.
>
> Rules thus tend to favor people who own property, entrepreneurs, people with good positions in society. The lash of criminal justice, conversely, tends to fall on the poor, the badly dressed, the maladroit, the deviant, the misunderstood, the shiftless, the unpopular.

In other words, the law is the problem, as is argued in this book.

The law, according to Shelden, is written to reflect the interests of the powerful and to maintain status quo arrangements in society. Similar to the argument of Alexander—who wrote that racial caste systems have always existed in America—Shelden shows that "the management of the dangerous classes is not a recent phenomenon" but instead that control of the poor has always been a primary function of criminal justice (p. 18). Perhaps it is thus not surprising that today, prisons and jails have been referred to by many criminologists, sociologists, historians, and other social scientists as the poorhouses of the twentieth and twenty-first centuries (Wright & Herivel, 2003). In fact, Reiman & Leighton (2013) show that prisons have always been reserved for the poor (p. 118).

Criminal Justice as a System Evolving Toward Pure Justice

Sam Walker, Cassia Spohn, & Miriam DeLone (2012) show that there are disparities through all of criminal justice, including in policing, judicial processes, and correctional outcomes, and they argue that these disparities arise from race *and* social class biases. These authors do not explicitly examine whether such disparities are intentional or not, yet they largely seem to conclude that they are not.

Walker et al. present five possible outcomes in criminal justice as part of a continuum of disparities in criminal justice, ranging from **pure justice** to **systematic discrimination**. This continuum is shown in Table 1.4.

Walker and colleagues argue that, as much as we've tried, pure justice still does not exist in the United States. Yes, we've come a long way since slavery, **slave codes**, **black codes**, **lynchings**, Jim Crow laws and the like, but neither the law nor enforcement of it is actually color-blind. **Disparities** and even **individual discrimination** still exist.

Yet, the type of discrimination that is most problematic, according to Walker and colleagues, is **contextual discrimination**. For example, Walker et al. write:

> Based on the evidence, we conclude that the system is characterized by *contextual discrimination*. Racial minorities are treated more harshly than whites at some

Table 1.4. The Discrimination Continuum

Systematic	Discrimination at all stages of the criminal justice system, at all times and places
Institutionalized	Racial and ethnic disparities in outcomes that are the result of the application of racially neutral factors such as prior criminal record, employment status, demeanor, etc.
Contextual	Discrimination found in particular contexts or circumstances
Individual	Discrimination that results from the acts of particular individuals but is not characteristic of entire agencies or the criminal justice system as a whole
Pure justice	No racial or ethnic discrimination at all

Source: Walker, S., Spohn, C., & DeLone, M. (2014). *The Color of Justice.* Beverly Hills, CA: Wadsworth.

stages of the criminal justice process ... but no differently than whites at other stages.... The treatment accorded racial minorities is more punitive than that accorded whites in some regions or jurisdictions.... Racial minorities who commit certain types of crimes ... or who have certain types of characteristics ... are treated more harshly than whites who commit these crimes or have these characteristics (p. 493).

Throughout their text, which presents an exhaustive review of studies of policing, courts, and corrections in the US, the authors conclude that contextual discrimination is documented by the following findings:

- Police in some jurisdiction use race and ethnicity to profile people (p. 156).
- African Americans and Hispanics are more likely to be stopped, questioned, searched, and arrested by the police than whites; they are also more likely to have force used against them, including excessive force and lethal force (p. 181).
- In some places, race and ethnicity impact pre-trial decision-making including bail, charging by prosecutors, and plea bargaining in the courts (p. 231).
- People of color are, in many jurisdictions, denied the right to serve on trial juries through the use of peremptory challenges based solely on their race (p. 273), even though this practice is explicitly illegal.
- African Americans and Hispanics who are convicted of certain types of crimes (e.g., drug crimes and violent crimes against whites) are treated more harshly than whites for those crimes (p. 274).
- Tougher sentences tend to be handed down to racial minorities than to whites in "borderline cases" where prosecutors and judges tend to have discretion about whether to pursue probation or a term of incarceration (p. 333).

The fact that discrimination is found only in some places, at some times, and in some contexts means that the criminal justice system is *not* plagued by *systematic discrimination*. Thus, the system cannot be accurately understood to be functioning as a racial caste system (as argued by Alexander and Tonry) or a lower class suppression system (as suggested by Reiman & Leighton and Shelden). Recall that Alexander (2012) suggested that policing *and* courts are biased against African Americans, suggesting systematic discrimination. And Reiman & Leighton (2013) argued that: "At each step, from arresting to sentencing, the likelihood of being ignored or released or treated lightly by the system is greater the better off one is economically" and: "For the same criminal behavior, the poor are more likely to be arrested; if arrested, they are more likely to be charged; if charged, more likely to be convicted; if convicted, more likely to be sentenced to prison; and if sentenced, more likely to be given longer prison terms than members of the middle and upper classes" (p. 119). The analysis by Walker et al. suggests that criminal justice practice is evolving away from the this kind of systematic discrimination that used to characterize all of American criminal justice toward the ideal of pure justice.

If systematic discrimination does exist anywhere in criminal justice, Walker and colleagues suggest it is in the practice of capital punishment:

> We contend that the type of discrimination found in the capital sentencing process falls closer to the systematic end of the discrimination continuum.... Racial discrimination in the capital sentencing process is not limited to the South, where historical evidence of racial bias would lead one to expect different treatment, but is applicable to other regions of the country as well. It is not confined to one stage of the decision-making process, but affects decisions made by prosecutors as well as juries. It is also not confined to the pre-*Furman* period, when statutes offered little or no guidance to judges and juries charged with deciding whether to impose the death penalty or not, but is found, too, under the more restrictive guided discretion statutes enacted since *Furman*.[1] Moreover, this effect does not disappear when legally relevant predictors of sentence severity are taken into consideration (p. 391).

Studies of dozens of criminologists and death penalty experts support this conclusion (Robinson, 2009).

Out-of-Class Activity:
Search the web for "Race and the death penalty" and read the main points of the Death Penalty Information Center, American Civil Liberties Union, Equal Justice Initiative, and Amnesty International.
Then answer these questions:

1) How does race impact capital punishment?
2) Is America's death penalty racist?
3) If you support the death penalty, does knowing there are serious issues of racial disparities in capital punishment impact your opinion? Why or why not?

---

1. *Furman* refers to the US Supreme Court case, *Furman v. Georgia* 408 US 238 (1972), which struck down capital punishment statutes across the US (new statutes were approved by the Court in *Gregg v. Georgia* 428 US 153 [1976]).

The final type of discrimination found in criminal justice is **institutionalized discrimination,** and it relates directly to the main argument of this book. This type of discrimination is common in American criminal justice, especially during the phases of arrest and sentencing (p. 492). For example, poor minorities are more likely to be arrested, convicted, and sentenced to correctional punishment because they disproportionately commit some crimes (meaning they commit more than their fair share of them). If African Americans are more likely to be arrested for crimes such as murder and robbery, part of the reason why is because they are more involved in these crimes.

Michael Tonry (2012) acknowledges this in his work with regard to street crimes, and data from the US government confirm it. For example, according to the US Department of Justice, Bureau of Justice Statistics (2004), African Americans made up 51% of people convicted of murder and nonnegligent manslaughter and 59% of people convicted of robbery in state courts in 2002; in 2002, African Americans accounted for only about 12% of the US population. So, clearly African Americans are committing more than their fair share of these crimes (but this does not make blacks more dangerous, as will be shown in Chapters 4 and 5).

Imagine living in a neighborhood where such crimes are common. These areas will obviously be of greater focus by the police. Thus, people living in such areas will be more likely to be arrested by the police. Then, at the time when they appear in court charged with the serious offense of murder or robbery, prosecutors will be more likely to file charges against them, juries will be more likely to convict, and judges will be more likely to hand down tougher sentences for *legal reasons* including **offense seriousness** and **prior criminal record.** Disparities in criminal justice will be found in police and court processes for these reasons, suggestive of institutionalized discrimination.

Now, you might reject the idea that this amounts to discrimination, because discrimination implies intent (as in having the intent to discriminate against people of color). But the term discrimination is appropriate here because police and court actions based on legal factors still demonstrate racial bias or discrimination, *if the law and policing are biased or discriminatory.* So, for example, if the law discriminates based on race, then the harmful behaviors of minorities will be more likely to be legislated as crimes and serious crimes, and if police discriminate based on race, then people of color will be more likely to be arrested for crime. Further, if the law discriminates based on social class, then the harmful behaviors of the poor will be more likely to be legislated as crimes and serious crimes, and if police discriminate based on class, then poor people will be more likely to be arrested for crime. It is called "institutional" discrimination because the discrimination has become part of the institutions of society (these institutions include the law and the media, as introduced earlier). If you accept the arguments of Reiman & Leighton and Shelden, you'd agree that the law is discriminatory when it ignores harmful acts simply because of who commits them.

This is not to say that murder and robbery are not serious crimes—they are. But, as will be shown in Chapters 4 and 5, there are other ways to kill people and take their property that are either not illegal or are, but aren't pursued vigorously by criminal justice agencies. It turns out the people who commit these other types of harmful behaviors tend to be older, white, rich men—the very people who make the law and own and operate the media (Robinson & Murphy, 2009). Further, as it turns out, it is not greater involvement in street crimes—especially violent ones—that explains racial

Table 1.5. Crime and Gender

Arrests of Women

Violent crime	20%
Murder	11%
Rape	1%
Robbery	12%
Aggravated assault	23%
Property crime	38%
Burglary	15%
Theft	44%
Motor vehicle theft	18%
Arson	17%
Drug offenses	19%

Source: http://www.albany.edu/sourcebook/pdf/t482010.pdf.

disparities in imprisonment, because what drives growth in imprisonment is not new admissions to prison for violent crimes, but instead for relatively minor offenses including drug offenses (Tonry, 2012).

A Patriarchal Criminal Justice System?

A *patriarch* is a man who rules or leads in a **patriarchal system** (Chesney-Lind, 2006). Is the criminal justice system a patriarchal system? When one looks at who makes the law in the US — older, rich, white men — one assumes the answer has to be yes (see Chapter 3). Indeed, scholars have long asserted that gender bias is prevalent in the criminal justice system (Leighton & Flavin, 2010; Mallicoat, 2011). Gender bias includes decisions that favor or harm individuals on the basis of sex. Overall, criminal justice activities are actually less punitive toward women, but this is because men are responsible for a much larger portion of street crime and violence in general.

Generally speaking, women are less likely to be victimized by crime, less likely to commit it, less likely to be arrested, less likely to be convicted, less likely to be sentenced to prison or jail, and generally are sentenced to less time in jail and prison than men. Table 1.5 illustrates arrests for serious street crimes by gender. As you can see, women (who make up 51% of the US population) are underrepresented among arrestees for every category of serious crime. Women are also underrepresented among those convicted for every crime — although court data are a bit outdated — and tend to receive more lenient sentences than men. It is thought that courts are more lenient to convicted female felons than convicted male felons because of legal factors — specifically, women tend to commit less serious crimes and have shorter criminal records.

Yet, when comparing sentences for certain types of crimes, women are sometimes sentenced to prison at a rate closer to and in some cases exceeding that of men. For example, African American females convicted of drug offenses—both possession and trafficking—are more likely to be sentenced to prison than white men and white women. Add on to this the fact that the rate of increase in imprisonment for females is larger than that of males since the 1970s and you start to see some evidence of potential biases against women.

Such findings may represent the fact that we are becoming more of an equal society, whereby women are being treated with less chivalry and more equality. It might also owe itself to the **evil woman hypothesis**, posited by Joanne Belknap (2007). This suggests that women may be reacted to more harshly by courts when they do things that are not generally expected of them (Chesney-Lind & Pasko, 2004).

As one example, consider the case of serial killer Aileen Wuornos. Wuornos, a white woman, killed seven men in the state of Florida. She claimed that all the men she killed were men who either raped her or attempted to rape her while she worked as a prostitute along truck stops in the state. Though after her arrest, Wuornos depicted herself as a victim, she ultimately admitted being responsible for her crimes, saying: "I killed those men, robbed them as cold as ice. And I'd do it again, too. There's no chance in keeping me alive or anything, because I'd kill again. I have hate crawling through my system ... I am so sick of hearing this 'she's crazy' stuff. I've been evaluated so many times. I'm competent, sane, and I'm trying to tell the truth. I'm one who seriously hates human life and would kill again" (Zarella, 2002). Further, Wuornos had a long criminal record including numerous acts of violence such as assault and robbery. She was executed by lethal injection in Florida in October 2002.

The increasingly punitive response of our criminal justice agencies to female offenders does not owe itself to a female crime wave. Instead, women are simply more likely to be sent to prison for offenses that typically did not receive imprisonment in the past. It is likely that there are, in fact, some biases against women in criminal justice, at least for some types of crimes in some places (i.e., contextual discrimination) Some of these biases are connected solely to gender; most operate in conjunction with race and class. In fact, one must consider the intersections of race, class, and gender to fully understand bias in criminal justice; the most prominent biases in criminal justice against women harm poor women of color.

Yet most of the "clients" of the criminal justice system are men, even above and beyond their representation in the criminal population. For this reason, most of the focus of this book is on the effect of criminal justice policies on poor men of color — the typical client in criminal justice. Stated simply, the war on crime has an enemy, and that enemy is poor men of color.

Which Argument Is Most Accurate?

All extra-legal factors—race, social class, and gender—impact criminal justice (HoSang, LaBennett, & Pulido, 2011; Omi & Winant, 1994). The works of all the authors reviewed in this chapter agree about this, in spite of their different focus. Race, class, and gender impact criminal justice independently of one another. Built-in biases against the poor and people of color will help explain why the nation's jails and prisons are filled with poor African Americans and Hispanics; again, most of those incarcerated are men.

Yet it is important to keep in mind that race, social class, and gender also interact to impact criminal justice processing. That is, no extra-legal factor exclusively determines the behaviors of personnel in policing, courts, and correctional agencies. Take the example of drug policy discussed earlier. Since the 1980s, police have devoted far more

Figure 1.3. Homicide by Circumstance, 1975–2005

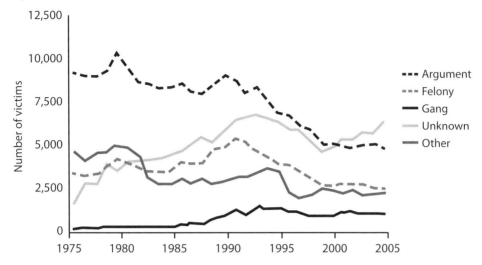

Source: http://bjs.gov/content/pub/pdf/htius.pdf.

energy and resources to "fighting" crack cocaine than they have to powder cocaine. Why? Crack cocaine was characterized by the news media as more dangerous than powder cocaine. Specifically, it was argued that crack cocaine was more closely linked to violent crime than powder cocaine, even though there is just as much violence, if not more, associated with the distribution of powder cocaine than there is with crack cocaine. As explained by Ted Gest (2001: 120): "The basic concept was simple: crack was more associated with violence than powder, it appeared, so those who sold it deserved a higher penalty." In an effort to reduce violent crime, lawmakers got much tougher with crack cocaine than powder cocaine.

Were lawmakers explicitly targeting African Americans with the intent of creating an unfair and unjust law? Unlikely. Ted Gest (2001: 121) reports a quote from a staff person of the Congressional Black Caucus, many of whom supported tougher sentences for crack cocaine in the 1980s: "Crack was so new and there was no data, so it wasn't debated in racial terms." In fact, no member of Congress objected to potential sentencing disparities based on race, even though, again, such disparities were not unforeseeable (Tonry, 2012).

Were lawmakers targeting poor people? Probably not. Also, not a word about social class was spoken on the floor of Congress. And it'd be hard to imagine this had much to do with gender, other than the use of pregnant women using crack and so-called "crack babies" that were used to justify getting tough with (some) drug users (Reinarman & Levine, 1997).

It is more logical to assume that lawmakers, ignorant of the realities of crack cocaine and powder cocaine noted above, reacted to heightened media attention to crack cocaine in the 1980s, which suggested that the illicit crack cocaine market was a major source of murder in the nation. In fact, studies show that when crack cocaine hit the streets of the nation's major cities, dealers sought out and obtained guns as means to protect their investments in the illegal marketplace (Robinson & Scherlen, 2013). And, starting in

Figure 1.4. Homicide Offending by Age, Race, and Gender, 1976–2005

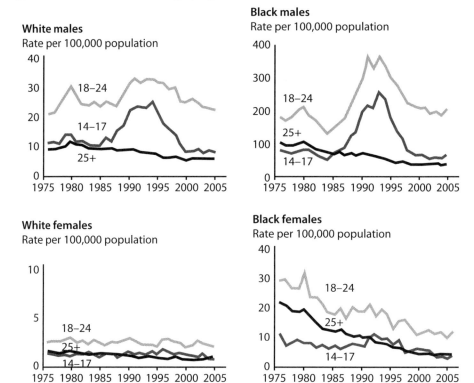

Source: http://bjs.gov/content/pub/pdf/htius.pdf.

the mid-1980s, murders preceded by arguments and initiated in felonies increased, as shown in Figure 1.3. Many of these and probably most were drug deals gone bad and rival drug dealers fighting for the right to establish the right to sell illegal drugs in pursuit of wealth and the American Dream (Contreras, 2013).

The goal of crime reduction (i.e., crime control) may have thus motivated the war on crack cocaine. Yet, without question, this war has had its greatest impact on the poor and minorities. Turns out, the largest share of murders in the 1980s preceded by arguments and felonies were being committed by young, urban black males, as shown in Figure 1.4.

So, the criminal justice system may not be intentionally biased against the poor, people of color, or either men or women. Yet criminal justice in the United States may achieve certain functions—even ones we might not like, such as discriminating against some people without actually intending to achieve them. This is an important distinction to understand. Yet it's also quite likely that when legislators were trying to reduce murder by getting tough on crack cocaine, images of young black men were in their minds— the very type of person Alexander (2012) and Tonry (2012) says are synonymous with "criminal" and the type of person identified by Reiman & Leighton (2013) as the "typical criminal."

How can outcomes of criminal justice occur, even when they are not intended? The answer lies in the influence of politics and ideology, which is addressed is the next chapter.

Summary

Assuming the values of crime control and due process are still important to American citizens, criminal justice is an important mechanism to achieve these goals. Ideally, criminal justice aims to reduce crime and to preserve our rights. Yet, when one examines the outcomes of criminal justice practice in reality, one sees that the system is often ineffective at reducing crime and tends to produce unfair outcomes. Specifically, the criminal justice system does not even target the most harmful behaviors in society, and it has its greatest detrimental effects on poor people, people of color, and young men.

The argument of this book is that criminal justice is ineffective at reducing crime and that it tends to produce unfair outcomes. This is not necessarily intentional but instead results from the political and ideological nature of lawmaking and criminal justice policy more generally. Lawmakers create laws and policies that benefit them and their financial backers by creating myths about who is dangerous and who is not. Media coverage of crime and criminal justice reinforces these perceptions of dangerousness, helping to maintain the focus of criminal justice agencies on street crime rather than on other forms of harmful behavior that actually cause far more damage to society.

Some scholars have asserted that the criminal justice system is a racial caste system that aims to suppress people of color, is a social class suppression system that aims to keep poor people in their place, and is a patriarchal system that aims to keep men dominant over women. Yet it is also possible that criminal justice functions to control some segments of the population and to serve some interests more than others without being intended, at least by individual police, courts, and correctional officials.

Key Terms

- **Black Codes**: Black codes were laws passed by southern states after the Civil War, which restricted free blacks and ensured their availability as workers, including requirements to enter into long-term work contracts.
- **Carnival Mirror**: The carnival mirror is the term used by Reiman and Leighton to describe a distorted picture of crime; the law does not label the most harmful acts as crimes but instead focuses on the acts of the poor.
- **Contextual Discrimination**: Contextual discrimination is when discrimination is found in some contexts or circumstances but not in others.
- **Corrections**: Corrections carries out the punishments assigned by courts.
- **Courts**: Courts determine legal guilt and sentence the guilty to punishment.
- **Crime Control**: Crime control is reacting to crimes after they occur by arresting, convicting, and punishing offenders.
- **Crime Control Model**: The crime control model is a fictional model of criminal justice that emphasizes protecting people from crime even if it means restricting people's rights and liberties.
- **Crime Prevention**: Crime prevention is stopping crime from happening before it happens by deterring would-be offenders as well as addressing the sources of crime before they produce crime.

- **Criminal Justice System**: The criminal justice system is the term used to describe the police, courts, and corrections.
- **Disparities**: Disparities are differences in outcomes by extra-legal factors such as race, ethnicity, class, and gender that do not necessarily reflect intentional discrimination.
- **Doing Justice**: Doing justice refers to assuring that criminal justice practices are fair by protecting people's rights and liberties.
- **Downsizing**: Downsizing is when companies institute massive layoffs to save money.
- **Drug War**: The drug war is the term used to describe America's policy of eradicating drugs at their source, disrupting drug markets in the US, and arresting and incarcerating drug offenders.
- **Due Process Model**: The due process model is a fictional model of criminal justice that emphasizes protecting people's rights and liberties even if it means that some guilty criminals go free.
- **Economic Inequality**: Economic inequality refers to the gap between the wealthy and the poor.
- **Evil Woman Hypothesis**: The evil woman hypothesis predicts that women will be treated more harshly for similar crimes than men when they violate prescribed gender roles in society.
- **Historical Inertia**: Historical inertia is the argument of Reiman and Leighton that the failures of criminal justice do not result from a conspiracy of wealthy, old white men but instead evolved over time and are maintained because they serve important functions.
- **Individual Discrimination**: Individual discrimination is when particular individuals act based on racist values or beliefs.
- **Innocent Bias**: Innocent bias is bias in criminal justice practice that comes from the criminal law and is thus not intended by individual criminal justice actors such as police officers.
- **Institutionalized Discrimination**: Institutionalized discrimination occurs when disparities in criminal justice outcomes are accounted for by race-neutral factors such as offense seriousness and prior criminal record.
- **Jim Crow**: Jim Crow refers to the system of segregation between blacks and whites by law and custom that was common in America from the late 1870s to the 1960s.
- **Lynchings**: Lynchings were an extra-legal form of justice where blacks suspected of crimes were rounded up and murdered by whites as a means of keeping white control of society.
- **Offense Seriousness**: Offense seriousness refers to how serious a crime is according to the criminal law.
- **Outsourcing**: Outsourcing refers to sending jobs overseas to save money.
- **Patriarchal System**: A patriarchal system is one that is ruled or dominated by men, as in when a country is ruled or controlled by men.
- **Police**: Police investigate crimes and make arrests.
- **Population Control**: Population control is one of the goals of criminal justice suggested by Reiman and Leighton. These authors argue that criminal justice is aimed at controlling certain segments of the population—poor people of color—by focusing on street crime.

- **Prior Criminal Record**: Prior criminal record refers to how many times a person has been arrested by the police and convicted by the courts.
- **Procedural Justice**: Procedural justice is concerned with assuring that due process is followed as people are processed through the criminal justice system.
- **Pure Justice**: Pure justice exists when there is no discrimination at all against any group in society.
- **Pyrrhic Defeat Theory:** The Pyrrhic defeat theory asserts that criminal justice does not effectively reduce crime or achieve fairness, and asserts that these failures amount to a victory for those who benefit from them.
- **Racial Caste System**: A racial caste system exists when a stigmatized racial group is locked into an inferior position by law and custom.
- **Racial Profiling**: Racial profiling is using race or ethnicity or color of skin rather than behavior to identify people as suspicious or dangerous and worthy of being stopped, questioned, and searched.
- **Retributive Justice**: Retributive justice is concerned with holding the guilty accountable and punishing them.
- **Serving Limited Interests**: Serving limited interests is one of the goals of criminal justice suggested by Reiman and Leighton. These authors argue that by controlling certain segments of the population — poor people of color — this serves the financial and moral interests of the powerful.
- **Slave Codes**: Slave codes were state laws giving masters complete control over the slaves and specifying specific rules for slaves that did not apply to free people.
- **Systematic Discrimination**: Systematic discrimination exists when discrimination against some groups is found in every stage of criminal justice at all times.
- **Three Strikes Laws**: Three strikes laws are specific mandatory sentencing laws that mandate long prison sentences upon conviction of a second or third felony, often including a life sentence.
- **Truth-in-Sentencing Laws:** Truth-in-sentencing laws require inmates to serve a large portion of their sentences, usually 85% of their prison terms, before release.

Discussion Questions

1) What is racial profiling? Why is it a problem in criminal justice?
2) What is innocent bias? Where does it come from?
3) What is the criminal justice system? Why do we have it?
4) Compare and contrast the crime control model of criminal justice and the due process model of criminal justice. Which do you prefer? Why?
5) Compare and contrast retributive justice and procedural justice. Which would you prefer the government emphasize more? Why?
6) What is the main argument about criminal justice of Michelle Alexander?
7) What is a racial caste system? Is the criminal justice system a racial caste system?
8) What was Jim Crow and how did it impact people of color?
9) What is the drug war and how does it impact people of color?
10) What are three strikes laws and truth-in-sentencing laws and how do they impact people of color?

11) What is the main argument about criminal justice of Jeffrey Reiman and Paul Leighton?
12) Summarize the pyrrhic defeat theory and the idea of historical inertia.
13) Does criminal justice control some segments of the population more than others and serve limited interests? If so, how?
14) What is the carnival mirror and why is it important?
15) What is economic inequality and how is it related to crime?
16) What are downsizing and outsourcing and how do they produce crime?
17) Define the major types of discrimination outlined by Walker, Spohn and DeLone. Compare and contrast these with disparities.
18) Define slave codes, black codes, and lynchings and explain how these played a role in subjugating blacks.
19) What are the main legal reasons that help explain racial disparities in criminal justice?
20) What is a patriarchal system? Is the criminal justice system a patriarchal system? Why?
21) What is the evil woman hypothesis and how is it relevant for criminal justice?

Chapter 2

Politics, Ideology, and Crime

"There is nothing wrong with describing Conservatism as protecting the Constitution, protecting all things that limit government. Government is the enemy of liberty. Government should be very restrained."

—Ron Paul

Criminal Justice Practice Is Impacted by Politics and Ideology

In the last chapter, I suggested that the criminal justice system ideally aims to reduce crime (crime control) and do justice (due process), but argued that it generally ignores the crimes that pose the greatest threats to us, and is disproportionately harmful to the poor and people of color, especially men. Unlike other scholars who assert that such outcomes are intended, the argument of this book is that they are merely functions served by a criminal justice system that is political and ideological in nature.

Most criminal justice texts state the ideal goals of the criminal justice system and ignore the reality that the system is highly impacted by politics and ideology. Yet, it should be obvious that criminal justice is political given that all criminal justice processes start with the criminal law, which is made by politicians! As explained by Richard Quinney (2000: 138): "The administration of justice, contrary to common belief, is not 'above politics,' but is by its very nature political." And given that politicians have very strong ideological beliefs, it should therefore be obvious that criminal justice is impacted by ideology.

Ignoring the political and ideological aspects of criminal justice is unfortunate because it is only with an understanding of politics and ideology that we can fully understand why criminal justice tends to fail to achieve its ideal goals and achieve the values found in the Declaration of Independence and the US Constitution. That is, without considering politics and ideology, it's not possible to understand why criminal justice in the US operates in ways contrary to American ideals of crime control and due process.

What Is Politics?

The word politics has several, related meanings. First, **politics** is often defined as "the art or science of government," as in elected officials governing citizens (Merriam-Webster, 2012). Politics thus means governing. Second, politics is understood to be " … concerned with guiding or influencing governmental policy" (Merriam-Webster, 2012), whereby **policy** is a "rule or set of rules or guidelines for how to make a decision" about some issue (Welsh & Harris, 2012: 4). Politics is therefore also about coming up with approaches to effectively solve problems in society, including crime. So, for example, whether we pursue policies of crime control or crime prevention is a political decision.

Third, politics is often understood as being synonymous with the actions, practices, and policies of government itself (Merriam-Webster, 2012). Often when people talk about politics they are literally discussing what the government is doing (or not doing)—which policies it is creating (or not creating).

Fourth, politics is obviously related to "winning and holding control over a government" as in the case of political races and elections. For many Americans, their understanding of politics is limited only to this aspect of politics, and only to what they learn during the campaign season; most people are largely unaware of the realities of lawmaking and other political processes. This is probably because they don't pay attention to politics up until election time. As one example, only about one-third of Americans were closely following the political campaigns process in June 2012, just months prior to a very important election (Flock, 2012). And it is widely known that Americans lack even basic information about the founding of their nation and the institutions of government that run it (Loewen, 2007). So it is a small minority of citizens who are actually informed that regularly participate in the political process. The implications of this are discussed in Chapter 3.

The idea of winning and holding control of the government brings up the important issue of the role of competition in the political process, leading to a fifth definition of politics: "competition between competing interest groups or individuals for power and leadership" (Merriam-Webster, 2012). Americans are at least vaguely aware of the reality of American politics that two major political parties in the US compete to win elections, and the winners get to make policies and thereby enjoy enormous benefits of power (Holyoke, 2011). *Power* is generally understood to mean the ability to influence the behavior of people without interference—to get them to do things that you want them to do (Gillens, 2012).

In-Class Activity:
Discuss as a class: who is the most powerful member of the criminal justice system? If you included lawmakers, who is the most powerful member?

A sixth definition of politics is a classic in the academic discipline in political science—the means used to decide who gets what economic benefits in society, when they get them, and how they get them (Lasswell, 1936). It is determinative of outcomes such as who gets to keep most of the income generated in the United States and how that income will be used (Harrigan, 2000). For example, it is politicians who also determine how much we are taxed and how those tax dollars are spent.

It is also politicians that get to define acts as criminal, which is an effective way to exercise power over people. Interestingly, legislating behaviors as crimes also has significant impact on who earns and gets to keep income. For example, some forms of property-seeking behaviors are illegal (e.g., selling marijuana) while others are perfectly legal (e.g., selling tobacco). Thus, people who want to sell marijuana are not only *not* permitted to earn profits by selling their drug of choice but also face the possibility of being incarcerated and thus prevented from achieving any income during the term of their punishment, in addition to the very real possibility of seeing even future job opportunities diminished as a result of their convictions (Alexander, 2012). Further, lawmakers obviously have the power to *not* legislate behaviors as crimes, even outlandish and harmful behaviors of the powerful that "are regarded as little more than the American way of doing business" (Quinney, 2000: 230). Legislating an act as a crime (or not) is thus a political act.

Politics is also about allocating society's values (Easton, 1953), at least for those who have the ability to have their values enacted into law. This is a seventh definition of politics. Then, resources are allocated by politicians to determine purposes of legitimating these values through government authority. Clearly, deciding which behaviors get called crimes and which don't has enormous influence on what society views as normal or abnormal, decent or deviant, right or wrong, etc. As an example, some forms of property-taking are called theft while others are not; even some forms of killing are called murder while, incredibly, others are not. So, again, criminalizing behaviors is a political act.

Then, it is politicians who decide whether to spend money on a particular approach to reduce crime, and how much. It is politicians who thus decide whether to fund criminal justice, how much, and for what purposes. In this book, I will demonstrate relationships between politics, crime, and criminal justice, and show how this impact tends to interfere with the ideal goals of criminal justice in America, distorting America's ideals.

What Is Ideology?

Ideology is a term closely related to politics. Generally speaking, the term refers to beliefs about how things are, how they should be, and why. It refers to things people believe to be true that are often self-evident (Hanson & Jost, 2012).

Ideology also is often defined as a collection of beliefs, values, or assumptions that underlie political policies or practices (Freeden, 2003). That is, it is those beliefs, values, and assumptions that politicians use to justify the policies they pursue and enact, as well as ignore. Benjamin Ginsberg, Theodore Lowi, Margaret Weir, & Caroline Tolbert (2013: 205) define ideology as "a cohesive set of beliefs that forms a general philosophy about the role of government."

Here it is useful to distinguish between politics and ideology, two very similar terms. Politics refers to the *what* of governing—competing for office, winning or losing, and then for the winners—maintaining power and making policies that ultimately decide who gets economic benefits and has their values enacted into law. Ideology is the *why* of governing—the beliefs and values that justify the policies that are made (and not made) and that help them make sense. So, politics can be thought of as what politicians do, and ideology as why they do it.

Conservativism versus Liberalism

According to Benjamin Ginsberg and colleagues (2013), American political culture today stresses the importance of three values—liberty, equality, and democracy (Ginsberg et al., 2013: 23), whereas:

- **Liberty** can be understood as "freedom from government control" (p. 24).
- **Equality** can be understood to mean either equal opportunity in society where "all people should have the freedom to use whatever talents and wealth they have to reach their fullest potential," or *political equality*, meaning "the right to participate in politics equally, based on the principle of 'one person, one vote'" (p. 25).
- **Democracy** is a system of government where "political power ultimately comes from the people" (p. 28).

Of the two major political ideologies that dominate America today—the liberal ideology and the conservative ideology—there are major differences in how each stresses or emphasizes these values (Ellis & Stimson, 2011). While a full examination of liberalism and conservatism is beyond the scope of this book, these terms are used throughout the book and thus some brief definitions are in order.

Liberalism is the political ideology that most values equality in society and that believes a strong government is necessary to assure equal opportunity for all (Ellis & Stimson, 2011). **Conservativism** also values equality but believes the best way to achieve it is not through government involvement or interference but instead through the "free market" of capitalism and business (Sandel, 2010). Whereas liberals favor government intervention in business to assure it is free from discrimination and protective of equal opportunity for all, conservatives believe the market itself is best equipped to achieve this through supply and demand processes; in this way, conservatives tend to see themselves as defenders of liberty or freedom from unnecessary government interference in their lives. Conservatives believe all will benefit when capitalism thrives, whereas liberals believe capitalism must be constrained in order to reduce the harmful impact of inequality in society and to benefit the least advantaged members of society (Rawls, 2005).

Further, liberalism is generally associated with keeping the government out of personal decisions pertaining to things such as what people put in their own bodies (e.g., drugs) or do with their own bodies (e.g., prostitution, abortion); in this way, liberals tend to see themselves as defenders of liberty or freedom from unnecessary government interference in their lives. Conservativism is generally associated more with the belief in strong government involvement in the lives of individuals in order to maintain control of society and promote traditional values. Thus, conservatives tend to believe the government has a vested interest in stopping people from putting drugs in their own bodies as well as engaging in prostitution and having abortions (Ginsberg, Lowi, Weir, & Tolbert, 2013). Their "small government" rhetoric is thus not entirely consistent. Yet, liberals, who generally reject big government when it comes to police, prisons, and the military, favor large government when it comes to providing social services (e.g., welfare to the poor).

Out-of-Class Activity:
Go online and find one of the many quizzes or tests you can take to find out how liberal or conservative you are. Examples include http://www.gotoquiz.com/conservative_or_liberal and http://www.politicalcompass.org/test.
Then share your findings with the rest of the class. How many students in the class are liberal, how many conservative, etc.?

One issue about which conservatives and liberals vehemently disagree is how much the government should be involved in helping people. Recall from the preface of this book that the US Constitution states that one purpose of establishing the United States of America was to "promote the general Welfare." Benjamin Ginsberg, Theodore Lowi, Margaret Weir, & Caroline Tolbert (2013: 566) expand on the idea of welfare, writing:

> One of the most important activities of the federal bureaucracy is to promote the general welfare. Americans often think of government welfare as a single program that goes only to the very poor; but a number of federal agencies provide services, build infrastructure, and enforce regulations designed to enhance the well-being of the vast majority of citizens (p. 566).

So government aims to "protect against the risks and insecurities that most people face over the course of their lives. These include illness, disability, temporary unemployment, and the reduced earning capability that comes with old age." Most spending on social welfare in the United States goes to programs that serve these purposes (p. 689). These authors also add that government is around to provide services to people that they cannot effectively provide for themselves, things like "defense against foreign aggression, maintenance of public order, enforcement of contractual obligations and property rights, and a guarantee of some measure of social justice" (p. 13). Generally speaking, such activities tend to be more favored by liberals than conservatives.

Finally, there are clear differences between liberals and conservatives when it comes to democracy. At the present time it is conservatives who are pushing for and often implementing policies that restrict people's ability to vote (e.g., voter ID laws that require certain kinds of people to produce certain kinds of identification, reduce the number of days that people can vote, make it harder for college students to vote, etc.), while simultaneously embracing the ability of corporations to impact the law and public policy. As an example, take a new law just passed by the state of North Carolina: the law reduces early voting, denies people the ability to register on the same day that they vote, "weakens the disclosure of so-called independent expenditures, disenfranchises felons and the 'mentally incompetent,' authorizes vigilante poll observers, and penalizes families of college students who vote out of state." Further, the voter ID component "cuts to seven the forms of permissible identification ... no county or municipal government or public employee IDs will be valid proof of voter identification. Nor will any photo ID issued by a public assistance agency, or any student ID from any college" (Lithwick, 2013).

This is a law passed by a conservative legislature that has a veto-proof majority over the state's governor (who is also a conservative). Liberals generally oppose such policies and favor wider access to voter registration and voter rights.

Table 2.1. Conservative and Political Ideology and Crime

	Conservativism	Liberalism
Humans have	Free will	No free will (bounded rationality)
Motivation for crime	Pleasure-seeking (hedonism)	Numerous (external and internal factors)
Approach to reduce crime	Punishment Crime control	Rehabilitation Crime prevention

Conservative and Liberal Ideology on Crime

Of most importance to this book are the differing views of conservatives and liberals in terms of the etiology of crime and the proper societal response to it. While scores of books have been written about the wide variety of theories of crime, the theories that are most appealing to conservatives are **rational choice theory** and **cultural deviance theories**. These theories assert, respectively, that criminal behavior is chosen by people using their free will or emerges out of subcultures which value, celebrate, and reward deviant behavior. For liberals, a much larger range of theories is appealing, including those that revolve around sociological, psychological, and biological determinism. These theories assert that factors outside and inside individuals—things beyond the control of individuals—*cause* or at least *increase the probability* of criminal behavior. While many liberals believe in free will and personal responsibility, liberalism embraces the idea that crime is more likely to occur due to **risk factors** such as poverty, stress, mental illness, difficulty coping, certain personality traits (e.g., impulsivity), hormonal imbalances, and so forth (Robinson & Beaver, 2009). Conservatives tend to dismiss these influences as "excuses" for bad behavior.

Table 2.1 depicts the differences between the liberal and conservative ideologies when it comes to crime. Whereas conservatives embrace free will without question, liberals often at least question it when they acknowledge that factors beyond people's control do impact the choices people make; this is called bounded rationality. The motivation for criminal behavior according to conservatives is pleasure and pain, meaning criminals are viewed as **hedonistic** and thus they can be deterred through punishment. Liberals see numerous motivations for criminal behavior, including factors inside and outside people (i.e., some things that impact people are in their biology, others are in their environment). Given this, rehabilitation makes more sense than punishment to liberals; people should be treated for what ails them, and their environments should be cured of whatever plagues them.

Given their divergent views of crime, conservatives tend to favor crime control whereas liberals tend to support crime prevention; to liberals it makes more sense to prevent crime rather than to react to it. For conservatives, it makes more sense to utilize police and prosecutors to get "tough on crime" so that people will not choose to engage in it through the exercise of their free will; prevention comes in the form of coercion— threatening would be lawbreakers with the threat of punishment.

A similar point is made by Katherine Beckett & Theodore Sasson (2000: 48) when they explain that "to the extent that crime is seen as a consequence of lenience within the criminal justice system, policies that 'get tough' with criminal offenders seem most appropriate." This would be the conservative argument. Yet "frames that depict crime as a consequence of poverty, unemployment, or inequality suggest the need for policies that address these social and economic conditions." This would be the liberal argument.

Finally, while conservatives and liberals both value freedom, as noted above, liberals are generally more interested in protecting due process rights of individuals confronted with the power of criminal justice agencies. Conservatives tend to be more comfortable with erosions of due process rights in order to assure public safety; as such, they tend to be more supportive of expanding police powers in order to facilitate the wars on crime, drugs, and terrorism (whereas liberals are far more skeptical of such efforts).

Both views of criminal behavior have impacted policy in the United States to some degree, but the conservative views of free will, rational choice, subcultural deviance, and crime control over due process have had the greatest impact on American criminal justice practice, especially during the last four decades (Barker, 2009; Beckett & Sasson, 2000; Gest, 2001; Hagan, 2010; Simon, 2007; Tonry, 2011). This helps explain why America has moved toward more and more punishment, which after all only makes sense if criminals are morally responsible for their crimes and does not make sense of all if they are influenced by factors beyond their control. As explained by Vanessa Barker (2009: 3): "Across much of the United States, rehabilitation, the underlying principle of punishment, has been replaced by retribution as many policy makers, politicians, and correctional officials have given up efforts to reform inmates and instead simply punish them, sometimes quite harshly."

Who is responsible for this outcome? Katherine Beckett & Theodore Sasson (2000: 48) write that "today's 'tough-on-crime' policies reflect the success of conservative efforts to frame crime as a consequence of excessive lenience or 'permissiveness' in government policy and in society more generally." This is the work of conservative politicians who "have worked for decades to alter popular perceptions of problems such as crime, delinquency, addiction, and poverty and to promote policies that involve 'getting tough' and 'cracking down.'" These authors claim that this is not just for the purpose of controlling the direction of criminal justice policy but also "to realign the electorate and to define social control rather than social welfare as the primary responsibility of the state." That is, instead of making efforts to help the less fortunate before they turn to crime (like liberals would favor), the government has shifted its approach toward just punishing people who commit crime without regard to the circumstances that prompted their criminality (as conservatives prefer). Vanessa Barker (2009: 12) also points out that citizen withdrawal from political participation shares some of the blame for America's shift away from rehabilitation toward mass incarceration. Chapter 3 shows how little Americans actually participate in their own democracy, supposedly such an important part of our political culture identified earlier.

When it comes to crime and criminal justice practice, the conservative ideology dominates, and has for decades—starting in the 1960s and picking up in the 1980s. Although this reality resulted from efforts of state- and national-level Republican Party politicians, both Republicans and Democrats ultimately embraced the conservative ideology when it comes to crime control. In fact, prominent Democrats share much of the responsibility for the shift toward crime control values over due process values in criminal justice, as will be shown in this chapter. This book demonstrates relationships between ideology, crime, and criminal justice, and show how the conservative crime control ideology interferes with the ideal goals of criminal justice in America, thereby distorting the ideals of reducing crime (i.e., crime control) and doing justice (i.e., due process).

How Politics and Ideology Impact Criminal Justice

Politics, ideology, and criminal justice are intimately linked and inseparable. Because of influence of politics and ideology on the law, it is easier to understand how some behaviors get legislated as crimes and serious crimes, while others are ignored. Further, it is easier to see how some interests get served while others are ignored or even harmed. Stated simply, those with political power get to make the criminal law, and in this way, they are more likely to have their ideology reflected in it and thus their interests served at the expense of others.

Politics and ideology are involved in criminal justice in numerous ways. The most significant way is in deciding which behaviors should and should not be considered "crime." Crime is defined through a political process by a very small group of people in the United States (lawmakers or legislators) who, ideally, are representative of the people but who, in reality, are not at all representative of the people in demographic terms. The implications of this are discussed in Chapter 3.

Another way that politics and ideology impact criminal justice is through the creation of criminal justice policies. The criminal justice policies we have pursued over the past four decades grew out of a particular ideological view of the world—the conservative ideology—that has led to likely unintended consequences in criminal justice witnessed in Chapter 1—a criminal justice system that fails to pursue the most dangerous acts in society and that predominantly catches and punishes poor men of color.

The Power to Define (Harmful) Acts as Crimes

Although criminal justice policy development is affected by groups other than lawmakers—including the media, voters, lobbying groups, and other special interests—politicians play the largest role in setting the crime control agenda. Because of their power, politicians have the largest ideological influence on what we do in criminal justice. They decide which harmful behaviors are illegal and which remain legal.

The US Congress, for example, has the power to define crimes, create criminal justice agencies, provide or withhold funding from criminal justice programs, and act as a public forum for public debate (Marion & Oliver, 2011). State legislatures share this power and actually have the largest impact on defining crimes since most crimes are violations of state laws (Rosenthal, 2008; Squire & Moncrief, 2009). Yet it is the federal government that sets national trends in criminal justice, largely due to its power to coerce states and state-level agencies and actors to pursue policies viewed to be in the national interest, often by providing or withholding federal funding.

Jonathan Simon (2007: 101) clarifies that it is mostly states that pass laws: "Criminal law has always formed a much larger share of state governance than federal governance."

And he adds that "legislatures have devoted an increasing share of their time since the 1970s to enacting laws creating new criminal offenses, increasing the punishment of existing ones, and producing innumerable procedural laws designed to promote the other processes." Still, it is clear that crime became a *national* concern in the twentieth century and it is predominantly candidates for major national office that made this so, as will be shown in this chapter (Gest, 2001).

According to Richard Quinney (2000) it is powerful individuals and groups who promote their conceptions of crime so that they can justify and maintain their authority and create policies that promote their own interests. Crime and criminal justice practices are thus efforts by the powerful to control others and maintain power. If true, this makes the arguments of Alexander (2012), Tonry (2012), Reiman & Leighton (2012) and Shelden (2007) introduced in Chapter 1 more believable; after all, these authors argued the criminal justice system is really aimed at controlling others — the poor and people of color — in order to maintain the current power structure of wealthy whites dominating US institutions.

Assuming for the moment it is true that criminal justice is used by the powerful to control other people and to maintain power, how would we know? One way would be to examine who makes the law, who votes for, and who pays for it, and then examine the behaviors they legislate as crimes (as well as those they don't). If the lawmaking process is representative of the people — and the people are represented by it — the law should be in our interests, and those things we define as crimes and serious crimes would be the behaviors that most threaten us and our interests. If not, perhaps it makes sense to see the law as a tool of the powerful to control the rest of us. These issues are addressed in Chapter 3.

As shown in Chapter 1, it is the criminal law that is the beginning of all criminal justice practice. Legislators define behaviors as illegal, police arrest people suspected of engaging in those illegal behaviors, courts determine the legal guilt of those accused of crimes and sentence those found guilty to some form of punishment, and correctional agencies carry out the punishment. Thus, everything the police, courts, and corrections do is dependent on lawmaking. That is power. Clearly it is lawmakers who have this power.

The Power to Create Criminal Justice Policy

Politicians also create policies of criminal justice. For example, lawmakers determine what the possible range of punishments can be for any given crime. Thus, whether people who break the law are put on probation, incarcerated in jail or prison, even put to death, or given some other wide range of possible punishments, is determined by lawmakers.

Lawmakers also create specific policies that are enacted by criminal justice agencies. For example, legislators created mandatory sentencing laws (such as the "three strikes" laws discussed earlier) and **sentencing guidelines** (Walker, 2011). And lawmakers launched the current drug war, not to mention prohibition of alcohol before that (Robinson & Scherlen, 2013). So it is legislators who literally decide *what* criminal justice does and *how* it does it.

Beyond deciding possible punishments and creating specific policies, it is legislators that also decide which general direction we as a nation move — either towards crime control or crime prevention, and either toward or away from due process. That is, do we invest more heavily in crime prevention programs and techniques to try to stop crime from happening in the first place or do we ramp up the criminal justice apparatus to catch and punish more and more lawbreakers after the fact? And do we protect civil liberties of Americans and thereby make it more difficult to attain and sustain criminal convictions or do we ease civil liberties protections and empower the police and prosecutors to zealously fight crime? It is lawmakers who make these decisions.

Richard Quinney (2000) claims that the most powerful interest groups have the greatest ability to influence criminal justice because they have the most access to decision-makers and thus the most opportunity to actually influence policy. Again, if this is true, it makes the arguments of scholars reviewed in Chapter 1 more believable. In Chapter 3, you'll see who makes the law, who votes for it, and who funds it in order to see if Quinney's argument is accurate.

Before turning to these key issues, it is important to understand how the conservative ideology took root in and began to dominate US criminal justice practice because it is this ideology, as noted earlier, that has led us away from our own values of crime control and due process. In the sections that follow, you'll see how the dominance of conservative ideology in American politics explains why we don't focus on those acts that create the greatest harms (i.e., white-collar and corporate crime) as well as why we pursue ever-expanding crime control policies that do most harm to poor people and people of color.

How and When Did the
Conservative Ideology Take Over?

For the most part, it is the people who have embraced the conservative ideology of crime and criminal justice who get to define acts as crimes and to create criminal justice policies. Thus, criminal justice policy is based on the assumptions that people have free will, are motivated by hedonism, and can be deterred by swift and severe criminal punishment. Further, criminal justice is motivated by law and order and crime control goals more than due process and crime prevention goals. But how did this become so?

As noted earlier, the shift to conservative, get tough on crime approaches in criminal justice began in the 1960s. Since then, politicians — especially governors, candidates for president, presidents, and their attorney generals — have focused on heinous, violent street crimes (the rarest of all crimes) in order to promote policies "aimed at 'getting tough' and 'cracking down'" on street crime. "As a result, the criminal justice system has become more and more punitive, and its scope and expense are now unparalleled among Western democracies" (Beckett & Sasson, 2000: 4–5). Politicians find this easy to do because first, punitive criminal justice policies seem to them to be supported by the public, and second, the deleterious outcomes of such policies mostly impact poor people of color — people with the least power in society who are thus unlikely to be heard if and when they complain.

Of course, crime was politicized long before the 1960s, including during Reconstruction when states attempted to integrate freed slaves into their societies but legislated behaviors of blacks and whites differently, and during the New Deal when the US government pursued bandits, back robbers, highway bandits, gangsters, and other "roving criminals" (Simon, 2007: 48). But it was the 1960s when crime became such a central issue that major politicians, including presidents, could use it to win elections and gain power in America. In fact, it was crime that eventually became *the* issue used by mostly state governors to become President of the United States starting around this time (Simon, 2007). Without the crime issue, there may not have ever been a President Richard Nixon (1969 to 1974), President Ronald Reagan (1981 to 1989), President George H.W. Bush (1989 to 1993), President Bill Clinton (1993 to 2001), or President George W. Bush (2001 to 2009)—each of them made crime issues central to their campaigns. Below a summary of national campaigns focused on crime is presented in chronological order.

Barry Goldwater, Lyndon Johnson, and Richard Nixon (1963–1974)

The conservative dominance in crime control policy was initiated in 1963, when conservative politicians of both major political parties criticized then President John F. Kennedy for supporting national civil rights legislation. To his critics, Kennedy and others promoting civil rights were rewarding law-breaking behavior by supporting civil rights because some civil rights activists promoted and engaged in acts of civil disobedience, many of which violated the criminal law.

Yet, most attribute the politicization of crime at the national level to charges made by Republican Senator Barry Goldwater, who ran for president in 1964 against Democratic president Lyndon Johnson. As noted by Ted Gest (2001: 5): "Barry Goldwater started it. [He] was the first to put crime on the national agenda in response to soaring rates of violence in the 1960s." Goldwater blamed Johnson for rising crime rates and characterized the president as "soft on crime." According to Michelle Alexander (2012: 42), Barry Goldwater "aggressively exploited the riots and fears of black crime, laying the foundation for the 'get tough on crime' movement that would emerge years later." In one speech, he urged voters not to choose opponent Lyndon Johnson because that choice was "the way of mobs in the streets."

Johnson had initiated his Great Society programs, aimed at reducing poverty and racial inequality by investing in the nation's infrastructure. Yet, the struggle for equality in society was still a struggle, and thus people did take to the streets to make their voices heard. Although Goldwater lost to Johnson, Johnson ultimately made a "war on crime" part of his **Great Society** programs (Simon, 2007). And it was Goldwater that assured Johnson would devote serious attention—in the form of a blue ribbon commission—to studying and addressing street crime.

Goldwater, a true conservative, also attacked public assistance programs by linking them to crime:

> If it is entirely proper for the government to take away from some to give to others, then won't some be led to believe that they can rightfully take from anyone who has more than they? No wonder law and order has broken down,

mob violence has engulfed great American cities, and our wives feel unsafe in the streets (quoted in Beckett, 1997: 35).

Goldwater probably never explained how helping out the less fortunate actually leads to a breakdown of law and order and sudden mob violence in the streets. Yet he used such rhetoric to promote policies that would help assure successful implementation of policies consistent with the conservative political ideology of limited government intervention in matters of state affairs.

In 1964, Goldwater said:

> Tonight there is violence in our streets, corruption in our highest offices, aimlessness among our youth, anxiety among our elderly ... Security from domestic violence, no less than from foreign aggression, is the most elementary form and fundamental purpose of any government, and a government that cannot fulfill this purpose is one that cannot command the loyalty of the citizens. History shows us that nothing paves the way for tyranny more than the failure of public officials to keep the streets safe from bullies and marauders. We Republicans seek a government that attends to its fiscal climate, encouraging a free and a competitive economy and enforcing law and order (printed in Beckett & Sasson, 2000: 50).

Rarely have we seen a clearer articulation of the conservative ideology — small government when it comes to economic issues and big government when it comes to dealing with street crime. And, as noted in Chapter 1, the "law and order" movement and statements about "crime in the streets" were efforts by politicians to equate legitimate complaints associated with unequal opportunity in society made by civil rights leaders as well as understandable dissent with crime.

In-Class Activity:
Pull up a video of Barry Goldwater on YouTube. Watch him talk about crime or liberty or the conservative ideology. Many short videos are available online. Then discuss how his ideas relate to the key concepts introduced in this book.

Also during this time, former Vice President Richard Nixon (who served with President Eisenhower and who would later become president himself) argued that "the deterioration of respect for the rule of law can be traced directly to the spread of the corrosive doctrine that every citizen possesses an inherent right to decide from himself which laws to obey and when to disobey them" (reported in Beckett & Sasson, 2000: 50). Given the major scandal of criminality that would later rock the Nixon White House in the form of Watergate, this is an ironic statement to be sure.

During this same time period, segregationist senators such as Sam Erwin, Strom Thurmond, and John McClellan helped push to restrict defendants' rights (i.e., due process) in order to get tougher on crime (i.e., crime control). According to Michelle Alexander, this was not housed in racial terms given that what passed as acceptable discourse had changed, so: "They developed instead the racially sanitized rhetoric of 'cracking down on crime'—rhetoric that is now used freely by politicians of every stripe to create and pursue policies that have their greatest impact on people of color" (p. 43).

Katherine Beckett (1997: 28) also claims that "the discourse of law and order was initially mobilized by southern officials in their effort to discredit the civil rights movement." Clearly, southern agencies of criminal justice—in particular law enforcement agencies—characterized and fought civil rights activities as acts of crime rather than as struggles for civil rights. Peaceful protests, sit-ins, marches, and similar methods of civil disobedience were characterized as evidence of disrespect for law and order rather than as struggles for basic human rights. This characterization permitted and even mandated government intervention against civil rights leaders and led to the characterization by the Federal Bureau of Investigation (FBI) of Martin Luther King, Jr., as the most dangerous man in America.

Out-of-Class Activity:
Listen to the story, "COINTELPRO and the History of Domestic Spying" on NPR: http://www.npr.org/templates/story/story.php?storyId=5161811. Then discuss to what degree it is appropriate to spy on US citizens in order to reduce crime.

Jonathan Simon (2007) suggests not only that "getting tough" through a conservative crime control model became the "correct" approach to reducing crime but also argues that our country has become literally obsessed with crime so that we are now being "governed through crime," a phenomenon he suggests started in 1968. That was the year that Congress passed the **Omnibus Crime Control and Safe Streets Act**, a law that provided more funding for police, increased the odds that confessions could be used in courts against defendants, empowered police to eavesdrop and wiretap without court approval under certain circumstances, and regulated gun sales and ownership in some cases. The bill, championed by President Lyndon Johnson, was part of his Great Society Program, as noted earlier. According to Simon (2007: 91):

> Johnson understood intuitively how dangerous violent crime was to the post-New Deal coalition he was seeking to reestablish. Barry Goldwater had invoked 'crime in the streets' in his campaign, and although LBJ succeeded in turning the campaign on Goldwater's own extremism, not Democratic permissiveness, he recognized presciently that crime was driving a stake through the heart of the Democrats' urban coalition even while leading liberal criminologists of the day continued to doubt the seriousness of the surge in armed robberies in the very largest cities.

Simon adds that serious street crime remained in the news at the time and notes:

> The apparent rise in violent street crime, primarily armed and unarmed robberies, was concentrated in the big cities that were the traditional anchors of the New Deal style of government. This kind of one-on-one crime linked the term 'violent' to the riots and antiwar protests that had become common for the first time in a century during the mid-1960s (p. 91).

As noted in Chapter 1, these riots and protests were associated mostly with blacks, the poor, and other powerless groups in society (as well as "liberal" college students). In this way, resulting criminal justice policies can be seen as efforts to restrain liberalism and protect status quo arrangements in society. Jerome Miller (2011: 64) agrees, writing that the Nixon presidential campaign later took the same approach as Goldwater before him, "linking riots and disorder associated with assassinations of Martin Luther King and Robert Kennedy to violent crime—all with a distinctly black face to it."

Although President Johnson could not really launch an all-out war on crime—in part due to Vietnam fatigue—he did consistently address crime "as a political problem of growing proportions to his liberal coalition" (Miller, 2011: 91). Jerome Miller explains: "With a war in full swing in Vietnam, there was little stomach for inflated rhetoric on a parallel war on crime. Wars on errant citizens would have to wait" (p. 81). Jonathan Simon explains that Johnson expressed solidarity with crime victims, embraced technical solutions to crime based in social science research (through the **Commission on Law Enforcement and Administration of Justice**), and worked to help start the creation of more efficient and effective criminal justice agencies (through the **Law Enforcement Assistance Agency**—LEAA). Because of LEAA, funding for law enforcement over other branches of criminal justice immediately became imbalanced in favor of police and corrections (Gest, 2001). In Chapter 1, it was suggested that this imbalance illustrates politicians' preference for crime control over due process.

As a result of governing through crime, "crime has now become a significant strategic issue. Across all kinds of institutional settings, people are seen as acting legitimately when they act to prevent crimes or other troubling behaviors that can be closely analogized to crimes." As a result, political leaders "deploy the category of crime to legitimate interventions that have other motivations." And "the technologies, discourses, and metaphors of crime and criminal justice have become more visible features of all kinds of institutions, where that can easily gravitate into new opportunities for governance" (Simon, 2007: 4–5).

Jonathan Simon thus suggests that our approach to dealing with crime has bled into other institutions in society; significantly weakened families and schools by diverting their attention to safety rather than love and education, respectively; and created a more hostile and fearful populace, especially toward people of color and the poor. He explains: "Governing through crime is making America less democratic and more racially polarized; it is exhausting our social capital and repressing our capacity for innovation ... it fuels a culture of fear and control that inevitably lowers the threshold of fear even as it places greater and greater burdens on ordinary Americans" (p. 6). Another result, according to Simon, is a less free country, with Americans sacrificing both civil liberties as well as much of their peace of mind. Further, American policy more broadly has shifted from a welfare state aimed at helping people in need to a penal state that punishes people for any transgression, no matter how small.

When Richard Nixon became President, he had the chance to nominate several Justices to the US Supreme Court, and Warren Burger, William Rehnquist, and Harry Blackmun (at least for the first ten years on the Court) proved reliable conservatives. They moved to erode and replace gains made for the rights of criminal defendants under the more liberal Court of Chief Justice Earl Warren (who provided over the Court through 1950s and 1960s). President Nixon saw advances for civil liberties by the Warren

Figure 2.1. Murders and Nonnegligent Homicides per 100,000 Inhabitants

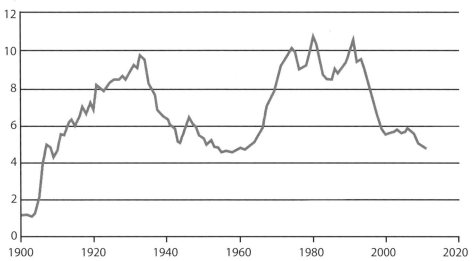

Source: http://www.americanthinker.com/articles/assets/Murders%201.bmp.
Used courtesy of Randy Mogoid.

Court as a threat to public safety. As it supposedly became harder for police to arrest and courts to convict suspects and defendants, respectively, politicians believed it would be harder to deter would-be offenders, thereby increasing crime. This is a good reminder of the tension between crime control and due process discussed in Chapter 1.

Yet Jerome Miller (2011: 80) claims it is a great myth that criminal justice in the 1960s and 1970s was overly permissive. Further, while it is generally agreed that crime did increase in the 1960s, such an increase had been witnessed in the US before—in the late 1920s and early 1930s. An examination of crime rates in Figure 2.1 shows, for example, that murder rose significantly during the 1920s and 1930s. One likely result of this increase in murder was the creation of the Uniform Crime Reporting system by the Federal Bureau of Investigation (FBI) for the purposes of tracking the most "serious" crimes in America. Before this could be done, of course, the government had to decide which crimes they thought were the most serious. The US government ultimately chose seven street crimes as **serious crime**—murder, rape, robbery, assault, theft, motor vehicle theft, and burglary. Many others, including those that actually pose the greatest harms to Americans, were not included. The implications of this decision for justice are discussed in Chapter 3.

So, the first rapid increase in crime in the US (1920s–1930s) led to the creation of an explicit list of serious crimes by the US government—crimes that are generally committed by people on the streets of America—which is why criminologists tend to refer to them as "street crime." This led to the explicit focus of all criminal justice agencies on these crimes, to the near exclusion of other harmful behaviors (more on this in Chapter 3)—this is the source of innocent bias illustrated in Chapter 1. And the second rapid increase in crime in the US (1960s) led to conservative dominance in politics and crime control policy. Even as America has witnessed episode after episode after episode of corporate crime committed with government complicity (more on this in Chapters

4 and 5, as well), there has been no similar focus on these crimes or a takeover of criminal justice policy by liberals. Combined, our focus on street crime and our conservative approach to criminal justice has produced results inconsistent with American ideals of crime control and due process, as will be shown in the book.

According to Jonathan Simon (2007: 53–54): "Much of Nixon's actual program on crime paralleled Johnson's goal of funding improvements in law enforcement, but he visibly moved closer to a prosecutorial role, advocating (even if not implementing) longer prison sentences, preventive detention for 'dangerous' offenders, and criminal code reform to strengthen prosecutorial power." With the help of his Attorney General John Mitchell, Nixon "helped turn the Kennedy-Johnson war on crime into a Vietnam-like conflict with federal funding and training of state and local police to fight the war" (p. 54).

All of this should be housed in the larger political context of trying to roll back gains for normal Americans that were part of the New Deal coalition of white southerners and urban minority groups that successfully controlled American politics from the 1930s to the early 1960s, as well as President Johnson's Great Society program which vastly expanded social welfare services to poor people and families who were disproportionately African Americans.

The progressive impulse of Democratic America would be severely obstructed by the Republican plan now referred to as the Southern Strategy. Stated simply, the **Southern Strategy** was a coordinated plan by Republican Party leaders to win back the South for the purposes of gaining power and eroding social welfare programs. According to Michelle Alexander (2012: 44):

> The success of law and order rhetoric among working-class whites and the intense resentment of racial reforms, particularly in the South, led conservative Republican analysts to believe that a 'new majority' could be created by the Republican Party, one that included the traditional Republican base, the white South, and half the Catholic, blue-collar vote of the big cities. Some conservative political strategists admitted that appealing to racial fears and antagonisms was central to this strategy, though it had to be done surreptitiously.

It was Richard Nixon that was behind the Southern Strategy, and his advisors and strategists later admitted that this plan was explicitly about subtly using race to encourage whites to vote Republican. Republican strategist Kevin Phillips, for example, wrote that a new Republican majority could be achieved if candidates ran on issues of race but using "coded antiblack rhetoric" (Alexander, 2012: 45). Earlier, Barry Goldwater used terms like "states' rights" to try "to appeal to white supremacist voters" (Tonry, 2011: 108).

The plan was to tap into white anger and alienation caused by the Democratic Party's embracing of civil rights. Characterizing crime as emanating from a dangerous black subculture that emerged out of an overgenerous federal government was part of the effort to convince whites to vote for the party that would put an end to disorder and (black) crime in the streets once and for all. Further, depicting the poor as lazy and undeserving was part of the effort to convince the working and middle classes to vote for the party that would supposedly protect the interests of the common man. So the Southern Strategy had both racial and social class elements to it.

Nixon denied that crime was caused by social forces such as poverty or unequal opportunity in society and instead insisted that "insufficient curbs on the appetites or impulses that naturally impel individuals towards criminal activities" were to blame (reported in Beckett & Sasson, 2000: 55). In fact, the official Republican Party platform at the time included words clearly stating that criminals are themselves solely responsible for bad behaviors. Consistent with the conservative view of crime, Kevin Stinson (1991: 5) adds that Nixon "promised to reverse the soft approach to crime control" promoted by "'bleeding-heart,' 'do-gooding' liberal Democratic administrations."

The Southern Strategy only worked because of how crime was framed in both racial and social class terms. According to Katherine Beckett & Theodore Sasson (2000: 10): "By emphasizing the severity and pervasiveness of 'street crime' and framing the problem in terms of immoral individuals rather than criminogenic social conditions, conservative politicians effectively redefined the poor—especially the minority poor—as dangerous and undeserving." This message was attractive to socially conservative voters who began identifying with the Republican Party and "legitimated (their) efforts to redirect state policy toward crime control rather than social welfare."

Nixon would make 17 speeches on law and order and would devote entire television commercials to the supposed disrespect of law and order by civil rights activists. So, according to Michelle Alexander (2012: 47): "Race had become, yet again, a powerful wedge, breaking up what had been a solid liberal coalition based on economic interests of the poor and the working and lower-middle classes." Looking forward several decades, where America leads the world in its rate of incarceration (see Figure 2.2), one realizes this may not have occurred without the Southern Strategy. Whether intended or not, Michelle Alexander (2011: 11) calls today's mass incarceration "the most damaging manifestation of the backlash against the Civil Rights Movement."

Whereas party identification was once framed around issues such as social class and a desire to take care of the least advantaged members of society, the 1968 election cycle saw race become "the organizing principle of American politics, and by 1972, attitudes on racial issues rather than socioeconomic status were the primary determinant of voters' self-identification" (Beckett & Sasson, 2003: 5). During this time, there was a "dramatic erosion in the belief among working-class whites that the condition of the poor, or those who fail to prosper, was the result of a faulty economic system that needed to be challenged" (Alexander, 2011: 46). Instead, the problem was lazy, good-for-nothing people of color.

An added bonus of refocusing the nation on race rather than class was that it would now be easier for politicians to dismantle social programs meant to help the poor. Even if crime went up as a result, the poor would be "handed an expensive gift—a new and improved criminal justice system," one that would supposedly most benefit the poor as well as people of color (e.g., by protecting them from street crime victimization). Jerome Miller (2011: 1) writes: "No expense was spared in crafting and delivering it inside the city gates. It proved to be a Trojan horse" because what happened is America shifted from a welfare state to a penal state, one that has its worst impacts on poor people of color.

Using race as such an effective political tool "had broken up the Democratic New Deal 'bottom up' coalition—a coalition dependent on substantial support from all

Figure 2.2. World Imprisonment Rates

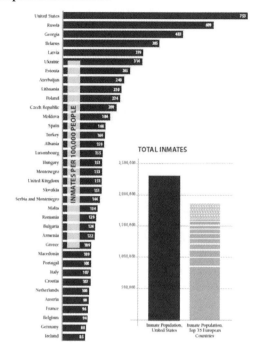

Source: International Centre for Prison Studies at King's College, London, "World Prison Brief," http://www.kcl.ac.uk/depsta/law/research/icps/worldbrief/wpb_stats.php.

voters, white and black, at or below the median income" (Alexander, 2011: 47). Similarly, Beckett & Sasson (2000: 57–58) write that the Southern Strategy:

> enabled the Republican Party to replace the New Deal cleavage between the 'haves' and the 'have-nots' with a new division between some (overwhelmingly White) working and middle class voters and the traditional Republican elite, on the one hand, and 'liberal elites' and the (disproportionately African American and Latino) poor on the other. As the traditional working class coalition that buttressed the Democratic party was ruptured along racial lines, race eclipsed class as the organizing principle of American politics.

Framing social problems like crime as problems of race rather than class would make it easier to develop and implement punitive responses to them, because as it turns out, there is a well-established relationship between racial resentment and hostility toward people of color and support for tough on crime legislation. This is true across numerous cultures and for the most severe sanctions (Unnever & Cullen, 2010).

Keep in mind that, to some degree, major Democratic Party politicians were also at least partially on board with the get tough on crime movement. For example, President Johnson, who signed major civil rights legislation and helped expand welfare, also established the Law Enforcement Assistance Administration (LEAA) to support local police organizations and created the **Bureau of Narcotics and Dangerous Drugs**, forerunner to the **Drug Enforcement Agency** (DEA, the lead federal agency in the nation's war on drugs). These organizations were part of Johnson's efforts to "arrest and reverse the trend toward lawlessness" (Beckett & Sasson, 2000: 54).

Katherine Beckett & Theodore Sasson (2000: 54) note: "These initiatives represented a shift away from the view that the most important crime-fighting weapons were civil rights legislation, **War on Poverty** programs, and other policies aimed at promoting inclusion and social reform." This did not mean these long-term efforts would be abandoned, only that they needed to be "balanced by the 'short-term' need for increased law enforcement and more efficient administration of justice." John Hagan (2010: 22–23) agrees that it was the campaign against Goldwater which led Johnson to include punitive responses to crime: "Johnson attempted to co-opt the law and order attack on his own presidency, which refused to disappear with Goldwater's defeat."

Yet, it was President Nixon who most shifted the nation's attention to a war-like crime control approach. For example, Nixon officially declared the war on drugs in 1971, calling drugs "public enemy number one," and created the DEA in 1973. Prior to this, Nixon spoke publicly about the dangers of drugs, like in 1968 at Disneyland when he said that drugs were "decimating a generation of Americans" (reported in Gest, 2001: 110) and in 1969 to Congress when he said drugs were a "serious national threat" in need of a national level agency to fight drugs. Nixon also "used the war on drugs to build a new political network, linking the highest levels of national government with local government through law enforcement. By investing federal money in local criminal justice agencies, Nixon was establishing links that bypassed the traditional structures of congressional representation and party machines" (Simon, 2007: 262). And politically, the war on drugs was such a success for Nixon that it allowed him to defeat George McGovern for a second term. Nixon advisor Egil Hrough asked: "Was [the war on drugs] a success from a political perspective?" And he answered: "Heck yes, it was a slam-dunk great success" (reported in Gest, 2001: 110).

In-Class Activity:
Pull up a video of Richard Nixon on YouTube. Watch him talk about drugs as the public enemy number one. Many short videos are available online. Then discuss how his ideas relate to the key concepts introduced in this book.

Ronald Reagan and George H.W. Bush (1981–1993)

Although the wars on crime and drugs never seemed to become major issues in the 1970s for Republican President Gerald Ford (likely because he took over after Nixon was embarrassed by the major criminal scandal of Watergate) or Democratic President Jimmy Carter (who actually favored decriminalizing marijuana), Republican Presidents Ronald Reagan and George H. W. Bush stepped up the wars on crime and drugs like never seen before. For example, Reagan criticized his predecessor, Jimmy Carter, as being "soft on drugs" (Gest, 2001: 113).

Figure 2.3. Nancy Reagan and "Just Say No"

Courtesy of the Ronald Reagan Library.

Ronald Reagan re-launched the drug war in the mid-1980s, creating a resurgence of media coverage and leading Americans to become very concerned about illegal drugs, even as only a tiny fraction of people were actually abusing them (Robinson & Scherlen, 2013). In 1985, first lady Nancy Reagan also started the "Just Say No" campaign. She appeared on television promoting personal responsibility and denouncing drug use. Her simple message, directed to children and spoken both on TV and on radio, as well as in print in popular magazines, on tee shirts, buttons and bumper stickers, was "Just Say No" (see Figure 2.3). Of course, the message of "Just Say No" to drugs did not apply to the most harmful drugs of tobacco or alcohol or prescription drugs—all produced and marketed by large corporations—which tend to be empowered by conservative politicians.

President Reagan also refocused the nation's attention on "crime in the streets" while simultaneously urging federal law enforcement agencies to not focus on white-collar and corporate crime in favor of street crime enforcement. John Hagan (2010) analyzed the era of Ronald Reagan and clearly demonstrated that President Reagan simultaneously stepped up enforcement of street crime while he successfully deregulated the financial industry, thereby assuring that acts of white-collar and corporate crime would increase. **Deregulation** refers to "a policy of reducing or eliminating regulatory restraints on the conduct of individuals or private institutions" (Ginsberg et al., 2013: 664). In other words, deregulation amounts to a reduction in the role of government in business, and is highly favored by political conservatives.

According to Benjamin Ginsberg, Theodore Lowi, Margaret Weir, & Caroline Tolbert (2013: 664): "President Reagan went about the task of changing the direction of regulation by way of 'presidential oversight.' Shortly after taking office, he gave the OMB [Office of Management and Budget] authority to review all executive branch proposals for new regulations. By this means, Reagan reduced the total number of regulations issued by federal agencies. Without proper regulations on corporations, they would be freer to engage in deviant acts as part of their profit-seeking ventures, putting American dollars as well as lives at risk" (Robinson & Murphy, 2009). Meanwhile, the nation's attention would be placed squarely on street crime, causing fear of behaviors that are less likely to harm us while ignoring those that are most likely to harm us (this issue is revisited in Chapters 4 and 5). Hagan (2010: 137–138) puts it this way:

> The policies of the age of Reagan may have led Americans to fear both too much and too little. On the one hand, the Reagan Administration pursued stricter drug policies and sentencing laws in response to a crack cocaine epidemic that it failed to avert or contain. It failed by allowing a surge in the flow of cocaine into the United States. The Reagan administration responded to its failed interdiction mission with a fear-driven trajectory of mass incarceration focused on the drug abuse of young minority males.

So, on the one hand, Americans became afraid of drugs and street crime. Hagan continues:

> At the same time, the Reagan administration deregulated investment and financial services, freeing these institutions to indiscriminately alter lending practices, resulting in large losses that were passed on to taxpayers and compensated with government bailouts. These programs and practices disproportionately victimized the minority working poor as well as others by facilitating the unfettered expansion of an unregulated and undercapitalized financial sector. This model was further abetted by a reckless "too large to fail" policy of corporate immunity providing a nearly fail-proof freedom for many financial institutions to expand risks that led to massive losses.

Thus, on the other hand, Reagan's policies at the very least permitted widespread fraud on Wall Street, and Americans were not only *not* made to fear this move (which would later lead to several huge corporate crime scandals from the 1980s through the early 2000s as well as the near collapse of the entire US economy in 2008), but they largely celebrated freeing up businesses to make greater profits and would ideally benefit all Americans.

Not only did President Reagan reduce regulations on business, he also reduced the number of specialists working on white-collar crime while ramping up the war on drugs (Beckett & Sasson, 2000). Yet, according to Ted Gest, "the main issue of the 1980s did not revolve around spending more money and enlarging local police forces. Rather, a broad conservative thrust to turn the criminal law to the right ended up crystallizing into a highly debatable campaign to extend prison terms, especially for drug-law

Figure 2.4. State Prison Population by Offense Type, 1980–2006

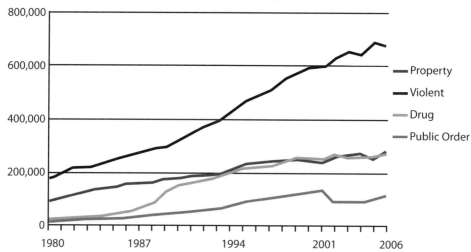

Source: Bureau of Justice Statistics.

violations" (p. 41). So it was in the 1980s that imprisonment started being used for even relatively harmless non-violent offenders (see Figure 2.4). This would ultimately impose and enormous financial burden on taxpayers as prisons and jails would become over-crowded.

President Reagan's attorney general, William French Smith, appointed a task force on violent crime. Its recommendations were to increase the role of the federal government in many kinds of crime (Gest, 2001), which is ironic given the supposed positive conservative view of states' rights and a smaller federal government. Yet, as explained by Ted Gest:

> The Republicans who dominated the Reagan panel did not call for a massive infusion of federal funds—with one glaring exception: $2 billion to help states build prisons. The GOP favored more incarceration, but party leaders were ever more emphatic about not spending federal tax dollars to help states do the job. So the prison plan went nowhere during Reagan's presidency. (States expanded their prison populations without help from Washington; a much larger version of federal support for prison construction ended up in the big federal anticrime law of 1994) (p. 44).

That law was supported by Republicans and Democrats (including then Senator and now Vice President Joe Biden), and signed into law by Democratic president Bill Clinton.

While turning the nation back to the approaches designed and initiated in the 1960s, President Reagan was explicitly motivated to do so by his conservative ideology. He said, for example: "Here in the richest nation in the world, where more crime is committed than in any other nation, we are told that the answer to this problem is to reduce our poverty. This isn't the answer … Government's function is to protect society from the criminal, not the other way around." He even stated that Americans had "lost patience with liberal leniency and pseudointellectual apologies for crime" and asserted: "Choosing a career in crime is not the result of poverty or of an unhappy childhood or of a misunderstood adolescence; it is the result of a conscious, willful choice made by some who consider themselves above the law, who seek to exploit the hard work and, sometimes, the very lives of their fellow citizens" (printed in Beckett & Sasson, 2000: 61). Again, it is impossible not to note the irony of the assertion of personal responsibility and free will coming from a President who himself was later implicated in serious wrongdoing in the Iran Contra scandal.

Still, President Reagan explained how criminal justice was necessary to deter bad behavior by people who make rational choices:

> The crime epidemic threat has spread throughout our country, and it's no uncontrollable disease, much less and irreversible ride. Nor is it some inevitable sociological phenomenon ... It is ... in large measure, a cumulative result of too much emphasis on the protection of the rights of the accused and too little concern for our government's responsibility to protect the lives, homes, and rights of out law-abiding citizens ... the criminal element now calculates that crime really does pay (reported in Beckett & Sasson, 2000: 61–62).

Such statements by our political leaders help explain the shift toward a crime control model of criminal justice over a due process model, with increased emphasis on fighting street crime and reduced emphasis on the due process rights of Americans.

In-Class Activity:
Pull up a video of Ronald Reagan on YouTube. Watch him talk about crime or poverty or conservativism. Many short videos are available online. Then discuss how his ideas relate to the key concepts introduced in this book.

President Reagan also literally blamed government for poverty, saying that government welfare programs amounted to "crippling poverty trap(s)" that destroy families and condemn generations to dependency on the government. Reagan also described a fictional "welfare queen" to help turn public opinion away from helping the less fortunate: "There's a woman in Chicago," Reagan said. "She has 80 names, 30 addresses, 12 Social Security cards.... She's got Medicaid, getting food stamps and she is collecting welfare under each of her names. Her tax-free cash income alone is over $150,000." The story was not true, and Reagan never mentioned race, but, according to John Hinshaw: "The Welfare Queen driving a pink Cadillac to cash her welfare checks at the liquor store fits a narrative that many white, working-class Americans had about inner-city blacks. It doesn't matter if the story was fabricated, it fit the narrative, and so it felt true, and it didn't need to be verified" (reported in Blake, 2012).

Such statements about crime and welfare exemplify the conservative view of government, as did Reagan's stance on drugs. Reagan said that "one of the best things

Figure 2.5. Four Measures of Serious Violent Crime

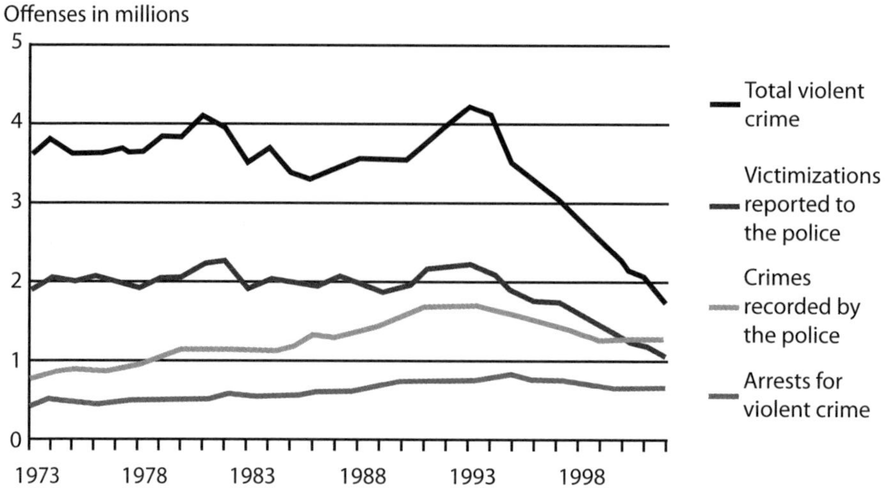

Source: http://www.4uth.gov.ua/usa/english/trade/whstats/crime1.htm.

we can do for families is obliterate drug use in America" and thus it was necessary to practice intolerance to drugs and to use tough and swift criminal punishments to deter drug use (quoted in Beckett & Sasson, 2000: 62).

Though President Reagan did not mention race, Michelle Alexander (2012: 205) illustrates how race was (and is) instrumental to the drug war:

> The War on Drugs was declared as part of a political ploy to capitalize on white resentment against African Americans, and the Reagan administration used the emergence of crack and its related violence as an opportunity to build a racialized public consensus in support of an all-out war—a consensus that almost certainly would not have been formed if the primary users and dealers of crack had been white.

Jerome Miller (2011: 28) agrees, writing that Reagan (as well as Clinton) refocused the nation on urban violence, and that focus was "implicit, if not blatant [on] youthful black male offenders" who also tended to be universally poor. Supposedly callous and amoral, young offenders would come to be known in the mainstream media as "superpredators" and crime in the US was expected to increase in society as their numbers increased; ultimately this did *not* occur as serious violent crime begin to decline in the 1990s (Robinson, 2013), as shown in Figure 2.5.

Ronald Reagan's "tough on crime" stance actually goes as far back as the 1960s when, as candidate for Governor of California in the 1960s, he defeated incumbent Pat Brown in part because Brown had taken a moral stance against the death penalty (even though he continued to enforce the state's death penalty statute). As noted by Jonathan Simon (2007: 56): "Against the background of the nation's rising homicide rate, Reagan modeled what would become a familiar circuit in suggesting that Brown's moral calculus represented a choice to identify with the killer rather than his victim." Reagan and his staffers also attacked the "liberal" US Supreme Court who had expanded defendants' rights under the US Constitution under Chief Justice Earl Warren, as noted earlier. This was a clear attack on due process, supposedly an American virtue.

Such rhetoric clearly demonstrates how candidates for major political office at the state and federal levels of government use issues of crime and criminal justice to achieve office, empowering them to implement policies driven by their conservative ideology. Beliefs about race and class were, and are, part of this ideology. Simply stated, the conservative ideology views poor people of color not only as dangerous but also as completely responsible for their behaviors as well as for the conditions of poverty and despair in which they reside.

Probably the most well-known use of a crime as a political issue was seen in the "Willie Horton" charges made against Democratic presidential hopeful Michael Dukakis by future Republican president George H.W. Bush in 1988. Bush, who had of course been Reagan's Vice President, ran a campaign that "for the first time, [made] ... the war on crime ... a primary basis for choosing a president" (Simon, 2007: 57). As governor of Massachusetts, Dukakis had supported early release programs from prison as a means to reduce prison overcrowding and as a low-risk way to reintegrate offenders into the community through meaningful employment. An inmate from Massachusetts named Willie Horton, on his tenth furlough from prison, committed a brutal rape and assault.

This incident led Bush to attack Dukakis as "soft on crime"; Bush assured citizens that if he was elected president, he would continue to expand criminal justice powers to fight crime. Bush campaign strategists masterfully created a television commercial frequently referred to as "Weekend Passes" that showed Horton's face—a black man— with a voiceover that described Horton's crimes committed against a white man and his wife. This is what the voiceover said:

> Bush and Dukakis on crime. Bush supports the death penalty for first-degree murderers. Dukakis not only opposes the death penalty, he allowed first-degree murderers to have weekend passes from prison. One was Willie Horton, who murdered a boy in a robbery, stabbing him 19 times. Despite a life sentence, Horton received 10 weekend passes from prison. Horton fled, kidnapped a young couple, stabbing the man and repeatedly raping his girlfriend. Weekend prison passes. Dukakis on Crime.

In-Class Activity:
Pull up a video of the Willie Horton ad on YouTube. Then discuss why you think this ad was so effective. Also discuss whether you think this ad was racist in nature.

Even though the "Horton case was atypical and exaggerated," it worked: support for Dukakis plunged and Bush was successfully elected president of the United States (Merlo & Benekos, 2000: 14). Alida Merlo & Peter Benekos (2000: 14–16) claim that the Willie Horton incident taught all politicians some important lessons about winning and losing:

- Don't be portrayed as being "soft on crime";
- Portray your opponent as "soft on crime";
- Simplify the crime issue; and
- Reinforce messages with emotional context.

According to Jerome Miller (2011: 67), "The Willie Horton ad was so successful in the Bush-Dukakis campaign that Bush's campaign manager, Lee Atwater, facetiously proposed nominating Willie Horton as Dukakis' running mate." In fairness to the Republicans behind the ad, it was actually Democratic rival Al Gore who first raised the Horton issue! This is a good reminder that prominent Democrats share responsibility for the politicization of crime.

Another ad, titled "Revolving door," shows convicts walking in and out of a revolving door outside of a prison. The voiceover in this ad said:

> As governor, Michael Dukakis vetoed mandatory sentences for drug dealers. He vetoed the death penalty. His revolving door prison policy gave weekend furloughs to first-degree murderers not eligible for parole [the words "268 Escaped" were superimposed on the screen]. While out, many committed other crimes like kidnapping and rape. And many are still at large. Michael Dukakis says he wants to do for America what he's done for Massachusetts. America can't afford that risk!

This ad had the largest impact on viewers and voters according to studies. For example, viewers picked this as the most influential of Bush's ads, and those who saw it were more than twice as likely as those who did not see it to say that crime was a major problem facing the country. Further, the percentage of people seeing Bush as tough on crime tripled and the percentage who saw Dukakis as not tough enough on crime increased significantly (Inside Politics, 2013).

What was the significance of race in these ads? Susan Estrich, campaign manager for Michael Dukakis, noted: "The symbolism was very powerful ... You can't find a stronger metaphor, intended or not, for racial hatred in this country than a black man raping a white woman.... I talked to people afterward.... Women said they couldn't help it, but it scared the living daylights out of them" (Inside Politics, 2013). In fact, women were more impacted by these ads than men and became more likely than men to thus see crime as a national issue. And of course, Willie Horton was also undoubtedly poor, as he had been incarcerated for years and thus was unable to earn income through work.

Dukakis did not help himself during one of the presidential debates, when he was asked by CNN's Bernard Shaw if he *would* support the death penalty for a man if he raped and murdered his wife, Kitty. Dukakis did not answer whether he *would* in such a case support a death sentence, but instead answered that he did not support the death penalty in general. He replied: "No, I *don't*, Bernard, and I think you know that I've opposed the death penalty during all of my life. I don't see any evidence that it's a deterrent and I think there are better and more effective ways to deal with violent crime" (Stephey, 2013).

Dukakis, of course, lost the election to Bush, becoming yet another governor from a state without the death penalty to *not* become President. Jonathan Simon (2007: 69) notes that "no governor from a state that has outlawed executions was elected president" during the "tough on crime" period that started in the 1960s and continues today. This is pretty clear evidence of the role that crime and criminal justice play in political races.

According to Jonathan Simon (2007: 58), when President Bush gave his acceptance speech in 1988, it was hinted that "crime was not just another social problem, but rather a metaphor around which a whole range of popular needs might be expressed, a metaphor whose crucial entailment was punishment and a punitive state." Further, he used the language of crime to speak about another issue about which conservatives care greatly—inflation:

> There are millions of older Americans who were brutalized by inflation. We arrested it—and we're not going to let it out on furlough. We're going to keep the Social Security trust fund sound and out of reach of the big spenders. To America's elderly I say: 'Once again you have the security that is your right—and I'm not going to let them take it away from you' (reported in Simon, 2007: 58).

That President Bush (see Figure 2.6) used terms like "arrest" and "furlough" when discussing inflation is clear evidence of the use of criminal justice terminology to address totally unrelated economic issues. Yet, like President Reagan before him, President Bush focused only on street crime while ignoring white-collar and corporate crimes. This is consistent with the conservative ideology which favors corporations above even their workers and consumers.

President Bush also made drugs a major priority during his presidential administration, even as drug use was apparently declining during the time. For example, Bush gave a nationally televised speech in 1989 to re-focus the nation's attention on crack cocaine. He held a bag of cocaine to the TV camera, supposedly purchased near the White House, in order to convince Americans that the drug was everywhere, even just outside the White House! Incredibly, the whole thing was a ruse! As explained by Ted Gest (2001): 124):

> To capture viewers' attention, Bush focused on a crack arrest in Lafayette Park, across from the White House. The president displayed a plastic package marked 'evidence' that had been seized in a 'sting' involving a 19-year-old dealer who had been lured to the site by undercover agents, supposedly against the orders of White House aides who had merely wanted to borrow some cocaine so that television viewers could see what it looked like.

Stephen Duke & Albert Gross (1993: xv) add that the young man "needed travel directions from his sham 'customers' to enable him to find the White House" allowing President Bush "to suggest that drugs were being deal virtually on [his] steps … and thus that the country was in grave peril."

Bush also moved for longer prison sentences for drug dealers and even death sentences for "drug kingpins" convicted of murder. Further, he reminded Americans that: "We must show less compassion for the criminal and more for the victims of crime" (reported in Miller, 2011: 76), another swipe at due process in America. Further, after taking office in 1988, President Bush organized a study of violent crime that made 24 recommendations. The 25th recommendation reportedly dealt with **community policing**, but was removed because it sounded "too liberal," "soft on crime," and "too much like

Figure 2.6. President George H. W. Bush

360b / Shutterstock.com

social work" (Gest, 2001: 168). Interestingly, Bush appeared frequently with police officers on stages when running for office against Michael Dukakis (Bill Clinton would do that same later when he went on to defeat George Bush for the presidency).

In the 1980s, Republican presidents Reagan and Bush (the first) not only stepped up the nation's wars on drugs and crime but also wanted more efficient, tougher criminal justice agencies (in line with a crime control model) and helped shift the perception of the causes of crime from society to the individual. Ted Gest (2001: 41) describes this period as the "get tough 1980s." Gest's insider account of federal criminal justice legislation concluded:

> The get tough theme permeated anticrime policy in the 1980s. Whether it was Washington's extended reach in drug control, the rise of the victim-rights movement, or the spread of sentencing guidelines, it seemed that a policy could survive only if it could be portrayed as more punitive. The flurry of major federal anticrime laws during the decade reflected a drive to federalize criminal law that gained strength relentlessly as crime dominated the national agenda (p. 62).

Bill Clinton and George W. Bush (1993–2009)

In each election since Bush (the first) and Dukakis, it has been hard to tell Republicans apart from Democrats on crime control issues, because both have supported more police, more power for prosecutors, more prisons, more money for the war on drugs, more executions, limiting appeals for death row inmates, and so forth (Beckett, 1997; Gest, 2001; Marion, 1995; Oliver, 2003). As noted by Steven Donzinger (1996: 13): "Since 1968, six major anti-crime bills have passed Congress and been signed into law by presidents. In one way or another, all of these bills have been used by elected officials to convince the public that Washington was getting 'tough' on crime by increasing sentences for certain types of offenses."

So, for example, under Democratic president Bill Clinton in the 1990s—who would successfully end 12 consecutive years of Republican rule of the White House—the focus was heavily on crime control, including more police on the streets and tougher sentences for convicted criminals. As Governor of Arkansas and candidate for president, Clinton made it clear that he supported more police and prisons. And the Democratic Party platform in 1992 stated: "The simplest and most direct way to restore order in our cities is to put more police on the streets" (reported in Platt, 1994).

Recall that then Senator Joe Biden was the prominent Democrat pressing for tougher crime control policies. He reportedly said: "Give me the crime issue, and you'll never have trouble with it in an election," an obvious admission of the role of politics in criminal justice policy (reported in Gest, 2001: 45). He also reportedly stated that "the Republicans always would take the least important but more controversial aspect of crime control—like the death penalty or the *Miranda*[1] ruling—and beat us about the head with it." He followed that up with, "If you do it my way, it will be the last time that Republicans will be able to run at the Democrats for being soft on crime" (reported in Gest, 2001: 224). And it was Biden, now Vice President, who originally proposed a **drug czar**, an executive level position eventually created in 1988 as Director of the Office of National Drug Control Policy (President Reagan actually vetoed a crime bill in 1983 that tried to create such a position).

As a presidential candidate, Bill Clinton was governor of a southern state with an active death penalty. Jonathan Simon gives the example of how Clinton interrupted his campaign for president in New Hampshire to oversee the execution in Arkansas of a mentally impaired man, Ricky Ray Rector. Rector, a black man, was executed in 1992 for the 1981 killing of a white police officer. The officer, Robert Martin, was known to Rector and had come to his house to negotiate a surrender of Rector for the murder of a different man. Either accidentally or on purpose after killing Martin, Rector shot himself in the head, resulting in serious brain damage and mental retardation. Rector was convicted, sentenced to death, and ultimately executed for his crime.

Rector was so impaired that, for his last meal before his execution, he asked for his slice of pecan pie to be saved until *after* his execution. Today, such an execution would likely be illegal for the US Supreme Court has ruled it unconstitutional to execute a

---

1. *Miranda* refers to the US Supreme Court case, *Miranda v. Arizona* 384 U.S. 436 (1966), which requires that for statements made by suspects to be admissible in courts, suspects must first be informed of their right to remain silent.

Figure 2.7. Public Concern over Violent Crime

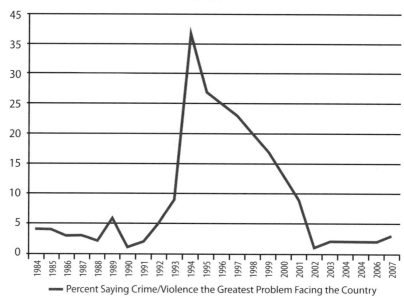

Source of data: http://www.albany.edu/sourcebook/pdf/t212008.pdf.

mentally impaired person under certain circumstances,[2] but in 1992 it was legal and Bill Clinton oversaw the execution likely as a political ploy to convince voters that he was very tough on crime.

While campaigning for president, Bill Clinton also said: "We ought to have 100,000 more police officers on the street ... Thirty years ago there were three police officers in this country for every serious crime. Today there are three serious crimes for every police officer" (reported in Gest, 2001: 171). It is probably obvious the political ramifications of such statements, for who would likely oppose such a plan, especially during a time when public concern over violent crime was peaking in the US due to intense media coverage of several sensational killings (see Figure 2.7)? As explained by Ted Gest (2001: 178): "Most members of Congress realized that adding local police officers during a time of public concern about crime could only be a political winner."

To this day, former President Clinton talks about having put 100,000 more police officers on the streets of America. Yet, while the 1994 crime bill provided all that additional funding for police, never did agencies actually hire 100,000 more police officers, but instead used the money for additional purposes such as technology and training (Walker, 2011).

Bill Clinton's 1994 crime bill allocated $13.8 billion for law enforcement, $9.8 billion in state prison grants, and only $6.9 billion for crime prevention (much of which was removed in 1996 when Republicans took control of the US House of Representatives as part of Rep. Newt Gingrich's "Contract with America"). In fact, the bill, pushed

---

2. The US Supreme Court ruling in *Atkins v Virginia* 536 U.S. 304 (2002) held that executing people with mental retardation is cruel and unusual punishment, in violation of the Eighth Amendment to the Constitution.

through Congress by then Senator and now Vice President Joe Biden, led to "the largest increases in federal and state prison inmates of any President in American history" (Justice Policy Institute, 2008). Further, the law

> created dozens of new federal capital crimes, mandated life sentence for some three-tier offenders, restricted the scope of court-ordered settlements in lawsuits seeking improved prison conditions, limited inmates' rights to sue over these issues, expanded federal prosecutors' capacity to use illegally obtained evidence, restricted prisoners' ability of file habeas corpus petitions, and strengthened measures to provide for the swift deportation of illegal aliens (Beckett & Sasson, 2000: 72).

So, President Clinton was succeeding politically on crime control issues the same way his predecessors had done in the 1980s. In the 1980s and 1990s, significant increases occurred in incarceration rates, and both parties sold being "tough" on crime to the masses (Merlo & Benekos, 2000).

Yet, it should be pointed out that the Democratic bill came one week later than the Republican plan in Congress, which also called for greater spending on law enforcement, prisons construction in states willing to adopt "truth-in-sentencing" laws (requiring inmates to serve at least 85% of their prison terms prior to release), as well as tougher punishment generally through measures such as mandatory sentencing and limiting death penalty appeals at the federal level. So this can be seen as a competition between Democrats and Republicans to be the toughest on crime.

In terms of drugs, Clinton expanded the nation's drug war, and he appointed an Army General to lead the Office of National Drug Control Policy (i.e., the Drug Czar's Office), and funding for treatment and prevention continued to lag behind funding for war-like measures of interdiction, eradication, and crime-fighting. Clinton had been criticized by Republicans for earlier cutting funding and staff of the Office of National Drug Control Policy in the early years of his presidency, but his appointment of General Barry McCaffrey to step up the drug war in 1996 showed he was in fact willing to vigorously pursue drugs. Interestingly, candidate Clinton famously admitted to having tried marijuana as a 22-year-old in a foreign country, saying: "I've never broken a state law. But when I was in England I experimented with marijuana a time or two, and I didn't like it. I didn't inhale it, and never tried it again" (reported in Ifill, 1992).

In spite of his own drug use, the drug war marched on and expanded under President Clinton. And in spite of ramping up the drug war, he criticized President Bush's drug war policy, saying things like: "Bush confused being tough with being smart, especially on drugs. He thinks locking up addicts instead of treating them before the commit crimes … is clever politics. That may be, but it certainly isn't sound policy, and the consequences of his cravenness could ruin us" (quoted in Beckett & Sasson, 2000: 70).

Although to this day, many Americans still see Bill Clinton as a liberal president, he in fact was quite moderate, even conservative, when it came to criminal justice policy as well as welfare reform. For example, Clinton signed into law the **Personal Responsibility and Work Opportunity Reconciliation Act**, limiting the amount of time people can receive welfare in consecutive years to two as well as placing a lifetime limit of five years that a person can receive federal benefits. Clinton also approved replacing **Aid to Families with Dependent Children (AFDC)** with **Temporary Assistance to Needy Families**

(TANF), a block grant program to states whereby assistance is determined by means testing, "a procedure that requires applicants to show a financial need for assistance" (Ginsberg et al., 2013). Finally, Clinton cut funding for public housing $17 billion while increasing spending on corrections $19 billion. All of this is consistent with the conservative ideology.

If there is any difference between Democrat Clinton and his Republican predecessors, it is that Clinton was able to still speak to and about the poor and disaffected, reminding us of their plight. Here is one example:

> We have to rebuild families and communities in this country. We've got to take more responsibility for these little kids before they grow up and start shooting each other. I know the budget is tight, but I'm telling you, we have to deal with family, community and education, and find jobs for members of society's underclass to bring structure to their lives (reported in Beckett & Sasson, 2000: 70).

This type of statement has not been recently uttered by a Republican, who instead insist as part of the conservative ideology that criminals are totally responsible for their own behavior and that government has no interest or responsibility for helping children in order to reduce the likelihood that they will grow up to be hardened criminals. Yet, in spite of such rhetoric, Clinton's criminal justice policies were no different than his Republican predecessors.

In the 2000 presidential debates between Republican nominee George W. Bush (the second) and Democratic nominee Al Gore—Vice President for Bill Clinton—both candidates had trouble separating themselves when it came to crime control policy preferences. When asked if he supported capital punishment, Bush —who was governor of Texas and oversaw more than 150 executions — said yes, "I believe it saves lives ... I'm proud that violent crime is down in the state of Texas." Similarly, Al Gore answered yes, "I think it is a deterrence (sic) ... I know that's a controversial view but I do think it's a deterrence (sic)." In a follow-up about whether they thought capital punishment is a deterrent, Bush replied: "I do, it's the only reason to be for it ... I don't think you should support the death penalty to seek revenge. I don't think that's right." Gore agreed, saying: "Yes. If it was not, there would be no reason to support it."

Such answers indicate how similar the positions of both candidates (one Republican, the other Democrat) were on the issue of capital punishment. Voters thus had the choice of a tough on crime Republican who supported the death penalty because he thought it was a deterrent or a tough on crime Democrat who supported the death penalty because he thought it was a deterrent. And it would be the closest presidential election in contemporary American history.

Of course, the answers of Bush and Gore could have simply been political—aimed at satisfying the public—because the available scientific evidence at the time, as well as since, suggests that the death penalty is not a deterrent. Nearly every study ever conducted has failed to find evidence of a deterrent effect of capital punishment (Robinson, 2009).

Interestingly, after being selected president, crime did not become a serious issue for George W. Bush. Instead, the presidency of George W. Bush will most be known for two major things: 1) huge tax cuts and a major economic collapse; and 2) the terrorist attacks of September 1, 2001, and America's response in the form of wars in Afghanistan and Iraq, as well as a broader war on terrorism.

First, President Bush signed into law two major tax cuts (which were meant to last only ten years but were actually extended by President Obama). According to Benjamin Ginsberg and his colleagues (2013: 224), these "tax cuts signed into law by George W. Bush in 2001, and extended by President Obama in 2010, provided a substantial tax break mainly for the top 1 percent of the nation's wage earners." Income inequality— the gap between the rich and the poor—thus grew in the United States during Bush's two terms in office. A major economic collapse would follow in 2008, in spite of the conservative rhetoric about how tax cuts and deregulation of business would generate economic growth (this collapse was caused by unethical and illegal behaviors of elites, and will be examined in Chapter 4).

Second, in October 2001, the Bush administration launched an attack on al-Qaeda in Afghanistan and the US remains there as of this writing, making the war the longest in US history. This invasion was understandable to most after the terrorist attacks of September 11, 2011 and was supported by countries around the world. Yet, in March 2003, the US also invaded Iraq, a country that had literally nothing to do with the 9/11 attacks. So this war was only supported by a handful of countries around the world and remains, to this day, a highly controversial subject in American politics (Bamford, 2005; Wright, 2007).

America's new obsession with terrorism after 9/11 meant that to some degree, *crime* took a back seat in terms of importance during the Bush administration. Public opinion polls showed that the things Americans used to worry about (e.g., school shootings and child abductions) were far less worrisome than terrorism. Congress, as well as President Bush, also took numerous steps domestically, that parallel America's approach to fighting crime.

For example, in the wake of 9/11, Congress quickly passed the USA PATRIOT Act and later created the **Department of Homeland Security**. It then passed the **Military Tribunals Act**, a law that allows the use of hearsay evidence and evidence obtained by coercion in military trials, and it excuses any abuses committed by US military officials in the war on terror. Further, President Bush authorized the indefinite detention of even American citizens as "enemy combatants" without criminal charges (Congress also passed the Military Commission Act of 2006 to give the President this authority). President Bush authorized—by executive order —a domestic spying program under the direction of the National Security Agency that tapped the phones and monitored the computer usage (i.e., email) of American citizens for the purpose of disrupting terrorist plots. Critics of the program claimed it violated American citizens' rights to privacy, as well as federal law. Lawsuits challenged the program, but the program was ultimately approved by Congress after the fact (Cole, 2009; Cole & Dempsey, 2006), and his successor (President Obama) pledged to look forward rather than backward.

The **USA PATRIOT Act** (an acronym for Uniting and Strengthening America by Providing Appropriate Tools Required to Intercept and Obstruct Terrorism) was signed into law with almost no debate on October 24, 2001 (only 45 days after the 9/11 attacks). The bill was 342 pages long, yet many members of Congress say they did not even read it before voting in favor of it.

The stated purpose of the law was: "To deter and punish terrorist acts in the United States and around the world, to enhance law enforcement investigatory tools, and for other purposes," but the majority of the time the law has been used against American citizens for non-terror related crimes. Legal experts have suggested that the law erodes elements of the First, Fourth, Fifth, Sixth, and Eighth Amendments to the US Constitution, because it is possible for the government to use its unlimited authority to spy on American citizens without any evidence of criminal activity, to do so in secret, without judicial oversight, and without any accountability to the American people. Perhaps this is why, at the time of this writing, more than four hundred towns and counties and eight states have passed resolutions against this law. The cities which passed resolutions include New York City and Washington DC, which witnessed the worst of the terrorist attacks on 9/11. Together, these "civil liberties safe zones" represent more than 85 million Americans. Other bodies, such as the National League of Cities, which represents 18,000 cities, towns, villages and 225 million citizens, also passed resolutions (Robinson, 2007).

These anti-terrorism laws and practices swung the pendulum farther toward a crime control model of criminal justice by eroding the Constitutional protections of Americans in order to make it easier for police, courts, and corrections (as well as the military and intelligence agencies) to investigate, arrest, detain, convict, and punish alleged terrorists.

President Bush also authorized **enhanced interrogation** techniques — which some referred to as torture in violation of federal and international law — and instituted targeted assassination of enemies using drones (Cole, 2009). The next President, Barack Obama, would continue (and step up) the latter program, while explicitly discontinuing the former.

In terms of criminal justice policy, President Bush continued the same crime control policies of his predecessors, but he did it with the words of a "compassionate conservative." For example, an analysis of his drug war policies shows that Bush urged people to seek treatment for drug abuse problems and sought to increase funding for that part of national drug control policy, even though about two-thirds of funding was allocated to the most war-like elements of the policy (Robinson & Scherlen, 2013). Some forms of drug use by young people declined during this time, while other (more dangerous) forms of drug use increased.

Meanwhile, major corporate crimes made the headlines during the early years of the Bush Administration. Giant corporations such as Enron, Tyco, WorldCom, and so many more, were charged with various forms of fraud that led to hundreds of billions of dollars in losses (Cullen, Cavender, Maakestad & Benson, 2006; Eichenwald, 2005; Friedrichs, 2006; McClean & Elkind, 2003; Rosoff, Pontell & Tillman, 2006; Schwartz & Watkins, 2004; Simon, 2006). Details of these crimes will be addressed in Chapter 4.

These crimes would not have been possible without the deregulation of the Reagan administration. Nor would have the near collapse of the US economy that emerged in 2008 occurred without it. Widespread fraud on Wall Street and in the banking industry cost Americans trillions of dollars in losses starting in 2008. Not only was no one punished for these crimes, Congress acted to force American taxpayers to bail out the companies that created the losses under the premise that the companies were "too big to fail" (McClean & Nocera, 2010). These crimes are also addressed in Chapter 4. The fact that people are not punished for these crimes, while millions of common street criminals are incarcerated every year is evidence of a serious source of bias in the US criminal justice system, a bias referred to in the preface of this book as "innocent bias"— biased created by the criminal law and thus not intended by individual actors in police, courts, and corrections.

Barack Obama (2009–present)

Has anything changed under President Obama? Obama, viewed as a liberal to some, is actually quite conservative when it comes to his crime control policies as well as the continuing war on terror. For example, President Obama has actually increased the number of drone strikes in Afghanistan and Pakistan (and of course authorized the team and plan that led to the death of Usama bin Laden) (Klaidman, 2012). Obama also signed the **National Defense Authorization Act of 2012** which allows American citizens even on US soil to be held indefinitely without charges or trial in military prison when suspected of terrorism. Further, he authorized by executive order the killing of US citizens without trial as part of the war on terrorism. Talk about an erosion of due process!

Obama also continues the national drug war, although his administration no longer uses the term "war on drugs." When running for President, Barack Obama promised to bring "change" to many American policies, including national drug control policy. And shortly after he was named Director of the Office of National Drug Control Policy (ONDCP), former police chief Gil Kerlikowske announced that White House officials would no longer use the term "war on drugs" to describe national drug control efforts. In April 2009, for example, Kerlikowske stated: "Regardless of how you try to explain to people it's a 'war on drugs' or a 'war on a product,' people see a war as a war on them. We're not at war with people in this country" (Robinson & Scherlen, 2013).

Obama and Kerlikowske have also regularly pledged to increase funding for treatment and prevention—the two demand-side elements of drug policy found to be the most effective—and this has started to occur (although about 60% of funding still is allocated to the supply-side elements of eradication, interdiction, and international spending), as shown in Table 2.2. Yet there has been no fundamental change in approach to America's prohibitionist stand with regard to illicit drugs. In fact, even as states have begun legalizing marijuana—Washington and Colorado did so in 2012—President Obama and his drug czar, Gil Kerlikowske, refuse to even discuss legalization of marijuana, now supported by more than half of Americans. They have repeatedly announced that Obama "firmly opposes the legalization of marijuana or any other illicit drug."

This is interesting, because just like Presidents Bill Clinton and George W. Bush before him, President Obama is a self-admitted drug user. In his autobiography, for example, he writes: "I had learned not to care. I blew a few smoke rings, remembering those years. Pot had helped, and booze; maybe a little blow when you could afford it. Not smack, though …" (Obama, 2007). Interestingly, Obama's yearbook photo identified him as part of the "Choom Gang" (chooming is Hawaiian slang for smoking marijuana). The hypocrisy of a former hard drug user leading the drug war, after the two previous presidents did the same, seems lost on lawmakers in the US.

Table 2.2. National Drug Control Policy Spending

Supply-Side Measures	$15.1 billion
Law Enforcement	$9.4 billion
Interdiction	$3.7 billion
International	$2 billion
Demand-Side Measures	$10.5 billion
Treatment	$9.1 billion (includes funds for research)
Prevention	$1.4 billion (includes funds for research)

Source: FY 2013 spending requests by the Office of National Drug Control Policy. http://www.white house.gov/sites/default/files/ondcp/fy2013_drug_control_budget_and_performance_summary.pdf.

More generally, President Obama is working to reform the criminal justice system in some important ways. As noted by Rafael Lemaitre (2012), Obama signed the **Fair Sentencing Act** into law which reduced the 100 to 1 disparity in sentences between crack cocaine and powder cocaine created in the 1980s (where five grams of crack cocaine mandated a five-year prison sentence but 500 grams of powder cocaine led to the same sentence). Obama also continues to promote drug courts, which provide treatment to people convicted of crimes as an opportunity to have their convictions removed and/ or to avoid prison time. The **Second Chance Act** is also being implemented to provide re-entry services for people leaving prisons as well as treatment programs, employment training, and other services for those re-entering free society.

Still, by his own admission, Obama is a "law & order" person. In an interview reported by Kara Dansky (2012), President Obama was asked: "One of the other things that I've heard being discussed is the idea of criminal justice reform. What would your goals be in that area?" His response was: "I tend to be pretty conservative, pretty law and order, when it comes to violent crime. My attitude is, that when you rape, murder, assault somebody, that you've made a choice; the society has every right to not only make sure you pay for that crime, but in some cases to disable you from continuing to engage in violent behavior." Note the terms used by President Obama: conservative, law and order, choice—right out of the conservative playbook.

Yet Obama continued:

> But there's a big chunk of that prison population that is involved in nonviolent crimes. And it is having a disabling effect on communities. You have entire populations that are rendered incapable of getting a legitimate job because of a prison record. And it boggles up a huge amount of resources. If you look at state budgets, part of the reason that tuition has been rising in public universities across the country is because more and more resources were going into paying for prisons, and that left less money to provide to colleges and universities. I think we have to figure out what are we doing right to make sure that that downward trend in violence continues, but also are there millions of lives out there that are being destroyed or distorted because we haven't fully thought through our process?

This is the more "liberal" side of President Obama, although many conservatives are today also realizing that we can save money and reduce crime by pursuing smarter criminal justice policies.

In a follow-up question about whether he might support alternative sentencing, Obama replied: "Potentially. You can't put a price on public safety; on the other hand, we're going to be in an era of fiscal constraint at the state, federal and local levels. It makes sense for us to just ask some tough questions." In other words, monetary concerns may very well be driving Obama's progressive impulses rather than an underlying liberal ideology. This, too, would be consistent with the conservative political ideology which stresses fiscal responsibility and small government.

Since the 1960s, street crime has been a national issue that has been used for political gain (and loss) in each presidential election and also in hundreds of elections at other levels of government. Meanwhile, we as a nation tend to ignore white-collar and corporate crime? Why? Because of who makes the law, which is examined in the next chapter. Amazingly, many criminologists now assert that this expansion of criminal justice policy actually has little to do with crime (Garland, 1990). According to Michael Tonry (2004: 14): "Government decides how much punishment they want, and these decisions are in no simple way related to the crime rates." In fact, a large amount of criminal justice research demonstrates that crime rates are largely unrelated to even the most serious sanctions, including imprisonment and even capital punishment (Robinson, 2009).

Further, although some polls suggest the public likes "getting tough on crime" in some cases, it is not public opinion that drives it (Beckett, 1997). A review of such research by Katherine Beckett & Theodore Sasson (2000: xii) led to this conclusion:

> The punitive turn in crime policy is not primarily the result of a worsening crime problem or an increasingly fearful or vengeful public. Rather, above all else, growing punitiveness reflects efforts by national politicians to shift public policy on a variety of social problems—including crime, addiction, and poverty—toward harsher and more repressive solutions.

Finally, the expansion of criminal justice—more police, more and tougher punishment—is not supported by empirical evidence, academic criminology, or what Miller (2011: xi) refers to as "best practice." These do not matter when policy is aimed at supposedly helping crime victims. Instead, what matters in criminal justice practice is sound bites that convince people you are tough on crime. As noted by Ted Gest (2001: 2), "high-pitched political rhetoric has drowned out serious public discussion on crime's root causes on a national level." So the tough on crime direction of US criminal justice policy owes itself to politics. And there is little political risk being "tough on crime" regardless of whether new policies are effective, necessary, or just.

Yet, even to the degree that criminal justice expansion is meant as some kind of service to crime victims, it is only to victims of some forms of street crime. Victims of white-collar, corporate, and corporate deviance are generally unassisted by criminal justice, as I'll show in Chapters 4 and 5.

Summary

Criminal justice is highly impacted by both politics and ideology. In fact, it might be wise to see criminal justice as a tool used to achieve certain political and ideology functions. As shown in this chapter, crime has been a political issue used by politicians (both Republicans and Democrats) to shift American politics and policies toward conservative "tough on crime" approaches that actually threaten the ideals of crime control and especially due process as found in the Declaration of Independence and the US Constitution.

The conservative ideology is threat to crime control because conservatives insist that we not only ignore white-collar and corporate crime but also that we enable those who commit them by easing regulation and oversight that is meant to prevent such acts. That is, conservative politics are dangerous because they promote crimes committed by elites, making it a direct threat to crime control values. The conservative ideology is a threat to due process because the Constitutional rights of suspects and defendants are weakened to enable the zealous pursuit of street criminals, drug users and dealers, and terrorists. That is, conservative politics also erode due process. As a result, Americans enjoy less freedom from government intrusion into their lives and less protections when they are processed through the criminal justice system.

Key Terms

- **Aid to Families with Dependent Children (AFDC):** Aid to Families with Dependent Children (AFDC) was created in 1935 and existed until 1996, which provided federal assistance to children who lived in poor families.
- **Bureau of Narcotics and Dangerous Drugs:** The Bureau of Narcotics and Dangerous Drugs was created in 1968 to try to control drugs in the US.
- **Commission on Law Enforcement and Administration of Justice:** The Commission on Law Enforcement and Administration of Justice was made up of 19 people appointed by President Johnson in 1965 to study the criminal justice system. Its report suggested reforms to make criminal justice more effective and fair.
- **Community Policing:** Community policing refers to an approach to law enforcement where officers partner with citizens in the community to reduce crime problems together.
- **Conservativism:** Conservativism refers to a political ideology that values personal freedom and free markets.
- **Cultural Deviance Theories:** Cultural deviance theories are theories of crime that assert that crime is endemic to certain subcultures within America, such as gangs.
- **Democracy:** Democracy is a form of government where the people self-rule or determine their own fate.
- **Department of Homeland Security:** The Department of Homeland Security is the largest bureaucracy in the US government, was created by executive order after the terrorist attacks of September 11, 2001, and then later by an act of Congress in 2002.

Its primary mission is to reduce the threat of terrorism to the continental United States.

- **Deregulation:** Deregulation is reducing regulations or rules on businesses so that they can operate more efficiently and earn more money.
- **Drug Czar:** The drug czar is the Director of the Office of National Drug Control Policy and directs the nation's efforts to reduce drug use and abuse in America.
- **Drug Enforcement Agency:** The Drug Enforcement Agency was created in 1973 to disrupt the illicit drug trade within the US.
- **Enhanced Interrogation:** Enhanced interrogation is the term used by US officials to describe efforts of extracting information from suspected terrorists that included methods such as waterboarding, stress positions, and hypothermia.
- **Equality:** Equality means being treated equally.
- **Fair Sentencing Act:** The Fair Sentencing Act was signed into law in 2010 and reduced the disparity between crack cocaine and powder cocaine from 100:1 to only 18:1 and eliminated the five-year mandatory sentence for possession of crack cocaine.
- **Great Society:** Great Society programs were initiated in the 1960s by President Johnson and were aimed at reducing poverty and racial inequality in society.
- **Hedonistic:** Hedonism means pleasure-seeking, and many criminologists believe that pursuit of pleasure leads to crime.
- **Ideology:** Ideology refers to beliefs about how things are, how they should be, and why.
- **Law Enforcement Assistance Agency:** The Law Enforcement Assistance Agency was created in 1968 to provide funding for law enforcement agencies and criminal justice research.
- **Liberalism:** Liberalism refers to a political ideology that values equality and equal opportunity.
- **Liberty:** Liberty means freedom and includes rights and liberties that Americans enjoy.
- **Military Tribunals Act:** The Military Tribunals Act was signed into law in 2006 and authorizes military commissions for those suspected of plotting acts of terrorism against the US government.
- **National Defense Authorization Act of 2012:** The National Defense Authorization Act specifies the budget of the US Department of Defense. In 2012, the law allowed for the indefinite detention of US citizens.
- **Omnibus Crime Control and Safe Streets Act:** The Omnibus Crime Control and Safe Streets Act of 1968 established the Law Enforcement Assistance Administration to provide funding for law enforcement agencies and criminal justice research, expanded the Federal Bureau of Investigation, strengthened some gun laws, and set rules for wiretapping suspects.
- **Personal Responsibility and Work Opportunity Reconciliation Act:** The Personal Responsibility and Work Opportunity Reconciliation Act was signed into law in 1996 and created the Temporary Assistance for Needy Families (TANF) to replace welfare with work after two years of federal assistance and placing a five-year lifetime limit of receiving federal benefits.
- **Policy:** Policy means rules or guidelines about making decisions about issues; an example is a law.

- **Politics:** Politics means governing and creating policies to make decisions about key issues. Politicians decide who gets what economic benefits in society, when they get them and how they get them.
- **Rational Choice Theory:** Rational choice theory is a theory of crime that asserts that criminals are rational and choose to commit crime because it leads to reward, and thus they can be deterred by the threat of severe punishment.
- **Risk Factors:** Risk factors are things that, when exposed to them, increase the odds or risk of criminal behavior.
- **Second Chance Act:** The Second Chance Act was signed into law in 2008 and uses federal money to provide support for people leaving prison so that they can be successfully reintegrated into society.
- **Sentencing Guidelines:** Sentencing guidelines provide guidance for judges about sentences for convicted offenders, making them more uniform based on the seriousness of the offense and the offender's prior record.
- **Serious Crime:** Serious crimes are those thought to be the most harmful, most common, and most widespread in America.
- **Southern Strategy:** The Southern Strategy was a deliberate effort to generate support among white voters in the South by appealing to racist sentiment in order to elect Republicans to office.
- **Temporary Assistance to Needy Families (TANF):** The Temporary Assistance for Needy Families (TANF) program requires people to find work after receiving two years of federal assistance and only allows them to receive federal benefits for five years over the course of their lives.
- **USA PATRIOT Act:** The USA PATRIOT Act was signed into law soon after the terrorist attacks of September 11, 2001, and empowers law enforcement and intelligence agencies to gather more information and communicate with one another in order to prevent acts of terrorism.
- **War on Poverty:** The War on Poverty was part of President Johnson's efforts to reduce poverty by providing more economic and employment opportunities for American citizens. Efforts included food stamps, social security, job corps, and many other programs.

Discussion Questions

1) What is politics? And how does it impact criminal justice?
2) What is a policy?
3) What is ideology? And how does it impact criminal justice?
4) What are the three values stressed by American political culture today according to Benjamin Ginsberg and colleagues?
5) Compare and contrast conservatives and liberals in terms of how they differ on the values of liberty, equality, and democracy.
6) What causes crime according to rational choice theory and cultural deviance theories?
7) What are risk factors for crime?
8) What is hedonism and how is it related to crime?

9) Compare and contrast conservativism and liberalism when it comes to causes and solutions to crime.
10) What are sentencing guidelines?
11) Summarize how Barry Goldwater, Lyndon Johnson, and Richard Nixon addressed crime and criminal justice. What was the role of race in their approaches?
12) What does the term Great Society refer to?
13) What was the Omnibus Crime Control and Safe Streets Act?
14) What was the Commission on Law Enforcement and Administration of Justice and the Law Enforcement Assistance Agency?
15) What makes a crime serious?
16) What was the Southern Strategy?
17) What was the Bureau of Narcotics and Dangerous Drugs and what is the Drug Enforcement Agency?
18) What was the War on Poverty?
19) Summarize how Ronald Reagan and George H.W. Bush addressed crime and criminal justice. What was the role of race in their approaches?
20) What is deregulation?
21) What is community policing?
22) Summarize how Bill Clinton and George W. Bush addressed crime and criminal justice. What was the role of race in their approaches?
23) What is the drug czar?
24) Discuss the Personal Responsibility and Work Opportunity Reconciliation Act, Aid to Families with Dependent Children, and Temporary Assistance to Needy Families (TANF), and explain their relevance for conservativism.
25) What are the Department of Homeland Security, Military Tribunals Act, USA PATRIOT Act, and enhanced interrogation? Do you support these? Why?
26) Summarize how Barack Obama has addressed crime and criminal justice. What was the role of race in his approaches?
27) What is the National Defense Authorization Act of 2012? Do you support it? Why?
28) What are the Fair Sentencing Act and the Second Chance Act? Do you support these? Why?

Chapter 3

The Law as a Source of Bias in Criminal Justice

"The law should be a shield for the weak and powerless, not a club for the powerful."

—Roy Barnes

Who Makes the Law?

In the last chapter, you saw that the criminal justice system is highly influenced by politics and ideology, and that it is politicians who have the power to define crimes as well as determine the general direction of criminal justice policy. You also learned that the conservative political ideology—which has come to dominate criminal justice practice in the United States—explains why we fail to hold those responsible for the worst crimes in America as well as why we are focused so heavily on street crimes, especially those committed by certain people under certain circumstances. It also explains the erosion of due process discussed in the last chapter.

We also entertained the possibility that the lawmaking process tends to serve the interests of the powerful at the expense of the rest of us. Yet Americans are generally under the impression that the law comes from them through the democratic process whereby we elect the people we want to represent us to make laws on our behalf. After all, we tend to operate on the assumption that this is a **democracy** (even though it is actually a **representative republic**). In this chapter, you'll see how little the law appears to actually represent the common interests of society.

Whose Interests Are Served by the Law?

There are at least three major arguments about whose interests are served by the criminal law. They include the consensus view, conflict view, and another which fits in the middle—the pluralist view. The major differences between these theories of the law are shown in Table 3.1.

Those who believe in the **consensus view of the law** believe that the law reflects societal interests and that "crimes" therefore are acts that a majority of the population view as immoral, wrong, and harmful. Crimes are thus deviations from the norm. This model is based on the belief that the "law reflects common consciousness and interests

Table 3.1. Views of the Law

	Consensus	Conflict	Pluralist
Law comes from	the people	the powerful	winner of competition
Law serves interests of	the people	the powerful	winner of competition (usually the powerful)
Crimes are	deviation of norms	acts of powerless	acts lobbied for by groups

of society" (Marion, 1995: 21). According to its proponents, the criminal law "serves as a banner to announce the values of society. It tells us where the boundaries of acceptable behavior lie and links those who violate the boundaries — criminals — with evil, pain, incarceration, and disgrace" (Kappeler, Blumberg & Potter, 2000: 216).

Proponents of the **conflict view of the law** believe that the law reflects the limited interests of powerful members of society. Thus, "crimes" are not necessarily the most harmful acts; instead, they are acts committed by relatively powerless people (e.g., the poor) (Vold, 1958). Those with political or economic power, as well as the most successful special-interest groups, are likely to have their beliefs reflected in the law. Recall the argument of Richard Quinney (2000) from Chapter 2, who claims that powerful individuals and groups are the ones that promote their own conceptions of crime so that they can justify and maintain their authority and create policies that promote their own interests. Quinney's theory of the criminal law is discussed more in Chapter 5.

Ronald Akers (1996: 142) seems to agree with this view, writing: "The dominant groups can see to it that their particular definitions of normality or deviance will become enacted as law, ensconced in public policy, and protected by the operation of the criminal justice system." Bruce Arrigo (1999: 6) also agrees, noting that all criminal justice policies that emanate from the criminal law are "merely definitions developed by people (authorities) who possess the power to shape, enforce, and administer such policies" (Arrigo, 1999: 6). Each of these assertions is consistent with the conflict view.

There is a middle-ground between the consensus view and the conflict view — the **pluralist view of the law.** Proponents of this view suggest that there is intense competition between various parties with regard to any issue based on the idea of **pluralism.** Compromise and moderation are necessary since no group will be able to achieve its goals "without accommodating itself to some of the views of its many competitors" (Ginsberg et al., 2013: 16, 435).

According to the pluralist view, the law reflects the interests of those who win this competition. As Erich Goode & Nachman Ben-Yuhuda (1994: 78) write: "Definitions of right and wrong do not drop from the skies, nor do they simply ineluctably percolate from society's mainstream opinion; they are the result of disagreement, negotiation, conflict, and struggle. The passage of laws raises the issue of who will criminalize whom."

Acts called crimes are those most lobbied for by interest groups. As it turns out, powerful groups and individuals are those most likely to win in this competition, making the pluralist view closer to the conflict view than the consensus view. In order to gain a clear understanding of why this is so, it is crucial to critically explore the legislative process in the United States, including who makes the law, who votes for the law, and how special interests shape the law.

This examination of who makes the law, who votes for it, and who pays for it, is quite revealing with regard to which of these views—the consensus, conflict, and pluralist— is most accurate when it comes to lawmaking in the United States.

Demographics of Lawmakers

To the degree that lawmakers are representative of all of society, it is likely that laws will represent all people in society, consistent with the idea of **sociological representation** (Ginsberg, Lowi, Weir, & Tolbert, 2013: 472). Do US lawmakers sociologically represent citizens? Table 3.2 compares demographic characteristics of state and federal legislators with those of the general US population. According to the US Census (2012), a majority of people in the US in 2011 were women (50.8%). They were also Caucasian, as whites made up 78% of the population of the United States in 2011; Hispanics or Latinos made up 17% and blacks made up another 13%. The remaining population was made up of Asians, American Indians, people of two or more races, and other groups. As for age, 26% of Americans were between the ages of 45 and 64 years, and only 13% of the US population was made up of people 65 years of age or older. And the average age in the US in 2011 was 37.1 years (CIA, 2012). Finally, the median per capita income in the US from 2007–2011 was $27,915, whereas the median household income during the same time was $52,762 (US Census, 2012). And a recent study found the average net worth of Americans in 2010 was only $57,000, down to its lowest level since 1969 (Wolff, 2012).

So it is clear that lawmakers are in no way representative of American citizens, making sociological representation impossible. When compared to the average person in the US, lawmakers tend to be wealthier, older, richer, and disproportionately male. Starting with the US Congress, federal lawmakers are not demographically representative of American citizens. For example, in both the US Senate and the US House of Representatives, 83% of lawmakers are men, and only 17% are women. Thus, men are vastly overrepresented among members of Congress. The US Senate is also 96% white, 2% Latino, and 2% Asian (with no African Americans whatsoever). The US House is 82% white, only 10% black, 6% Hispanic, and 2% other. Thus, whites are also greatly overrepresented among federal lawmakers. Benjamin Ginsberg and his colleagues (2013: 473) note that "African Americans, women, Latinos, and Asian Americans have increased their congressional representation in the past two decades … but the representation of minorities in Congress is still not comparable to their proportions in the general population."

As for age, the average age of House members is 57 years, and the average age of Senators is 62 years (Manning, 2011). Thus, members of Congress are much older than the average American.

Federal lawmakers are also generally far wealthier than the average person in the United States. First, the beginning salary for both Senate and House members in 2012 was $174,000. Party leaders in the House and Senate received salaries of $193,400, and the Speaker of the House earned a salary of $223,500 (Longley, 2012). Meanwhile, the average wealth held by a US Senator was about $13 million and for a House member

Table 3.2. Comparing Lawmakers and Citizens

	US population	US Senate	US House	State legislatures
Female	51%	17%	17%	24%
Male	49%	83%	83%	76%
White	78%*	96%	82%	86%
Hispanic	17%*	2%	6%	3%
Black	13%*	0%	10%	9%
Average age	37 years	62 years	57 years	56 years
Income	$27,915 per capita $52,762 per household	$174,000	$174,000	$7,000–$95,000 (85% are part-time)
Net worth	$57,000	$13 million	$6 million	not available

* People may report more than one "race" to the US Census

Sources
http://ballotpedia.org/wiki/index.php/Comparison_of_state_legislative_salaries; https://www.cia.gov/library/publications/the-world-factbook/geos/us.html; http://usgovinfo.about.com/od/uscongress/a/congresspay.htm; http://www.senate.gov/reference/resources/pdf/R41647.pdf; http://this nation.com/congress-facts.html; http://www.ncsl.org/legislatures-elections/legisdata/latino-legislators-overview.aspx; http://www.ncsl.org/legislatures-elections.aspx?tabs=1116,113,782; http://www.ncsl.org/legislatures-elections/legisdata/legislator-occupations-national-data.aspx; http://www.ncsl.org/legislatures-elections/legisdata/african-american-legislators-1992-to-2009.aspx; http://www.ncsl.org/legislatures-elections/wln/women-in-state-legislatures-2011.aspx; http://www.opensecrets.org/pfds/averages.php; http://quickfacts.census.gov/qfd/states/00000.html; http://www.census.gov/prod/cen2010/briefs/c2010br-02.pdf; http://washington.cbslocal.com/2012/11/30/study-american-households-hit-43-year-low-in-net-worth/.

about $6 million (Open Secrets, 2012). Compare this to the average income of US citizens and households. In 2012, per capita income was $27,915 and average household income was $52,762.

Further, as Americans have recently seen their wealth decline (e.g., Americans lost about 40% of their net worth during the latest recession), members of Congress actually got richer by about 5% (while the wealthiest one-third of lawmakers reported increases in wealth of about 14%). Now, between 40% and 50% of members of Congress are millionaires, compared to only 1% of all Americans.

Data from the National Conference of State Legislatures show that lawmakers at the state level are very much like members of Congress. For example, only 24% of state legislators are women, whereas 76% are men (National Conference of State Legislatures, 2012e). Thus, at the state level, women again are underrepresented as lawmakers. State lawmakers are also overwhelmingly white, as only 9% are African American and 3% are Latino (National Conference of State Legislatures, 2012a, 2012d). Further, the average age of lawmakers at the state level is 56 years, and the largest percentage of legislators (48%) is between the ages of 50 and 64 years. Another 24% are 65 years or older (National Conference of State Legislatures, 2012b). Recall that in the US, the average age is only 37.1 years, and smaller percentages of Americans are 50 years of age and older.

Average pay for legislators varies widely by state, from a low of about $7,000 per year to a high of more than $95,000 per year (Ballotpedia, 2012). Yet, keep in mind that about 85% of state legislators are part-time positions, and legislators tend to already be employed in other profitable businesses or industries as attorneys, business owners, business executives, and so forth (National Conference of State Legislatures, 2012c). Thus, we can be confident that even state lawmakers are significantly wealthier than the citizens they represent.

Since lawmakers are much whiter, older, richer, and "maler" than the average person, perhaps a suitable acronym for people who make the law is *WORMs* (white, older, rich males). While this is not meant as a derogatory term, *worms* will likely conjure up images of slimy creatures crawling around in the dirt. Certainly others have said worse things about lawmakers. Given that the approval rating for Congress is, at the time of this writing, lower than that of cockroaches (Stephens, 2013), hopefully you won't find the acronym offensive. Studies of state legislator approval are consistently higher than those of Congress but also consistently below 50% (Richardson, Kinisky & Milyo, 2011).

In-Class Activity

Look up the demographic characteristics of legislators in your state. Compare these with the demographic characteristics of citizens in your state. Are they sociologically representative of the population? Does it matter?

Voting Behavior

WORMs — our elected "representatives" — may still represent the voter, but most people do not regularly vote. Data from the US Census show that only about two-thirds of people eligible to vote (18 years or older) are registered to vote in any given year. Thus, about one-third of people who are eligible to vote cannot vote for the simple reason that they are not registered. Specifically, about 60% of eligible voters vote in presidential elections, about one-third vote in mid-term congressional elections, and turnout is even lower for local elections (Ginsberg et al., 2013: 306).

Before we move on to whether voters are representative of the population generally, think about this: If people do not vote, how do representatives know what normal citizens think? The law cannot represent the masses, and the **collective conscience** of society (Durkheim, 1893) cannot be incorporated into the criminal law, if people do not vote. That is, the set of values that are supposedly shared by people in society and that are expected to be reflected in the law in a representative democracy cannot be known to legislators if we do not participate in democracy.

Of those registered to vote, 58.2% voted in the 2012 Presidential elections, versus only 45.5% voted in the 2010 Congressional elections, and 63.6% voted in the 2008 Presidential election (US Census, 2013). Turns out these voters are also not representative of the US population. For example, data from the US Census show that whites are more likely to vote than blacks and Hispanics. There is also a positive relationship between voting and age — as age increases, so too does participation in voting. The same kind

Table 3.3. Money in Politics

	House of Representatives	US Senate	President
Number of candidates:	1,711	251	16
Amount raised:	$1,111,628,101	$699,077,040	$1,368,861,431

Source: http://www.opensecrets.org/overview/.

of relationship exists between voting and education—as education increases, so too does participation in voting.

This suggests the very real possibility that wealthier people are more likely to vote than poorer citizens. In fact, there is a positive relationship between income and voting behaviors. That is, the highest level of voter registration and reported voting is for people who earn more than $150,000 per year, and the lowest is for those earning less than $10,000 per year.

Voting is generally lowest in the South, where poverty and minority residence are very high. According to John Harrigan (2000), lower rates of voting by the poor should be attributed to the fact that poor people have been systematically shut out of the electoral process, not that they are bad citizens. In essence, economic stress threatens good citizenship.

In the 2012 Presidential and Congressional elections, voting was highest among whites (followed by blacks and Hispanics), 45–64-year-olds, and women (Kliff, Mathews & Plumer, 2012). From all these data, we see that voters tend to share three of the same demographic characteristics of lawmakers—they are whiter, older, and richer than the average person. Only on gender are they different since women are slightly more likely than men to participate in voting. Yet the conclusion is still the same when it comes to voting in the US—most people don't vote—and of those who do, they are not representative of the US population. This suggests the law will not likely represent all people equally well.

Voters can still have tremendous power to the degree that politicians fear voters will be antagonized. Yet, John Harrigan (2000) shows how very powerful interest groups have their will enacted into law, even when the interests of the voting public are not served. This is increasingly true in the era of big spending on political races.

Special Interests/Lobbying

Let there be no doubt about two key facts when it comes to American politics:

1) There is a lot of money involved in the political system; and
2) Money determines the outcomes of most elections.

Table 3.3 illustrates just how money is involved in the federal system. During the 2010–2012 election cycles, Republicans and Democrats received a total of $9.35 billion (Center from Responsive Politics, 2013).

According to the Center for Responsive Politics (2013), in 2012, 1,711 House candidates raised a total of $1.1 billion to run for office, and 251 Senate candidates raised a total of $700 million to run for office. And of the 11 candidates for President, they raised a combined $1.4 billion, including about $732 million raised just by one candidate—incumbent President Barack Obama. Incumbents in the House raised an average of about $1.6 million while incumbents in the Senate raised an average of $11.8 million. If candidates had to raise this money in one year in order to run, House incumbents would have to raise an average of $4,382 every single day, and Senate incumbents would have to raise $32,328 every single day! That gives you an idea of how much money is involved in federal politics.

From where does this money come? Well, it does not come from average Americans. According to the Center for Responsive Politics (2013): "Only a tiny fraction of Americans actually give campaign contributions to political candidates, parties or PAC [Political Action Committees]. The ones who give contributions large enough to be itemized (over $200) is even smaller. The impact of those donations, however, is huge." Specifically, far less than 1% of the US adult population (0.53% of adults) gave more than $200 to a political candidate, party, or lobbying group in 2012, and even less (0.1% of all adults) gave $2,500 or more. These donations made up 67.3% of all dollars raised in politics in 2012. Interestingly, consistent with what we already know about lawmaking activities, men were twice more likely than women (0.66% versus 0.31%) to have donated $200 or more.

The great bulk of money in federal politics comes from wealthy individuals, major corporations, interest groups, Political Action Committees (PACs) and now Super PACs in the form of campaign donations. Although Americans like to think of the law as representing them, in reality, both "voters and individuals making political contributions tend to be more affluent and educated than nonvoters" (Ginsberg, 2013: 242).

PACs

Political Action Committees (PACs), in operation since the 1940s, are groups organized to raise and spend money on political campaigns. PACs typically represent corporate, labor, and ideological interests, and are allowed to give $5,000 to a candidate committee per election (primary, general or special), up to $15,000 annually to any national party committee, and $5,000 annually to any other PAC. They may also receive up to $5,000 from any one individual, PAC or party committee per calendar year (Center for Responsive Politics, 2013).

Table 3.4 illustrates the top PACs between the years of 2011 and 2012 for federal elections. The data show that both major parties are well funded by PACs, and that Democrats are most represented by groups of workers and teachers, whereas Republicans are most represented by corporations. According to the Center for Responsive Politics, strongly Democratic industries include unions, lawyers, and entertainment (TV, movies, music), whereas strongly Republican industries include insurance, pharmaceuticals, and oil and gas. And the top ten industries donating to American politics through lobbying include pharmaceuticals, insurance, computers, business associations, electric utilities, education, real estate, hospitals, oil and gas, and entertainment (TV, movies, music).

Table 3.4. Top Political Action Committees

PAC Name	Amount	Dem/Rep Split	
National Assn of Realtors	$3,960,282	44%	55%
National Beer Wholesalers Assn	$3,388,500	41%	59%
Honeywell International	$3,193,024	41%	59%
Operating Engineers Union	$3,186,387	84%	15%
National Auto Dealers Assn	$3,074,000	28%	72%
Intl Brotherhood of Electrical Workers	$2,853,000	97%	2%
American Bankers Assn	$2,736,150	20%	80%
AT&T Inc	$2,543,000	35%	65%
American Assn for Justice	$2,512,500	96%	3%
Credit Union National Assn	$2,487,600	47%	52%
Plumbers/Pipefitters Union	$2,395,150	94%	5%
Northrop Grumman	$2,353,900	41%	58%
American Fedn of St/Cnty/Munic Employees	$2,279,140	99%	1%
Lockheed Martin	$2,258,000	41%	59%
Blue Cross/Blue Shield	$2,177,898	33%	67%
Machinists/Aerospace Workers Union	$2,173,500	98%	1%
American Federation of Teachers	$2,171,644	99%	0%
MINT PAC	$2,138,229	0%	100%
Every Republican is Crucial PAC	$2,086,000	0%	100%
Teamsters Union	$2,053,410	96%	4%

Source: http://www.opensecrets.org/pacs/toppacs.php.

In 2012, public-interest and ideological PACs were the most common, followed by corporate PACs, trade PACs, labor PACs, and other PACs. In 2010, corporate PACs gave the following amounts: finance, insurance and real estate—$63 million; health—$55 million; miscellaneous business—$38 million; energy and natural resources—$29 million; communications and electronics—$28 million; agribusiness—$23 million; transportation—$21 million; lawyers and lobbyists—$16 million; construction—$16 million; defense—$14 million. Ideological groups—conservative and liberal—gave $60 million, and labor groups donated $64 million (Ginsberg, 2013: 459). PACs contributed about 15% of all money spent in federal, state, and local elections in 2012, whereas 50% came from other interest groups (including 527s and 501(c)(4)s, discussed later) and Super PACs (Ginsberg et al., 2003: 458).

Super PACs

Super PACs are a new kind of political action committee created in July 2010 following the outcome of a federal court case, *SpeechNow.org v. Federal Election Commission* (No. 08-5223). This case, decided by the DC Circuit Court of Appeals, held that groups of individuals cannot be denied the right to engage in political speech in order to help or harm political candidates or organizations.

While legally referred to as "independent expenditure-only committees," Super PACs are allowed to "raise unlimited sums of money from corporations, unions, associations and individuals" and then can "spend unlimited sums to overtly advocate for or against political candidates." Unlike PACs, Super PACs are not allowed to donate money directly to political candidates. Instead, they "make independent expenditures in federal races— running ads or sending mail or communicating in other ways with messages that specifically advocate the election or defeat of a specific candidate." For such activities, no limits or restrictions are placed "on the sources of funds that may be used for these expenditures" (Center for Responsive Politics, 2013). That is, money can come from anyone and unlimited amounts of money can be spent to help or hurt political candidates.

When you combine the impact of the *SpeechNow* decision by the DC Circuit Court of Appeals to the decision reached by the US Supreme Court in the case of *Citizens United v. Federal Election Commission*, 558 U.S. 310 you get a crystal clear understanding of how much money can impact lawmaking in the United States. The 5–4 decision in *Citizens United* was hailed in a *Wall Street Journal* editorial as "a wonderful decision that restores political speech to the primacy it was intended to have under the First Amendment" but also assayed in a *New York Times* editorial as a "disastrous" and "radical" decision that "strikes at the heart of democracy" that will "thrust politics back to the robber-baron era of the 19th century."

The decision of the Court arose out of a documentary during a primary election cycle about Hillary Rodham Clinton (who was running for the Democratic nomination for president) that was produced by a conservative advocacy group called Citizens United. Citizens United sued the Federal Election Commission since the film was not allowed to be shown on television because of restrictions created through federal law meant to limit the impact of partisan speech in the final months of an election.

Specifically, parts of two laws—the Federal Elections Campaign Act of 1971 (FECA), and the Bipartisan Campaign Reform Act of 2002 (BCRA)—were struck down by the Court. FECA provided campaign finance reform but still allowed corporations and unions to establish political action committees (PACs) to finance campaign contributions. BCRA, according to the Court, prohibited "corporations and unions from using general treasury funds to make direct contributions to candidates or indirect expenditures that expressly advocate the election or defeat of a candidate, through any form of media, in connection with certain qualified federal elections." This includes any publically distributed electioneering communications such as "broadcast, cable, or satellite communication" referring to a candidate for federal office made within 30 days of a primary election or 60 days within a general election. Violations of this law amounted to crimes, punished as felonies in the federal court system.

The case dealt with whether corporations (as well as unions) could spend limitless amounts of money trying to sway voters through direct expenditures so close to election day; the Court held that they can. The reason? Any effort by the government to restrict a "person" (which the Court holds to include a corporation) from providing information to citizens amounts to "censorship to control thought," something unlawful according to the majority. The Court wrote that the "First Amendment confirms the freedom to think for ourselves" and the more information citizens have in this process the better.

The ruling was based in part on the Court's assertion that "the public begins to concentrate on elections only in the weeks immediately before they are held" and because there "are short timeframes in which speech can have influence." Thus, federally imposed limits of speech during the final two months of elections are particularly harmful to corporations (as well as unions) because it is only during this time that voters supposedly pay attention to elections.

An even more recent decision by the Court, in the case of *McCutcheon v. FEC* (2014), the Court struck down limits on how much any person or entity can donate to political candidates or parties. The limits had been set at $48,600 for the amount an individual could spend on contributions to all candidates, plus $74,600 on contributions to all political parties and committees. Chief Justice Roberts explained the majority's decision, writing: "There is no right more basic in our democracy than the right to participate in electing our political leaders. We have made clear that Congress may not regulate contributions simply to reduce the amount of money in politics, or to restrict the political participation of some in order to enhance the relative influence of others."

Of course, by elevating money to the status of speech, that is precisely what the Court has done: enhanced the relative influence of those who can spend more over those who cannot. Strangely, the Court did not overturn the limit on how much an individual can contribute to a specific candidate, currently set at $2,600 per election. Expect this limit to be challenged in a future case.

In the wake of these decisions, corporations, wealthy individuals (and to a much less degree, unions), have been empowered to spend endless amounts of money to sway elections in their favor. As a result, we've witnessed a flood of donations to political races at both the federal and state levels. This is a direct result of the US Supreme Court holding that corporations and people and that money is equivalent to speech. The Court is shown in Figure 3.1.

It is fair to say that American politics has essentially become a fundraising contest: whoever raises the most money (and spends it) is almost guaranteed to win. While some may claim that the best candidates are the ones most likely to raise the most money—meaning that money does not really determine the winner but merely reflects citizen perceptions of quality candidates—the fact remains that in order to even be heard by citizens through media coverage, candidates must raise enormous amounts of money in order to have their candidates covered by the mainstream media. For this reason, candidates for federal office must rely on wealthy individuals, interest groups, PACs, and Super PACs in order to be elected. Logically, this should make them less responsive to citizen influence, especially considering that most people don't vote.

The picture is the same at the state level, as well. The Center for Public Integrity (2013) claims that private interests basically govern our states. According to the National Institute on Money in State Politics (2012), candidates for legislative and statewide offices raised $2.3 billion during the 2012 election cycle. Again, most of this money comes not from normal, everyday citizens but instead from wealthy donors, corporations, PACs, Super PACs, and interest groups.

An analysis of the impact of these funds on state-level elections found that money was the second-best predictor of winning elections behind incumbency. According to the study, those candidates for office who raised more money than their opponents won 76% of the time in the 2009 and 2010 primary and general elections: "In other words,

Figure 3.1. US Supreme Court

Matt Snodderly / shutterstock.com

fundraising, and the ability to spend large sums of money to persuade voters, helped lead almost eight of 10 candidates to victory. In contested general elections, the fundraising advantage was similar—successful candidates won 77 percent of the time" (Casey, 2012).

Incumbency, or already holding a lawmaking seat, was the best predictor, as 87% of incumbents won re-election in the 2009 and 2010 primary and general elections: "And those incumbents in contested general election races saw a similar success rate of 85 percent" (Casey, 2012). Since incumbents tend to raise more money than challengers, this finding is also not surprising. According to the National Institute on Money in State Politics, between 88% and 94% of incumbents with the most money win elections.

Political scientists assert that incumbency "tends to preserve the status quo in Washington." Further, "incumbency advantage makes it harder for women [and people of color] to increase their numbers in Congress because most incumbents are [white] men" (Ginsberg et al., 2013: 479).

Out-of-Class Activity:
Research the legislators in your own state. How much money did they raise in the last election cycle and from where did it come? Whose interests do you think your legislator most represents?

Interest Groups

Even though PACs and wealthy individuals seem to have a stranglehold on lawmakers, groups other than powerful elites are involved in the codification of criminal law. For example, the general public makes demands, and events such as media reporting and tens of thousands of lobbying actions among more than a dozen interest groups affect legislation, including **interest groups**. Most of the lobbying groups in the United States represent corporations from the United States and abroad but some also represent average Americans. The latter are funded by their members and thus have greater difficulty raising funds.

Interest groups, include **527s**. According to the Center for Responsive Politics (2013):

> These groups represent a variety of positions on a variety of issues, but they have one thing in common: they influence how you look at the candidates. Their activities may not instruct you to vote for or against a specific candidate, but often they will try to shape your opinion of a political candidate or party in the context of a specific issue. Such "issue advocacy" won't explicitly tell you to elect or defeat a particular candidate, but the advocacy group's view of the candidate's stance on their issue is clear.

Five hundred twenty-seven groups took in about $460 million in 2012 and spent about $416 million, mostly on state and local elections.

Another type of interest group is **501(c)(4)s**. As it turns out, wealthy individuals and corporations funnel money into these groups to elect candidates that will be more approachable and legislate in ways favorable to their interests. As noted by Benjamin Ginsberg and colleagues (2013: 458): "One powerful but little-known campaign finance tactic is the formation of strategic alliances between corporate interest groups and ideological or not-for-profit groups." Why? "Politicians are reluctant to accept money directly from what might have seemed to be unsavory sources, and corporate interests may find it useful to hide campaign contributions by laundering them through a not-for-profit." Groups use a tactic called **money swapping** to give money to candidates.

According to the Public Broadcasting System (2012):

> Social welfare nonprofits don't fall under the Federal Election Commission's standard definition of a political committee, which, under FEC guidelines, must disclose its donors. Because 501(c)(4)s say their primary purpose is social welfare, they can keep their donors secret. The only exception is if someone gives them money and specifically states the funds are for a political ad.
>
> And unlike political committees, social welfare nonprofits have a legal right to keep their donors secret. That stems from the landmark 1958 Supreme Court case, *NAACP v. Alabama*, which held the NAACP didn't have to identify its members because disclosure could lead to harassment.
>
> Fast forward to the post-*Citizens United* world of campaign finance where outside groups can now spend unlimited amounts of money to influence elections so long as they are independent of candidates. Seeing the advantages offered by groups that can engage in political activity while keeping their donors secret, both Democrats and Republicans have seized onto this opening in the tax code.

That's why in recent years, many new 501(c)(4)s have popped up right before the election season, focusing heavily on television advertising, usually attacking, though sometimes promoting, candidates running for office.

These nonprofits do have to report some of their activities to the FEC. When they run ads directly advocating for the election or defeat of a candidate, they have to tell regulators how much and what they spend money on—but not where the money comes from.

An investigation of these non-profit groups (which thus pay no taxes) by the media organization *Propublica* focused on documents filed with the Internal Revenue Service and the Federal Election Commission, and found "that dozens of these groups do little or nothing to justify the subsidies they receive from taxpayers. Instead, they are pouring much of their resources, directly or indirectly, into political races at the local, state and federal level." According to Kim Barker (2012):

> For this story, ProPublica reviewed thousands of pages of filings for 107 nonprofits active during the 2010 election cycle, tracking what portion of their funds went into politics. We watched TV ads bought by these groups, looked at documents from other nonprofits that gave them money, and interviewed dozens of campaign finance experts and political strategists.
>
> We found that some groups said they would not engage in politics when they applied for IRS recognition of their tax-exempt status. But later filings showed they spent millions on just such activities.

The investigation found that some groups "told the IRS they spent far less on politics than they reported to federal election officials" and others "classified expenditures that clearly praised or criticized candidates for office as 'lobbying,' 'education' or 'issue advocacy' on their tax returns." Still others donated to other 501(c)(4)s who then spent that money on political activities. Such financial donations to political activities have risen dramatically over the past several years and most of it comes from conservative groups, according to the analysis.

Ideally, interest groups are the "core of democracy, because they represent channels through which people can band together to counteract the advantages that the economic elite have in a political system" (Harrigan, 2000: 165). They can be comprised of "individuals who organize to influence the government's programs and policies" (Ginsberg et al., 2013: 435). But given that the poor are the least likely to belong to interest groups, and that the richest one-third of US citizens are nearly twice as likely as the poorest one-third to belong to such a group, interest group activity is biased in favor of the wealthy. David Simon & John Hagan (1999: 13) thus claim that "the richest 1 to 5 percent of the population pays for political campaigns. The resultant system is something of a corrupt gravy train that only the rich and powerful may board."

The voter is left with the realization that his or her vote, letter, phone call, fax, e-mail, or personal visit carries relatively little weight in a political process driven by money. Benjamin Ginsberg and colleagues (2013: 30) concur, explaining: "With the decline of locally based political parties that depend on party loyalty to turn out the vote, and the rise of political action committees, political consultants, and expensive media campaigns, money has become the central fact of life in American politics."

The Revolving Door

The point of lobbying by PACs, Super PACs, and other interest groups, obviously, is to get organized in order "to influence the passage of legislation by exerting direct pressure on members of the legislature" (Ginsberg et al., 2013: 445). But, careful study of the lawmaking process reveals a more perverse reality. According to Benjamin Ginsberg and his colleagues: "The influence of lobbyists, in many instances, is based on personal relationships and the behind-the-scenes services that they are able to perform for lawmakers. Many of Washington's top lobbyists have close ties to important members of Congress or were themselves important members of Congress or ... important political figures, thus virtually guaranteeing that their clients will have direct access to congressional leaders."

According to the Center for Responsive Politics (2013) close connections between lobbyists and lawmakers exist because of the **revolving door** between the two groups. They note that this revolving door "shuffles former federal employees into jobs as lobbyists, consultants and strategists just as the door pulls former hired guns into government careers. While officials in the executive branch, Congress and senior congressional staffers spin in and out of the private and public sectors, so too does privilege, power, access and, of course, money."

According to the Center, nearly

> every industry and special interest area hires lobbyists to represent and defend their interests in Washington, D.C. But some industries frequently employ a special breed of lobbyist: those who previously worked for the federal government they're now tasked with lobbying. Some of these "revolving door" lobbyists once toiled as low-level congressional staffers or entry-level bureaucrats. Plenty more, however, worked within government's upper ranks, serving as top agency officials, congressional chiefs of staff and even as members of the U.S. House and U.S. Senate.

Clearly, these lobbyists are effective at achieving their desired objectives, or else industries would not be willing to fund their salaries.

Lobbyists not only donate money but also set legislative agendas, help draft legislation, and "build broader coalitions and comprehensive campaigns around particular policy issues." Benjamin Ginsberg and colleagues (2013: 448) note: "These coalitions do not rise from the grassroots but instead are put together by Washington lobbyists who launch comprehensive lobbying campaigns that combine *simulated* grassroots activity with information and campaign funding for members of Congress" (emphasis added). In other words, most lobbyists serve limited interests rather than the common good, and the "common good" element that is sometimes seen in lobbying efforts is often simulated or artificial!

Lobbyists also have a huge impact on Presidents of the United States. For example, one advisor to a fund-raiser for President George W. Bush helped lobbyists prevent the Environmental Protection Agency (EPA) from placing further controls on the emission of mercury by power plants. President Barack Obama employs former lobbyists on his staff as well, including David Axelrod who, while a lobbyist, helped achieve a major rate hike on customers for a utility company (Ginsberg et al., 2013: 448–449).

Whereas none of this is illegal, many examples of **bribery** have been uncovered between lobbyists and politicians, even recently. One well-known example is the case of lobbyist Jack Abramoff, who was involved in a major corruption scandal involving excessive gifts to politicians.

Yet, as noted by Benjamin Ginsberg and colleagues (2013: 450),

> access to decision makers does not require bribes or other forms of illegal activity. In many areas, interest groups, government agencies, and congressional committees routinely work together for mutual benefit. The interest group provides campaign contributions for member of Congress, and it lobbies for larger benefits for the agency. The agency, in turn, provides government contracts for the interest group and constituency services for friendly members of Congress. The congressional committee or subcommittee, meanwhile, supports the agency's budgetary requests and the programs the interest group favors.

An **iron triangle** exists when a congressional committee, administrative agency, and interest group are connected and working together around a given issue. Citizens can and often do impact this process, as suggested by the pluralist view of the law. Yet, iron triangles tend to mostly serve the interests of the powerful.

Examples of Influence of the Powerful on the Law

Because of such close connections, the powerful are well-positioned to impact public policy. Common Cause (2013) calls our attention to a few examples:

> Some of the nation's largest and richest companies, including Koch Industries, ExxonMobil, and AT&T, have joined forces to invest millions of dollars each year to promote the careers of thousands of state legislators and secure passage of legislation that puts corporate interests ahead of the interests of ordinary Americans.
>
> The American Legislative Exchange Council, also known as ALEC, counts among its members some 2,000 state legislators and corporate executives. They sit side-by-side and collaborate to draft "model" bills that reach into areas of American life ranging from voting rights to environmental protection. They work in concert to get those bills passed in statehouses across the country.

By **Koch Industries**, Common Cause is referring to the activities of the Koch brothers—Charles and David—who have spent hundreds of millions of dollars of their own money to influence political races across the country. Charles and David Koch donate to conservative, libertarian, and "free market" candidates and causes in order to protect their own financial interests and to generate political support for pro-capitalist policies. Their organizations—*Freedom Works* and *Americans for Prosperity*—are used to try to get the "right" people elected as well as to fund specific, targeted initiatives including trying to first defeat and now repeal "Obamacare." They also played a key role in forming the so-called "Tea Party" movement.

The chairman of Freedom Works is Dick Armey, former speaker of the House of Representatives from Texas. It gets its funding from individuals, most of whom are quite wealthy, as well as oil, tobacco, communications, and insurance corporations. The group is also funded by the conservative Scaife family (which gives generously to numerous other conservative groups such as the *American Enterprise Institute, Americans for Tax Reform*, and the *Heritage Foundation*).

Out-of-Class Activity

Research Americans for Prosperity, the American Enterprise Institute, Americans for Tax Reform, and the Heritage Foundation. Would you describe these as conservative or liberal organizations? Why? Have these organizations impacted policy in the US? How?

Chairman Dick Armey also was a senior policy adviser for DC-based lobbying firm DLA Piper, whose recent clients include pharmaceutical maker Bristol-Myers Squibb, health care provider Metropolitan Health Networks, medical device supplier SleepMed, and the pharmaceutical firm Medicines Company. This is significant because it is Dick Armey who organized the anti-health care reform rallies at town halls across the country during the debates over health care reform in the US; these events were depicted as being spontaneous uprisings and thus created the perception that Americans were greatly upset about the health care reform passed by Congress and signed into law by President Obama. This is one example of the simulated or artificial grassroots activities noted earlier.

Although the vast majority of money from the Koch brothers in the 2012 election cycle went to losing candidates, their influence on politics simply cannot be understated. According to Source Watch (2013), Koch industries "owns a diverse group of companies involved in refining and chemicals; process and pollution control equipment and technologies; minerals; fertilizers; polymers and fibers; commodity trading and services; forest and consumer products; and ranching." Koch Industries is the largest provider of funds for political campaigns among all oil industry PACs, and about two-thirds of the incoming freshman class of GOP legislators received money from them. And although about 90% of their donations tend to go to Republicans, the point is they give to both sides of the aisle in order to assure their interests are served in Congress.

According to the Center for American Progress (2013), Koch Industries denies climate change while working to reduce regulations on polluting industries, repeal heath care reform, fight reform of Wall Street, and dismantle worker unions. One of its major successes was protecting Governor Scott Walker of Wisconsin, who narrowly defeated a recall election after private interests such as Koch Industries used their enormous pull to turn out large numbers of voters.

Koch Industries, founded by David and Charles Koch, is also closely aligned with the **American Legislative Exchange Council (ALEC)**, also noted above by Common Cause. Koch Industries is a member and funder of ALEC. ALEC is "a corporate bill mill. It is not just a lobby or a front group; it is much more powerful than that. Through ALEC, corporations hand state legislators their wish lists to benefit their bottom line. Corporations fund almost all of ALEC's operations. They pay for a seat on ALEC task forces where corporate lobbyists and special interest reps vote with elected officials to approve 'model' bills" (SourceWatch, 2013).

According to its website: "The American Legislative Exchange Council works to advance the fundamental principles of free-market enterprise, limited government, and federalism at the state level through a nonpartisan public-private partnership of America's state legislators, members of the private sector and the general public." ALEC began in the early 1970s, developed influential task forces and ultimately think tanks, which act "upon ALEC's long-time philosophy that the private sector should be an ally rather than an adversary in developing sound public policy."

Common Cause (2013) asserts that: "ALEC supports public subsidies for private schools, the development of privately-owned prisons, restrictions on the voting rights of thousands of college students and senior citizens and unlimited, secret corporate spending on behalf of political candidates and parties." Additionally, "ALEC has a lengthy list of things it opposes, including federal and state environmental regulations, the new federal health care reform law, state minimum wage laws, and trade and public employee unions."

ALEC writes resolutions and model bills that frequently become law. While ALEC does not always win, about 180 of its model bills are enacted in at least one state every year. According to its website: "To date, ALEC's Task Forces have considered, written and approved hundreds of model bills on a wide range of issues, model legislation that will frame the debate today and far into the future. Each year, close to 1,000 bills, based at least in part on ALEC Model Legislation, are introduced in the states. Of these, an average of 20 percent become law." Some of the recent successes of ALEC include "Stand Your Ground" laws like in Florida (which made the news in the shooting death of Trayvon Martin by George Zimmerman in the state of Florida), tough "Show Me Your Papers" anti-immigration laws as in Arizona, and "Voter ID" laws passed in many states.

Who is behind ALEC and how does ALEC work? ALEC receives nearly all of its money from wealthy individuals, foundations, and corporations in order to do legislative work on their behalf. The list of corporations behind ALEC is enormous, and includes or has included well-known brands including Anheuser-Busch, AOL, AT&T, Bank of America, Bayer, BP, Bristol-Myers Squibb, Charter Communications, Chevron, Comcast Cable, Cox Communications, Cracker Barrel, Dike Energy, EBay, Eli Lilly, Exxon Mobile, Farmer's Insurance, FedEx, Georgia Pacific, GlaxoSmithKline, Honeywell, Marathon Oil, Microsoft, Occidental Oil & Gas, Pfizer, Phillip Morris, Public Supermarkets, Qwest Communications, Rubber Manufacturers Association, Shell Oil, State Farm Insurance, TMobile, TASER International, Direct TV, Time Warner, UPS, United Health, Verizon, VISA, Yahoo, and many others (Common Cause, 2013).

Reviews of ALEC suggest that money donated to the organization gets donors a seat at the table with lawmakers, a level of access that is clearly greater than that of the average person in the United States. Further, when legislators, governors, and other officials work on behalf of ALEC, they receive money in the form of campaign donations as well as advertisements directed against their opponents.

Further, according to Common Cause, ALEC sends lobbyists on trips with lawmakers in order to influence what laws they pass and don't pass. ALEC "has raised and spent an estimated $4 million in funds from its corporate backers since 2006 to pay for state lawmakers' trips to meet with corporate CEOs and lobbyists at ALEC sponsored events at posh retreats, according to internal ALEC documents and other investigative work." According to its analysis, Common Cause found that ALEC funders pay to have legislators and corporate lobbyists sit together and write state laws as equals, with literally no input from normal citizens. At these meetings, legislators enjoy free meals and entertainment and their trips are paid for or reimbursed by corporations, including stays at beach resorts where lawmakers bring their families! More than 300 lawmakers have taken these trips, and more than 100 corporations have been involved in paying for them. The largest companies are pharmaceutical and tobacco companies, as well as energy and health insurance corporations.

While none of this activity can be considered bribery and most of it is legal, it is not necessarily in the public's interest. Common Cause provides an example:

> Two major tobacco companies on ALEC's private board, Altria [formerly Phillip Morris] and Reynolds American, have worked through ALEC to fight state regulations on second-hand smoke, increased state taxes on tobacco, and efforts to regulate tobacco sales nationwide through the Food and Drug Administration. In 2006 alone, those two firms put nearly $35.3 million into a successful campaign to stop a California ballot initiative that would have directed revenue from an increased tobacco tax to improve hospital care for children and bolster anti-smoking campaigns.

Deregulation of tobacco is not in the public interest, and tobacco literally kills hundreds of thousands of Americans every year and costs us more than one hundred billion in direct losses annually (more on this in Chapters 4 and 5). Yet, since Congress and state legislatures are impacted to a much greater degree by groups like ALEC than they are by regular, everyday citizens, powerful corporate interests tend to be protected even when they are detrimental to citizens. The state of North Carolina is currently considering a bill to remove restrictions on second-hand smoke exposure in public places and community colleges, a bill written by ALEC.

Because of negative publicity, several notable companies have quit ALEC, including Amazon.com, Hewlett Packard, Miller/Coors, John Deere, CVS Caremark, Best Buy, Coca-Cola, McDonald's, Dell Computers, Kraft Foods, Blue Cross-Blue Shield, WalMart, and the Bill & Melinda Gates Foundation. ALEC is also asking lawmakers *not* to use its name in discussions with others and is reportedly considering changing its name.

Here is a contemporary example of the impact that ALEC and its subsidiary corporations can have on the law. In 2010, the state of Arizona passed a law that required police officers to request proof of legal resident status from anyone they felt looks suspicious—i.e., not documented American citizens. The stated purpose of the law, titled, **Support Our Law Enforcement and Safe Neighborhoods Act**, was to crack down on illegal immigration and thereby make Arizona communities safer.

But from where did the law come? It turns out that the idea of the law came from private, for profit companies. The bill was introduced and sponsored by legislators who received financial donations from those same companies, and signed into law by a governor with close connections to the companies as well. It started in a meeting between Arizona legislators and corporate officials from ALEC, which included members of the **Corrections Corporation of America (CCA)**.

CCA's plan was to build and operate prisons for illegal immigrants, including both adults and children, and they sold this plan to Arizona as a positive gain for the community in terms of jobs. Reports by CCA show they believe illegal immigration to be the next big financial market for their company. So they helped drafted the model bill which became Arizona's immigration reform law.

Ultimately, 36 legislators joined to co-sponsor the bill, and two-thirds of them were members of ALEC or were at the meeting with ALEC when the bill was drafted. As the bill was being considered, CCA was lobbying the legislature to assure passage. Of these 36 co-sponsors, 30 received donations from prison lobbyists or companies within six months of the passage of the bill. Governor Jan Brewer then signed the bill into law. It turns out that two of her top advisers used to be lobbyists for private prison corporations.

The lesson of this story is simple: If private companies wrote this law, because they thought it would benefit them financially, then they clearly do not really want illegal immigration to go away. How do we know? Because they are in the business of making money; they would not write and push a law that would lead to monetary loss. Translation: As long as there is illegal immigration, private prisons will make money. If illegal immigration is stopped, they will not make money. That is the clearest proof that the Arizona immigration law (written by the private prison industry) will not reduce illegal immigration into the country, and that this was not its assumed purpose (in spite of claims by state officials).

Summary about the Law

Lawmakers tend to be white, older, rich males (WORMs). People who fund the elections process and who most lobby to have their interests served by the law also share the same characteristics.

Of course, lawmakers can still represent their constituents even if they do not look like them, as long as they serve as **representative agents** for them. According to Ginsberg et al. (2013: 475–476): "A good deal of evidence indicates that ... members of Congress ... *do* work very hard to speak for their constituents' views and to serve their constituents' interests." Yet, this does not mean they "always represent the interests of their constituents."

> In fact, a review of studies by Ginsberg and colleagues suggests that, even though shifts in public opinion on particular issues do in fact tend to lead to changes in public policy ... especially ... when there are wide swings in opinion regarding particularly high-profile issues that are relatively simple ... actual policies strongly reflect the preferences of the most affluent and show little or no relationship to the preferences of poor or middle-income Americans (pp. 241, 243).

These authors conclude that "every American citizen has an equal right to voice opinions in the political arena, but ... some voices receive a very attentive listening while others are hardly heard at all" (p. 243). Specifically, "government policy is much less responsive to public opinion on the issues that really count, and ... when the interests of elites are at stake, government officials are much more likely to represent the opinions of the affluent than the poor" (p. 243). As a general rule, legislators tend to be less responsive to low-income constituents than the well-off. This is simply because it is the well-off who engage in lobbying and interest group activity.

Voters also tend to be unrepresentative of the larger population, and most people don't regularly vote anyway. Given all this, it is hard to argue that the consensus view of the law is accurate; that is, the law does not come from or represent citizens. Yet it also does not mean that the conflict view of the law is correct, only that it is at least possible. The truth is that every day, average citizens can and do impact the law, but in the competition between many groups to have your will enacted into the law (as predicted by the pluralist view of the law) it is the powerful who tend to be the most successful at having their will reflected in the law.

A recent study, stunning in its findings and implications, supports the above statement. The study, examining whether American lawmaking more closely resembles the consensus, conflict, or pluralist views discussed earlier, suggests that American politics more closely resembles an **oligarchy** rather than a democracy (Gilens & Page, 2014). According to the authors: "When the preferences of economic elites and the stands of organized interest groups are controlled for, the preferences of the average American appear to have only a minuscule, near-zero, statistically non-significant impact upon public policy" (p. 21). The authors further note:

> Nor do organized interest groups substitute for direct citizen influence, by em-bodying citizens' will and ensuring that their wishes prevail ... Interest groups do have substantial independent impacts on policy, and a few groups (particularly labor unions) represent average citizens' views reasonably well. But the interest group system as a whole does not. Over-all, net interest group alignments are not significantly related to the preferences of average citizens. The net alignments of the most influential, business oriented groups are *negatively* related to the average citizen's wishes (p. 22).

The authors thus reject the consensus view (which they refer to as *Majoritarian Electoral Democracy*) as well as the notion of pluralism that favors common, everyday Americans (*Majoritarian Pluralism*).

Instead, their findings indicate support for *Biased Pluralism* (where "corporations, business associations, and professional groups predominate" [p.3]) and *Economic Elite Domination* (where "policy making is dominated by individuals who have substantial economic resources, i.e. high levels of income and/or wealth — including, but not limited to, ownership of business firms" [p. 6]). The authors thus state that "preferences of economic elites ... have far more independent impact upon policy change than the preferences of average citizens do. To be sure, this does not mean that ordinary citizens always lose out; they fairly often get the policies they favor, but only because those policies happen also to be preferred by the economically elite citizens who wield the actual influence" (p. 22).

The conclusion of the authors is that, in America:

> the majority does *not* rule — at least not in the causal sense of actually determining policy outcomes. When a majority of citizens disagrees with economic elites and/or with organized interests, they generally lose. Moreover, because of the strong status quo bias built into the US political system, even when fairly large majorities of Americans favor policy change, they generally do not get it (p. 23).

Given that lawmaking is a political process that helps determine whose ideology will become the dominant worldview, the above facts suggests it is at least possible that the criminal law will tend to serve the interests of WORMs—white, older, rich, men— more than any other group in society.

If this is true, then we'd expect the law to ignore the harmful acts of the powerful and to instead focus heavily on the harmful acts of the powerless—poor people of color—and thus be ineffective in terms of crime control. Why? Because why would lawmakers—WORMs—legislate harmful acts committed by other WORMs as crimes? Further, we would expect criminal justice policy to disproportionately harm poor people of color and thus fail to protect due process and equality in society. Why? The same reason—WORMs should logically be expected to define harmful acts of people different than them as crimes which would subject those people to greater involvement with the criminal justice system.

The only way to know for sure if this is true is to examine what the law does— specifically, those acts that are crimes and especially those acts that are deemed to be the most serious (as well as those that are not). Before moving on to this, it is first important to illustrate one final important fact: the media in American are owned and operated by the same types of people who make the law—WORMs. This is tremendously important because the media have an enormous impact on citizens in terms of influencing their worldview, including their views of crime and criminal justice. In fact, it is the media who largely determine America's perceptions of who is dangerous and who is not (Robinson, 2011).

Who Owns the Media?

The term **media** is a plural form of the word *medium*, which refers to the means of communication, information, and entertainment in society. The media are made up of the Internet, television, radio, newspapers, books, and so on. The media are often referred to as the "mass media" or the "mainstream media" which are "media that are easily, in-expensively, and simultaneously accessible to large segments of a population" (Surette, 1992: 10). These are the sources most commonly relied upon by citizens for information as well as entertainment.

Major Forms of Media

There are at least three kinds of media, not including advertising (which is present in all three media types). First, there are the news media. Second, there are the entertainment media. Finally, there is infotainment. The primary goal of the **news media** is to provide information on major events, issues, problems, and trends. The primary goal of the **entertainment media** is to entertain or divert our attention from more serious concerns. Finally, **infotainment** exists in-between the news and entertainment media; it is a blurring of the lines between the news and entertainment.

Crime and criminal justice make up a major part of each of these forms of media. Specifically, crime and criminal justice stories make up a large portion of local (and sometimes national) news, are common in all forms of entertainment, and even comprise a surprising share of infotaintment (e.g., television shows such as COPS). As you'll see in this chapter, this is problematic for at least two reasons. First, media coverage of crime and criminal justice is highly inaccurate. As will be shown in this chapter, the media tend to focus only on some forms of crimes committed under some circumstances, and/or committed by certain people.

Second, media coverage of crime and criminal justice is largely responsible for major misconceptions held by citizens. Since the media are the main source for news about crime and criminal justice policy for citizens, it makes sense that they would create misconceptions. As noted by David Krajicek (1998: 139): "The press provides our window on public problems, on the government's strategies to solve them, and on how well those strategies succeed (or fail)." When it comes to crime, since most Americans will not be victimized by serious crimes other than theft, they are far more likely to get their information from media sources than from personal experience.

However, not all media sources have the same impact on us. According to John Harrigan (2000: 120): "The organization at the top of the media hierarchy decides what counts as news." The top of the media hierarchy has been referred to as the **inner ring** of the media as well as the **first tier** of the media (Herman & Chomsky, 2002). It is the inner ring or first tier of the media that determines what is in the media. These media sources are discussed below.

Corporate Control of the Media

Most of our sources of information and entertainment are not owned or operated by the public. Nor are they necessarily run in the interests of the common citizen. While that last point is certainly debatable, it is beyond question that the media are owned and operated by elites — specifically for-profit corporations.

Ben Bagdikian (2004) chronicles the ever-growing stranglehold that major corporations have on news in the United States. In 2004, "five huge corporations — Time Warner, Disney, Murdoch's News Corporation, Bertelsmann of Germany, and Viacom (formerly CBS) — own most of the newspapers, magazines, books, radio and TV stations, and movie studios of the United States." Instead of local media control, the mainstream press are owned and operated by a handful of major profit-seeking corporations who have "more communications power than was exercised by any despot or dictatorship in history" (p. 3).

In a nutshell, NBC is owned by General Electric, ABC is owned by Disney, CBS is owned by the CBS Corporation, CNN is owned by Time Warner, and Fox News is owed by Rupert Murdoch's News Corporation. Viacom is another large media company that owns lots of channels including MTV, Nickelodeon/Nick-at-Nite, VH1, BET, Comedy Central, and many other media companies. Less and less corporations control the media over time, as shown in Figure 3.2. By the way, these media corporations are largely run by the same people who make the law — white, older, rich males.

All of these media companies are profit-seeking entities that are aimed at making money above all else. Noam Chomsky writes that the mainstream press consists of "major, very profitable, corporations." Since the media are "profit maximizing commercial

Figure 3.2. Number of Corporations that Control a Majority of U.S. Media*

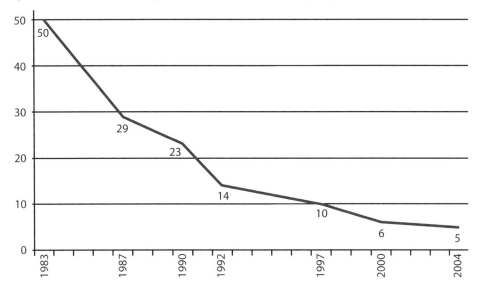

* Media include newspapers, magazines, TV and radio stations, books, music, movies, videos, wire services, and photo agencies.
Source: http://www.corporations.org/media/. Based on research compiled by Ben Bagdikian.

organizations," efforts to seek profit may interfere with honest and objective journalism that can result in people being unaware of key facts necessary to make informed choices on matters of social policy (McChesney, 2004: 17).

> **Out-of-Class Activity:**
> Find out who owns your local newspapers. What else do they own? Do they accurately cover crime and criminal justice?

Why does it matter when it comes to crime? Crime is often seen as a serious problem deemed worthy of significant media attention. Public policies are created to deal with, fight, solve, or prevent it. Citizens who see, hear, or read stories about crime and the policies created to address it may assume what they are seeing, hearing, or reading is accurate and objective. This is often untrue. That which is being depicted may be aimed at one simple goal—creating profit for the media corporation, whether true or not.

The argument from the top media scholars is that the media have become little more than profit-generating businesses. According to Edward Herman & Noam Chomsky (2002: xvii), bottom-line considerations of profit have become more important along with increased corporate power over the media through mergers and centralization. Herman & Chomsky point out that "the dominant media firms are quite large businesses; they are controlled by very wealthy people or by managers who are subject to sharp constraints by owners and other market-profit-oriented forces; and they are closely interlocked, and have important common interests, with other major corporations, banks, and government" (p. 14). In this environment, "the pressures of stockholders, directors, and bankers to focus on the bottom line are powerful" (p. 5). If what really matters to the media is money, it is clear that coverage of crime helps generate profit. Simply stated, crime sells. This is likely one significant reason why crime is such a popular topic in the media.

According to Robert McChesney, corporate owned media threaten the vital duties of journalists necessary for a healthy democracy, which include:

1) Acting as a watchdog of the powerful.
2) Separating truth from lies.
3) Presenting a wide variety of different opinions based on empirical information.

McChesney (2004: 57) concludes that the mainstream press fails in this regard because of "the system of profit-driven journalism in largely noncompetitive markets that began to emerge over a century ago."

The media have often been referred to as the **Fourth Estate** because they have been "uniquely capable by force of will, resources, and mission to uncover the misconduct, malfeasance, and hidden shame of the state" (Montross, Jr. & Mulvaney, 2009: 1444). Without the media acting as a watchdog of the powerful, the powerful can do and say things that American citizens will not be able to question or challenge due to being uninformed about the facts. This is especially problematic given that acts of the powerful tend to be so much more damaging than even serious street crime (see Chapters 4 and 5).

Three important outcomes of corporate ownership of media are: 1) a failure to focus on acts of the powerful; 2) relatively similar content across media outlets devoid of context; and 3) a lack of critical coverage of important issues. This is problematic for several reasons. First, it means that people generally do not learn important realities of corporate and white-collar crime (realities we will examine in Chapters 4 and 5). Second, it means the stories that appear as news will be roughly the same stories no matter where you live; there will be little variation even based on real differences across communities. Third, it means that stories will tend to be covered in the same superficial way; there will be little depth or context to the stories. Fourth, it means that many important issues will be ignored, which are typically issues that do not serve the interests of the corporations that own the media.

When it comes to media coverage of crime and criminal justice, this is exactly what studies tend to find—the same general focus on and fascination with certain types of crimes committed by certain types of people under certain circumstances covered in generally the same way, and a failure to focus on other types of crimes committed by the powerful.

Robert McChesney (2004: 4) also asserts that the mainstream media are an antidemocratic force because they help maintain a system of government where most important decisions are "the province of the corporate sector" and they "are influenced by powerful special interests with little public awareness or input." The culprit, according to McChesney, is *neoliberalism*, or policies such as deregulation of business that "maximize the role of markets and profit-making and minimize the role of nonmarket institutions" that are based on the belief that "society works best when business runs things and there is as little possibility of government 'interference' with business as possible" (p. 6).

McChesney goes further, suggesting that media activity is most consistent with the "needs and concerns of a handful of enormous and powerful corporations" that are run by very wealthy people whose "interests are often distinct from those of the vast majority of humanity" (pp. 29–30). Interestingly, it is the same people who own the media that make the law—white, older, rich men (WORMs).

Many consumers of media products (i.e., news and entertainment) are as unaware of this fact as they are that the crime and criminal justice news they see on TV and in the newspapers is the version that large corporations choose to air. Would it be logical to expect these corporations to focus on their own acts of deviance and harmful behaviors? Further, would it be logical to expect corporate media to broadcast many stories about corporate crimes at all, given their close ties to and vested in the welfare of corporations? Robert McChesney (2004: 93) answers no because "the corporate news media have a vested interest in the corporate system. The largest media firms are members in good standing in the corporate community and are closely linked to it through business relations, shared investors, interlocking directors, and common political values." Perhaps this is why street crimes are more likely to be the focus of news than acts like corporate and white-collar crimes.

In-Class Activity:
Go to the website of the Nielsen ratings. Examine the top rated television shows, movies, and video games. How many of these television shows, movies, and video games focus on crime and/or acts of violence?

With the rare exception of cases such as Enron (Williams, 2008) corporate crime is generally ignored by the mainstream press (Lynch, Stretesky & Hammond, 2000; McMullan, 2006). According to Sandra Evans & Richard Lundman (1983: 539), "newspapers protect corporate reputations by failing to provide frequent, prominent and criminally oriented coverage of common corporate crimes." When an act committed by corporations is dangerous or harmful but not covered by corporate owned media, a logical conclusion is that the mainstream media have some vested interest in making sure such acts continue to fly under the radar.

This may explain why "the most commonly suppressed news items each year are stories involving corporations" (Bagdikian, 2004: 161). While the media fail to report on harmful and culpable acts of corporations, the corporations themselves spend hundreds of millions of dollars each year in advertisements, brochures, web sites and public events in order to put forth a more gentle image. Apparently, this works, as throughout the 1990s, roughly 70% of Americans had a favorable view of corporations, although this figure has declined recently in the wake of the numerous stories of corporate fraud (Pew, 2005). Interestingly, a majority of Americans report thinking corporations make too much profit and hold too much power, yet Americans are evenly split on whether regulation of business is necessary or does more harm than good (Pew, 2002).

In summary, US corporations, through the inner ring of media outlets they own and control, define problems, identify crises, and thereby determine "what issues will be brought to the attention of political leaders" and US citizens, while other issues and problems are ignored (Harrigan, 2000: 124). This is an amazing power of the mainstream media.

Media Coverage of Crime and Criminal Justice

According to Steven Chermak (1995), certain kinds of crimes committed against certain kinds of victims are more likely to be featured in the media, especially when they are violent in nature, random, rare, and committed against victims perceived as innocent and vulnerable. Of all types of crime, serious, violent street crime generates more media coverage—acts like murder, rape, and robbery (Chermak & Chapman, 2007; Potter & Kappeler, 1998).

As David Krajicek (1998: 95) said about his own work as a crime reporter, crime reports focus on the miserable, the deviant, the strange, and the "particularly cruel." The common saying, "if it bleeds, it leads," accurately characterizes the philosophy of the media in the United States. Specifically: "Murder and sexual offenses are the marquee offenses ... and certain cases, generally based upon nubility or celebrity, are anointed for extravagant coverage" (p. 4). Roslyn Muraskin & Shelly Domash (2007: 1) agree, writing: "The cliché phrase, 'if it bleeds, it leads,' is unfortunately the case with the American media; the search for heinous, outrageous and even *sexy* crimes, no matter how rare the incident ... is sure to boost ratings."

By focusing on certain types of crimes over others, the media are involved in "constructing" the typical view of crime, even when they are only reporting "extreme, dramatic cases: the public is more likely to think they are representative because of the emphasis by the media" (Chermak, 1994: 580). That is, it is the media from where citizens get their views on and perspectives of crime.

Gary Potter & Victor Kappeler (1998: 7) explain: "Media coverage directs people's attention to specific crimes and helps to shape those crimes as social problems." This means Americans are much more concerned with violent crimes such as murder, even though they are much more likely to be victimized by property crimes such as theft and burglary (and especially acts of white-collar and corporate crime that receive virtually no coverage).

Recall the metaphor of the law and media as spotlights that determine on what Americans focus their attention and on what they do not. It is the law that determines who the criminals are (and who they are not); along with the media, the law determines who is seen as dangerous (and who is not), who we fear (and who we don't), as well as who we catch with criminal justice (and who we don't) (Hagan, 2010). Recall that these are decisions made by politicians in pursuit of their political ideologies.

Homicide, being violent and perceived as the most serious crime of all, is usually news. In fact, in some places, one-quarter of all news stories are focused on murder, even though murder regularly accounts for only a tiny fraction of 1% of all crimes known to the police. Although murder may be the most heinous of all crimes, this disproportionate focus creates misconceptions about which crimes are common and likely to happen to any given person. Reporters will inevitably go to the scene of a murder,

Figure 3.3. TV reporter

Originally posted to Flickr by Sister72. Available at: http://en.wikipedia.org/wiki/File:Reporter.jpg.

like in Figure 3.3, hours or even days after it occurs, which can result in fear of street crime among viewers.

Media coverage of murder is also problematic in that the types of murders that are most likely to be of focus by the media are not consistent with the typical murder. Most murders are committed against young men of color. Most murders are committed by people who know each other. Yet media coverage of murder tends to suggest that murder is mostly committed by strangers and against whites, females, and children. This creates misconceptions of not only who is dangerous but also who is most at risk of victimization (Robinson, 2009).

Media, Race, and Crime

The media generally are most focused on acts of people of color, especially African Americans (Dixon, 2007, 2008; Johnson, Bushman, & Dovidio, 2008; Johnson & Dixon, 2008; Wilcox, 2005). Specifically, black men are routinely depicted in the news as dangerous criminals (Russell-Brown, 2006). According to an exhaustive reviews of the evidence: "The media's representation of young Black men as criminal perpetrators is so uniform that most people treat them as imagined bogeymen. Studies indicate that Whites, Latinos, Asian Americas, American Indians, and even African Americans believe they are most likely to be victimized by Black men" (Russell-Brown, 2006: 29). Recall the argument from Chapter 1 of several scholars that blackness and criminality are synonymous in the minds of many. It is media coverage of crime that largely explains this. That is, we see crime as mostly a "black thing" because of how it's covered in the news and because of how it's depicted in entertainment and infotainment media. Also keep in mind a major point from Chapter 2 that it was prominent conservative politicians who conflated blackness with crime in the 1960s (e.g., George Wallace) and continuing in the 1980s (e.g., George H. W. Bush). Statements, speeches, and ads made by these politicians received major coverage across mainstream media outlets.

According to Donna Bishop (2006: 145):

> It is in the interest of the media to highlight violent crime, especially violence committed by young black males, because this is the kind of crime than the public fears most. This is not to suggest that the media intentionally try to generate fear or champion a punitive crime control agenda, but they exploit fear and inadvertently promote that agenda in the interest of profit. Dramatic accounts of the most feared crimes sell newspapers and magazines. They attract viewers to television news and other crime-related programming, and generate advertising revenues. Violent crime is cheap and easy to report (it does not require in-depth investigative reporting) and it has wide audience appeal.

In addition, there tends to be more media coverage of homicides when they are interracial in nature, even though most murders are committed within the same race (Perry & Sutton, 2006). This leads to increased fear of blacks, especially among whites (Wilcox, 2005). One study found that when offenders are not identified by race in the news, most viewers assume that the offenders are black and that police are white. This is especially true for heavy news viewers (Dixon, 2007). This may serve as evidence that when people think of crime, they tend to think of black crime, since this is so prevalent on television and in other media forms.

Interestingly, being exposed to black suspects on the news increases the odds that people will come to see criminality itself as a function of dispositional factors such as personality traits, consistent with the conservative crime control agenda introduced in Chapter 2 (Gilliam & Iyengar, 2000). This means viewers see blacks as responsible for their criminality rather than being promoted to act by structural impediments. Those who are heavy watchers of the news featuring blacks as suspects are more likely to view the world as dangerous (Dixon, 2007). Perhaps it is not surprising then that exposure to black suspects leads to increased support for punitive crime control policies such as capital punishment and three-strikes legislation. Travis Dixon (2007: 168) suggests this to the fact that blacks have been "so associated with criminality on news programs." Again, the conservative political ideology tends to conflate "black" with crime and that conservatives generally favor "get tough" approaches to criminal justice.

Those who hold negative stereotypes about African Americans are less likely to perceive blacks as facing structural limitations: "as news viewing increases, the perception that Blacks face structural limitations decreases" (Dixon, 2007: 239). Those who hold black stereotypes are also more likely to see offenders as culpable, especially when the stories feature black offenders (Dixon & Azocar, 2007). This is evidence of the media's impact on criminal justice policy; the media help create myths of black dangerousness, which ultimately results in an expansion of criminal punishment against blacks. Meanwhile, whites are overrepresented as victims and police officers (Dixon, Azocar & Casas, 2003). This fits well with the popular conception of whites as innocent.

Why do black crimes get so much attention in the press? Because those "crimes that receive the most attention—from the media, from politicians, and from criminal justice policy makers—are 'street crimes' such as murder, robbery, and rape" (Krajicek, 1998: 4). Robert McChesney's (2004: 87) review of the research leads to the same conclusion that media coverage has "overemphasized African Americans as criminals and whites as victims" and "has had the perverse effect of encouraging popular support for draconian measures to stem the bogus 'crime wave.'"

Not surprisingly, studies show that both demographic characteristics of those watching the news and those portrayed as offenders and victims have meaningful impacts on attitudes toward minorities in society. For example, in some cases, white women are more likely to see black males as guilty when they are shown as suspects of rape on television while white males are more likely to respond sympathetically to white male suspects on television (Mastro, Lapinski, Kopacz, & Behm-Morawitz, 2009).

According to a study by Jon Hurwitz & Marc Peffley (2010), African Americans are far more likely than whites to say that it is a serious problem that "police stop and question blacks far more often than whites" or that police "care more about crimes against whites than minorities" (70% versus 17%, respectively). Similarly, African Americans are far more likely than whites to disagree with the statement that "courts give all a fair trial" (60% versus 25%, respectively). These differences in perceptions were driven largely by personal experience, as African Americans are far more likely than whites to be stopped, questioned, and arrested by police and thereby processed through the courts.

Meanwhile, whites attribute racial disparities in criminal justice processing to their perception that African Americans commit more crimes and/or are more dangerous than whites. This belief emanates from stereotypes of blacks as violent and criminal. According to the authors:

> Social psychologists conducting controlled lab experiments … have demonstrated that merely thinking briefly about blacks can lead people, including police officers, to evaluate ambiguous behavior as aggressive, to miscategorize harmless objects as weapons, to shoot quickly and, at times, inappropriately, and to endorse harsh treatment of a black (versus a white) suspect.

And other examples are provided as well:

> In a series of survey experiments we found that when whites with negative stereotypes of African Americans were asked about black (versus white) perpetrators, they were much more likely to judge blacks as guilty of the alleged crimes, assume blacks would commit more crimes in the future, and favor much harsher punishments for black than white suspects.
>
> In another survey experiment, we manipulated race in a more subtle way: with a single phrase, "inner city," that carries strong racial connotations. A random half of white respondents was asked about spending money for prisons (versus anti-poverty programs) to lock up "violent criminals," while the other half was asked about "violent *inner city* criminals." As expected, whites' racial stereotypes were much more important in boosting support for prisons to lock up criminals in the inner city (reported in Sides, 2013).

Generally speaking, media coverage of crime also tends to be most focused on acts of the poor, young, as well as men. Thus, those people depicted as most dangerous tend to be young, poor men of color (Robinson, 2009). Because of this media spotlight, people believe these people to be the most dangerous, even though they are not. As it turns out, harmful acts of these groups are also the most likely to be legislated as crime, whereas the harmful acts of wealthy whites are least likely to be identified by the law as crimes (see Chapters 4 and 5). Yet, media focus on poor men of color reinforces support for criminal justice policies promoted by conservative politicians; as Americans came to fear street crime more, it became easier to promote and institute "get tough" policies that promise public safety even while they generally failed to do so and also imposed enormous costs on society.

Media Coverage of Criminal Motivation

Media coverage generally tends to depict criminal motivation as individualistic, meaning it leaves citizens with the impression that criminality is motivated by individual-level factors such as jealously, emotional instability, mental illness, greed, and so forth (Cavender & Bond-Maupin, 1993). According to Robert Bohm & Jeffery Walker (2006: xxi), crime is seen in the United States largely as an individual phenomenon, meaning it arises due to individual-level causes, "the result of a personal defect — especially of poor, young males between the ages of 15 and 24.... there is no social or structural solution to the problem of crime." As such, media coverage of crime tends to reinforce conceptions of the etiology of crime that is comprised within the conservative ideology. Recall that the conservative political ideology holds that crime results from free will and rational choice.

Ray Surette concurs (2007: 209), writing: "With its individually rooted causes, crime is constructed as an autonomous plague on society, its genesis not associated with other historical, social, or structural conditions." These are criminals of their own will, "certainly not of society's will. Such criminals can, therefore, be guiltlessly battled and eliminated" (p. 230).

According to Kenneth Dowler (2004: 584), "crime reporting is criticized for ignoring the relationship between crime and broader social conditions." While news reports associate criminal violence with youth, maleness, and minority group membership, the news media ignore "how labor markets, employment opportunities, poverty and so forth as they relate to crime." That is, the liberal view of crime is largely ignored and the conservative view dominates. Dowler explains:

> Ultimately, the tendency to portray crime as perpetrated mainly by pathological individuals precludes alternative explanations ... Consequently, crime portrayals are almost based exclusively on individual characteristics rather than on social conditions, and the causes of crime are perceived to be rooted in individual failings rather than social explanations. Deviant behavior is viewed as an individual choice, while social, economic, or structural explanations are ignored or deemed irrelevant.

The typical characterization of the individually responsible offender is consistent both with the dominant narrative of the innately evil criminal in the media as well as the cultural belief in American society of free will, which underlies most criminal justice practice.

Even though the media tend to cast motivations for crime as emanating from within individuals, more Americans suggest that "attacking the social and economic problems that lead to crime through better education and job training" comes closer to their own views about what should be effective at reducing crime than "improving law enforcement with more prisons, police, and judges" (65% versus 31%, respectively) (Sourcebook of Criminal Justice Statistics, 2009). Higher portions of certain groups are more likely to say "attacking the social and economic problems that lead to crime through better education and job training," including non-whites (especially blacks), younger people (especially under the age of 30), people with college degrees (especially those with post graduate degrees), those living in urban areas, and Democrats (especially liberals). Yet, since lawmakers do not represent the common person—as shown in this chapter— lawmakers generally do not pursue crime prevention policies favored by the public.

One important outcome of the media's focus on individual motivations for criminality is greater pressure for crime control solutions to the crime problem. For example, Ray Surette (2007: 218) explains that given that the "repeated message in the media is that crime is largely perpetrated by predatory individuals who are basically different from the rest of us; that criminality is predominantly the result of individual problems; and that crimes are acts freely committed by individuals who have a wide range of alternate choices" crime control responses such as arrest, conviction, and punishment are entirely logical.

The Media Ignore Corporate Crime

As noted earlier, corporate crimes are virtually ignored by the media. Since mainstream media tend to ignore white-collar and corporate crime, this is a serious bias in mainstream media.

Ignoring corporate and white-collar crime is troubling precisely because the harms associated with such acts clearly dwarf those resulting from all street crimes combined in any given year (evidence of this is shown in Chapters 4 and 5). Americans do not know this, however, largely due to media coverage of violence. According to David Friedrichs (2006: 20):

> Perceptions of violence and fear are often shaped by the media. Conventional forms of violence are pervasively featured in film, television, newspapers, and most other media … The public has been socialized to think of violent crime principally in terms of either individual offenders or a small group of offenders (e.g., a gang); violent crimes are disproportionately associated with deranged or manifestly evil offenders, and are most readily thought of in terms of murder, rape, or felonious assault. Overall, it has been easier to portray the crimes of individual psychopaths than those of corporations, and such crime makes for much more colorful copy than corporate crime. When the media expose unsafe, harmful, and destructive activities of corporations, they risk, as well, losing advertising revenue from such corporations; this is only one of the more obvious reasons why the media focus on conventional violence.

If Friedrichs is correct, the media have a vested interest in *not* covering corporate crime.

While it is true that acts of white-collar and corporate crimes do occasionally make the news, it is only the worst of the worst cases that do. Robert McChesney (2004: 73) provides an example:

> The intense coverage of the widespread corporate malfeasance in 2002–2003 was very unusual. Careful analysis of the coverage provided evidence of how unusual; after all, the fraud that led to the collapse of major corporations like Enron and WorldCom had been going on for years with the knowledge of some pretty powerful people, yet it had never come to our attention until it was too late.

Ben Bagdikian (2004: 131) points out that the "unprecedented magnitude of corporate fraud, theft, and collusion was not by fly-by-night sleazy operations but by some of the country's largest corporations" aided by conspirators in the auditing and banking industry. Perhaps this explains the lack of serious investigation into what caused the fraud in the first place. Recall that mainstream media are owned by large corporations and have close connections with other large corporations.

A study of how mainstream television networks covered the corporate crime scandals of 2001–2002—discussed in Chapter 4—found that coverage of the crimes peaked in early 2002 (Center for Media and Public Affairs, 2002). From January to July 2001, there were 489 stories on ABC, NBC, and CBS about business, yet only 52 were about the scandals (11%). From January to July 2002 there were 613 stories about business and 471 centered on the scandals (77%). This is significant because the Enron scandal broke in the news at the end of November 2001; at the end of July 2002, WorldCom filed the largest bankruptcy in US business history. During this period, "the networks broadcast almost as many stories on corporate scandals as they did on business stories for the same period a year before." Further, 77% of the stories dealing with business were centered on the corporate scandals.

Ironically, some media companies committed the very same behaviors that got companies like Enron and WorldCom in trouble. Time Warner (owner of CNN), for example, who had joint business ventures with WorldCom and Qwest, allegedly distorted its books and inflated its revenues. Viacom (former owner of CBS) also had links to Enron. According to McChesney (2004: 94): "Media firms historically have been understandably reluctant to cover their own misdeeds in their news media, and they could hardly be enthusiastic about a no-holds-barred journalism that would uncover the entire corporate crime story." Logically, Time Warner and Viacom had pretty serious reasons for not providing in-depth analyses of the corporate fraud that rocked the country.

All of this is problematic precisely because the media serve as the major source of information about crime for most people (Beckett & Sasson, 2003). Crime stories funnel out to media viewers, but they are in no way accurate of what most crime really is; nor is public perception of crime.

The more people are unaware of the harms inflicted on them by corporations, the more this feeds the conservative political ideology of "hands off" corporations—i.e., the more deregulation of business makes sense and is favored by citizens. Logic suggests that, to the degree people become aware of corporate harms, the more they will favor regulation of business in the public interest. Yet, since mainstream media organizations are owned and operated by corporations, widespread and in-depth coverage of corporate crime is highly unlikely.

Summary about the Media

The media are largely owned and controlled by large, for-profit corporations. It is they who determine what is newsworthy and what is not, what is covered and what is not. Many media scholars now claim that the media are no longer as interested in telling the truth as they are in making money. Further, given that the media are owned by very powerful interests, it is not logical to expect them to regularly focus their attention on harmful acts of the powerful. This might explain the relative absence of corporate crime from the news.

Instead of focusing on harmful acts of elites, the media instead focuses heavily on street crime, especially certain kinds of street crimes committed by certain kinds of people under certain circumstances. The result is that Americans have false conceptions of what is actually the most dangerous and most likely to harm them. Regularly exposed to random acts of violence committed by strangers, Americans live in fear of street crime, even as the likelihood of being victimized by serious street crime is actually quite low for most Americans.

Further, given the news media's focus on crimes committed by people of color and its predominant focus on individual motivations for crime (such as free will or rational choice), it is easy to understand how the media tend to promote the conservative political ideology, especially when it comes to criminal justice practice. Ultimately, this leads to an expansion of criminal justice in America, one more consistent with the crime control model and less consistent with a due process model.

Summary

There are serious problems with major institutions in the US. First, the law fails to define the acts that actually pose the greatest threat to Americans as crimes and especially as serious crimes. Second, the media fail to cover them, thereby assuring they will be largely unknown to or understood by Americans.

Given the two major institutions in society that first determine which behaviors are illegal (and which are not) and that second highly influence people's perceptions of who is dangerous (and who is not) are not representative of the people, should we expect definitions of crime and serious crime and popular conceptions of crime and serious crime to be in the people's interests? Or should we expect them to be defined in ways that serve the interests of the people who make the law and own the media?

In fact, as you'll see in Chapters 4 and 5, it can be demonstrated empirically that the behaviors we identify as crimes and serious crimes are *not* the most harmful behaviors in society; they are, however, the acts that tend to be disproportionately committed by the powerless—poor people of color, and especially younger, poor, minority men. This, as it turns out, is the major source of bias in American criminal justice, a form of bias introduced earlier in the book as *innocent bias*, which is further examined in Chapters

4 and 5. Recall that innocent bias refers to unfairness in criminal justice that exists because of unfair criminal laws. It is called "innocent" because it does not emerge from intentional discrimination on the part of individual police officers, prosecutors, or other agents of criminal justice. Instead, innocent bias occurs when criminal justice agents innocently enforce biased criminal laws.

Key Terms

- **501(c)(4)s:** 501(c)(4)s are non-profit groups and corporations, supposedly set up for the common good, which can not only lobby for legislation but can also participate in the elections process by making donations to political campaigns.
- **527s:** 527s are a type of interest group that aims to promote particular candidates or ideas within politics.
- **American Legislative Exchange Council (ALEC):** The American Legislative Exchange Council (ALEC) consists of a group of corporations that write and promote bills in their own interests.
- **Bribery:** Bribery is a crime that consists of giving or receiving money or gifts in exchange for a vote.
- **Collective Conscience:** The collective conscience refers to the shared norms, values, and beliefs that bond citizens together.
- **Conflict View of the Law:** The conflict view of the law suggests that the law comes from the powerful and represents their interests.
- **Consensus View of the Law:** The consensus view of the law suggests that the law comes from the people and represents their interests.
- **Corrections Corporation of America (CCA):** The Corrections Corporation of America (CCA) is the largest private prison company in America.
- **Democracy:** Democracy is a form of government where power and decision-making reside in the hands of the people.
- **Entertainment Media:** Entertainment media entertain or divert our attention from more serious concerns.
- **First Tier:** See **inner ring**.
- **Fourth Estate:** The Fourth Estate refers to the media as a political force in society whose primary role is to challenge authority and power.
- **Infotainment:** Infotainment provides information through an entertaining format.
- **Inner Ring:** The inner ring or first tier media are the largest and most powerful members of the mainstream media and have the largest impact on audiences.
- **Interest Groups:** Interest groups are collectives of individuals with a common interest or goal who seek to influence public policy.
- **Iron Triangle:** An iron triangle consists of a connection or partnership between a congressional committee, an administrative agency, and an interest group.
- **Koch Industries:** Koch Industries consists of many large business interests owned and operated by brothers Charles and David Koch.
- **Media:** The media are our primary means of communication, information, and entertainment in society.

- **Money Swapping**: Money swapping is making large contributions to seemingly unrelated groups who then lobby for or against legislation in the former group's interests.
- **News Media**: The news media provide information on major events, issues, problems, and trends.
- **Oligarchy**: An oligarchy is a government or entity ruled by a small, powerful group.
- **Pluralism**: Pluralism is the idea that all interests should be free to compete for influence in the government.
- **Pluralist View of the Law**: The pluralist view of the law suggests that the law comes from numerous competing interests and serves the interests of whomever wins in the competition to have varied interests served.
- **Political Action Committees (PACs)**: Political action committees (PACs) are groups that represent a given interest or candidate that raise money for a candidate or party.
- **Representative Agents**: Lawmakers acts as representative agents when they work on behalf of and in the interests of their constituents.
- **Representative Republic**: A representative republic is a form of government where power and decision-making do not directly reside in the hands of the people but instead are in the hands of others who pledge to represent the people.
- **Revolving Door**: The revolving door is the term used to capture the reality that former federal officials often go to work in the lobbying world after serving as legislators.
- **Sociological Representation**: Sociological representation refers to an outcome in government where representatives have the same demographic and social characteristics as the people they represent.
- **Super PACs**: Super PACs are political action committees that are allowed to raise and spend unlimited amounts of money on candidates or parties.
- **Support Our Law Enforcement and Safe Neighborhoods Act**: The Support Our Law Enforcement and Safe Neighborhoods Act is a law passed by Arizona that requires police to determine the legal status of anyone they suspect to be in the country illegally during a routine stop or arrest.

Discussion Questions

1) Contrast the consensus, conflict, and pluralist views of the law.
2) Summarize who makes the law, votes for the law, and pays for the law.
3) Which view of the law is most accurate?
4) Provide real-life examples of how the wealthy and powerful have their interests protected in or served by the law. Focus on Koch Industries and the American Legislative Exchange Council.
5) What problems does corporate ownership of the media cause?
6) Summarize media coverage of crime and criminal justice.

Chapter 4

Property Street Crime versus Elite Deviance

"Corporate crime inflicts far more damage on society than all street crime combined. Whether in bodies or injuries or dollars lost, corporate crime and violence wins by a landslide."

—Russell Mokhiber, "Twenty Things You Should Know about Corporate Crime"

What Is Crime?

In the last chapter, you saw that the law is mostly created by white, older, rich men (WORMs). Further, political campaigns and elections are mostly funded by the same people. And most people are *not* registered to vote and do not regularly participate in the electoral process. Since it is the law that defines which behaviors are crimes (and which are not) as well as which are pursued by criminal justice agencies as serious crimes (and which are not), the fact that the law is not made by people representative of the US population raises the possibility that the criminal law might not serve our interests, meaning that the consensus view of the law is not accurate.

You also learned that the mainstream media are owned and operated mostly by the same people who make the law—corporations owned and operated by white, older, rich men (WORMs). And media coverage of crime and criminal justice tend to focus far more heavily and regularly on street crimes (that are disproportionately committed by poor people of color) while largely ignoring white-collar and corporate crimes (that are overwhelmingly committed by wealthy whites).

Given these facts, are definitions of crime and serious crime created in our interests (as suggested by the consensus view of the law), or do they serve the interests of the powerful (as suggested by the conflict view of the law)? An examination of what acts are defined as crimes and pursued as serious crimes may answer these questions.

Crime Is an Act That Violates the Criminal Law

When you think of the word *crime*, you probably have a good idea of what it means. Although there is a straightforward legal definition of crime, most of us think of crimes as any behaviors that are done intentionally and cause physical or financial harm to

Table 4.1. Crimes and Non-Crimes

Crimes	Non-Crimes
Theft	*Product shrinkage* (putting less product in containers and selling them for the same price as the original)
Murder	*Manufacturing and selling tobacco* (which kills 430,000 Americans a year)
Bank Robbery	*Risky securitization* (selling fraudulent loans to be invested on by unknowing consumers in the stock market)

another person. For example, if you were standing on a street corner minding your own business, and someone came up and poked a pencil into your eye, causing a loss of vision, you would probably feel that you had been victimized by crime. Even if it was not against the law, you would probably think it should be. If a corporation manufactured a toaster that shot sparks into your eyes, you might also feel like a victim of crime, even if it was not specifically a violation of the criminal law to manufacture such a toaster. Whether or not any act violates the law, you may feel like a crime victim when you are harmed by another.

Yet, from a legal standpoint, a **crime** occurs only when an act violates the criminal law. This means that there is no crime without law. Clearly, there are scores of behaviors that kill and injure us and take our property; many of them are committed intentionally but are not against the criminal law. Such acts are not legally considered crimes, even if we all think the act is wrong, immoral, deviant, or bad. What makes the act a crime is that it is written down as a crime by the government.

This means that crime is made up — invented — by people. Richard Quinney (2001: 15) makes this point clear in his book, *The Social Reality of Crime*, when he writes:

> Crime is a definition of behavior that is conferred on some persons by others. Agents of the law, representing segments of a politically organized society, are responsible for formulating and administering criminal laws. Persons and behaviors, therefore, become criminal because of the formulation and application of criminal definitions. Thus, crime is created.

Since crime is created by humans, it does not exist in nature. It is something that human beings have invented and continue to invent every day. Table 4.1 illustrates different kinds of harmful behaviors. Some of them are illegal (i.e., crime), while others are legal (i.e., not crimes). What makes some behaviors crimes and others not is not the degree of harms they cause or the culpability of the offenders, but instead is their status in the criminal law.

This is not to say that there is no harmful behavior in nature. Many behaviors in nature kill and lead to property loss. Yet, human beings are the only species to legislate killing and theft as crimes (and only under certain circumstances, because there are plenty of ways to kill people and take their property, even intentionally, without committing a crime). As noted in Chapter 2, only some forms of property-taking and only some forms of violence are legislated as crimes; many others are not. As it turns out, those harmful acts committed in the course of legitimate business (e.g., hazardous workplaces) tend *not* to be legislated as crimes even when they are viewed by larger society as abnormal or antisocial. Richard Quinney (2000: 230) explains:

> A capitalist economy, based on competition and free enterprise, promotes an ethic that stresses the rightness of any activity that is pursued in the interests of one's business or occupational activity. Consequently, other 'respectable' members of society engage in activities that have been criminally defined by various laws, but which are not considered by them or most of the public as criminal. Such business and occupational activities as misrepresentation in advertising, fraudulent financial manipulations ... misappropriation of public funds ... are regarded as little more than the American way of doing business.

You'll see in this chapter that Quinney is unfortunately right; major and widespread acts of fraud have occurred in the US, even recently nearly toppling the entire economy, and no one has been held accountable for it. In fact, legislators used taxpayer dollars to bail out the very companies that caused our recent economic woes!

Obviously, there are also ways to assault and kill that are perfectly legal. According to Quinney: "Violence that occurs in the interests of the dominant interests of society is ... legitimized violence. Assault and murder used on others in war, in military operations, in policing riots, and in the controlling of actions conceived as politically subversive are not defined as criminal. Such uses of violence are patriotic and as American ... as apple pie" (p. 232). Some of these kinds of acts will be discussed in Chapter 5.

Since crime is invented, then no behavior is inherently criminal, and any behavior can be defined as a crime. Because crime is a human invention, there will obviously be disagreement among citizens about what behaviors should constitute crime. Yet, several studies have shown a remarkable level of agreement among citizens about which behaviors should be called crimes and which crimes should be treated as the most serious. These studies typically reveal a higher level of perceived seriousness for the violent street crimes included in the Uniform Crime Reports—things like murder, rape, and robbery. That is, Americans generally believe the most serious crimes in America are murder, rape, robbery, and similar offenses (Bjornstrom, Kaufman, Peterson & Slater, 2010; Einat & Herzog, 2011; Green, Staerklé & Sears, 2006; Vogel & Meeker, 2001).

Out-of-Class Activity:
Go to the website of Loony Laws at: http://www.loonylaws.com/. Find some behaviors that are identified as crimes for your state. Discuss why you think these behaviors are banned. Does banning them serve the public interest?

Some would claim that this is evidence that the criminal law clearly serves the interests of the public. Given the evidence discussed in Chapter 3 with regard to whose interests impact the law, this is unlikely. And which came first—public support for the law or the law itself? It is likely that people perceive harmful acts as more or less serious based on their status in the criminal law and the degree to which they're covered in the media—

that is, people view the crimes identified by the government as the most serious precisely because they've been repeatedly told they are the most serious crimes for so long.

As you'll see in this chapter, the crimes considered serious in the US have been codified as serious since the 1930s; thus, Americans have been told for more than 80 years that some crimes are worse than others and our attention has been squarely focused on those crimes. Yet it should be noted that there are also studies showing that people generally think serious harmful acts committed by the wealthy and by corporations also ought to be illegal and subjected to criminal punishment (Almond, 2008; Brody & Kiehl, 2010; Cullen, Hartman & Jonson, 2009; Holtfreter, Piquero & Piquero, 2008; Jarrell & Ozymy, 2012; Piquero, Carmichael & Piquero, 2008; Rosenmerkel, 2001; Shelley, Chiricos & Gertz, 2011). The fact such acts are not pursued by criminal justice agencies is further evidence that the law does not serve us well.

As shown in Chapter 2, the interests of conservative politicians are the interests that are most reflected in the criminal law. And as shown in Chapter 3, it is rich, older white men (WORMs) who make the law and own the media. Therefore, it is possible that the acts that are defined as crimes (and those that are deemed to be the most serious) are *not* necessarily the most harmful behaviors in America but instead the ones that must be defined as crimes and serious crimes in order to serve their interests and the interests of the people who donate to their political campaigns.

Culpability

Of course, not all harmful acts are committed with **culpability.** For an act to be legally considered a crime, it must be committed with culpability, including acts that are committed under any of the following circumstances:

- **Intentionally**: Committed with a guilty mind on purpose (e.g., sticking a gun in someone's face and pulling the trigger with the intent to kill);
- **Negligently**: Committed as a result of a failure to meet normal or recognized expectations (e.g., failing to follow safety regulations meant to protect human life which results in death);
- **Recklessly**: Committed without due caution for human life or property (e.g., driving while intoxicated); and
- **Knowingly**: Committed with knowledge that an outcome is likely (e.g., continuing to manufacture a product after product testing reveals a high likelihood of a deadly defect).

Generally, acts committed intentionally are considered more serious in the criminal law than those committed negligently, recklessly, or knowingly. Considering that a person who is killed negligently, recklessly, or knowingly is just as dead as one killed intentionally, you may question the logic of such distinctions. You'll see in this chapter that dangerous acts of the powerful—elite deviance—are committed with culpability, yet many of them remain either legal or simply not vigorously pursued by criminal justice agencies.

Types of Crime

There are many different types of crime. There are also various ways to categorize the wide variety of crimes. In this book, *street crime* (those crimes on which we focus) will be compared and contrasted with *elite deviance* (those acts we tend to ignore).

Street Crime

The war on crime is a war on **street crime**, including some of the behaviors denounced by major politicians during the civil rights movement and of primary focus by the government since the 1980s. Street crime is synonymous with **serious crime**. What does "serious" mean?

The Uniform Crime Reporting Program (UCR) is a source of crime information compiled by the Federal Bureau of Investigation (FBI) each year. This source of data was created because of a need to gather and disseminate national crime statistics. In the 1920s, the International Association of Chiefs of Police (IACP) formed a committee to create a uniform system for recording police statistics. Crimes were originally evaluated on the basis of the following criteria:

- Harmfulness;
- Frequency of occurrence;
- Pervasiveness in all geographic areas of the country; and
- Likelihood of being reported to the police.

After a preliminary compilation in 1929 of a list of crimes that met these criteria, the committee completed their plan for developing the UCR. Statistics on these crimes were collected beginning in the 1930s.

As noted within each year's UCR publication: "Seven offenses were chosen to serve as an Index for gauging the overall volume and rate of crime." These offenses were known as **Part 1 Index Offenses**. In 1979, arson was added to the UCR list, for a total of eight "serious" crimes. These are defined in Table 4.2.

Given their own discussion of what constitutes a serious offense, you might expect that the street crimes listed above would be the ones that cause the greatest harm (either physical or financial), occur with great frequency, are pervasive throughout the country, and are likely to be reported to the police (although the majority of crimes overall are not reported to the police). In discussing the eight types of serious crime in each annual UCR report, it is claimed that "These are serious crimes by nature and/or volume." That is, these crimes supposedly cause the most harm, occur with the greatest frequency, and are the most widespread. As it turns out, this is not accurate because there are other acts that are more harmful, frequently occurring, and widespread, as will be shown in this chapter.

Table 4.3 shows data from 2011 on the extent of street crime in the United States. As you can see, there were 22.9 total criminal victimizations against people 12 years and older in the US that year. This includes 17.1 million property victimizations and 5.8 million violent victimizations. Also, understand that most of these people were *not* victimized by violent crimes but instead relatively minor acts such as theft. Even of the

Table 4.2. Serious Street Crimes of the Uniform Crime Reports

- **Criminal homicide**—a.) Murder and nonnegligent manslaughter: the willful (non-negligent) killing of one human being by another. Deaths caused by negligence, attempts to kill, assaults to kill, suicides, and accidental deaths are excluded. The Program classifies justifiable homicides separately and limits the definition to: (1) the killing of a felon by a law enforcement officer in the line of duty; or (2) the killing of a felon, during the commission of a felony, by a private citizen. b.) Manslaughter by negligence: the killing of another person through gross negligence. Traffic fatalities are excluded. While manslaughter by negligence is a Part I crime, it is not included in the Crime Index.
- **Forcible rape**—The carnal knowledge of a female forcibly and against her will. Rapes by force and attempts or assaults to rape regardless of the age of the victim are included. Statutory offenses (no force used—victim under age of consent) are excluded.
- **Robbery**—The taking or attempting to take anything of value from the care, custody, or control of a person or persons by force or threat of force or violence and/or by putting the victim in fear.
- **Aggravated assault**—An unlawful attack by one person upon another for the purpose of inflicting severe or aggravated bodily injury. This type of assault usually is accompanied by the use of a weapon or by means likely to produce death or great bodily harm. Simple assaults are excluded.
- **Burglary** (breaking or entering)—The unlawful entry of a structure to commit a felony or a theft. Attempted forcible entry is included.
- **Larceny-theft** (except motor vehicle theft)—The unlawful taking, carrying, leading, or riding away of property from the possession or constructive possession of another. Examples are thefts of bicycles or automobile accessories, shoplifting, pocket-picking, or the stealing of any property or article which is not taken by force and violence or by fraud. Attempted larcenies are included. Embezzlement, confidence games, forgery, worthless checks, etc., are excluded.
- **Motor vehicle theft**—The theft or attempted theft of a motor vehicle. A motor vehicle is self-propelled and runs on the surface and not on rails. Motorboats, construction equipment, airplanes, and farming equipment are specifically excluded from this category.
- **Arson**—Any willful or malicious burning or attempt to burn, with or without intent to defraud, a dwelling house, public building, motor vehicle or aircraft, personal property of another, etc.

Source: http://www.fbi.gov/about-us/cjis/ucr/crime-in-the-u.s/2012/crime-in-the-u.s.-2012.

violent victimizations, the largest portion of the violent crime victimizations were "simple assaults" and only 1.45 million were violent crime victims with injuries (in a nation with more than 300 million people). To these numbers, we must of course also add murder—data that are obviously not available from NCVS but instead from UCR. In 2011, 14,612 people were victims of murder.

Keep in mind that in that year, there were about 311 million people in the US. This gives you a rough idea of your risk of victimization from serious street crime: for property crime it was 17.1 million out of 311 million people (or one in every 18 people

Table 4.3. Extent of Street Crime in the US

Property crime	17.1 million
Theft	12.8 million
Burglary	3.6 million
Motor vehicle theft	628,000
Violent crime	5.8 million
Assault	5.0 million
Robbery	557,000
Rape	244,000
Murder	14,612

Sources: Federal Bureau of Investigation (2012). Crime in the United States. Murder. Retrieved May 2, 2013 from: http://www.fbi.gov/about-us/cjis/ucr/crime-in-the-u.s/2011/crime-in-the-u.s.-2011/violent-crime/murder; Truman, J., & Planty, M. (2012). Criminal Victimization, 2011. Bureau of Justice Statistics. Retrieved April 30, 2013 from: http://www.bjs.gov/content/pub/pdf/cv11.pdf.

were victims of serious property crime); for violent crime it was 5.8 million out of 311 million people (or one in every 54 people were victims of serious violent crime); and for murder it was 14,612 out of 311 million people (or one in every 21,284 people were murdered).

With regard to the odds of victimization reported above, they are actually *not* even distributed across the US population. Serious street crimes such as murder and robbery tend to fall heaviest on some segments of the population, especially young, urban, minority males (e.g., young African American men). Whites, the elderly, and women are actually least likely to be victimized by serious street crimes. Table 4.4 illustrates this reality, showing rates of victimization per 1,000 people — the higher the number, the higher the odds of victimization.

Out-of-Class Activity:

Go online and read the report "Criminal Victimization in the United States, 2012" to examine who is most likely to be victimized in the United States. http://www.bjs.gov/content/pub/pdf/cv12.pdf

Which groups are most likely to be victimized by street crime? Why do you think this happens?

One could argue that tough criminal justice policies benefit those most likely to be victimized by crime — sort of like a service to those victims — but keep in mind the other reality that these same populations also suffer most at the hands of these tough criminal justice policies. That is, it is largely young, minority men being arrested, convicted, and incarcerated in the US, as shown in Chapter 1. Meanwhile, acts of white-collar and corporate crime tend to harm people of all races, classes, ethnicities, and

Table 4.4. Street Crime Victimization by Age, Race, and Gender

Rates of Serious Crime Victimization (per 1,000 people ages 12 years and older)

Gender		
	Male	7.7
	Female	6.7
Race		
	White	6.5
	Black	10.8
	Hispanic	7.2
Age		
	12–17 years	8.8
	18–24 years	16.3
	25–34 years	9.5
	35–49 years	7.0
	50–64 years	4.3
	65 or older	1.7
Location		
	Urban	9.7
	Suburban	5.7
	Rural	6.7

Source: http://www.bjs.gov/content/pub/pdf/cv11.pdf.

genders, and yet they are largely ignored by criminal justice (more on this later in the chapter).

Finally, how much does street crime cost Americans? That is, how many dollars are lost due to victimization from serious street crime? In 2010, the serious property crimes of theft, burglary, and motor vehicle theft created about $15.7 billion in direct property losses (FBI, 2013). This cost only includes direct costs — actual property loss to victims; it does not include indirect costs — things like lost wages due to not being able to work or costs associated with pain and suffering, decreased quality of life, and distress. Further, the costs do not include costs attributable to violent crimes, as it is obviously difficult to put a dollar figure on the value of human life.

Here, researchers make estimates based on actual direct costs to victims as well as other likely financial losses due to lost income and other expenses. Research by Kathryn McCollister, Michael French & Hai Fang (2011) illustrates that, when these costs are included, street crime produces enormous harms. These scholars review the literature on victim costs (direct economic losses suffered by victims, such as medical care costs, property loss, lost earnings), intangible costs (indirect costs suffered by victims, such as pain and suffering, decreased quality of life, psychological distress), criminal justice system costs (expenditures on police, courts, and corrections), and crime career costs (income lost by offenders who are committing crime instead of working).

According to this research, the average cost of each murder to society is about $9 million, the average cost of an aggravated assault is about $107,000, the average cost of a rape is about $240,780, the average cost of a robbery is about $42,300, the average cost of motor vehicle theft is about $10,770, the average cost of burglary is about $6,460, and the average cost of theft is about $3,530. One can use these figures to calculate the costs of street crime in any given year. For example, in 2012, there were about 14,830 murders, 1 million aggravated assaults, 742,000 robberies, 347,000 rapes, 15.2 million thefts, 3.8 million burglaries, and 634,000 motor vehicle thefts. Multiplying these numbers of crimes by the figures above results in a total estimated cost to society of $133 billion for the crime of murder, $107 billion for the crime of aggravated assault, $82.6 billion for the crime of rape, $31.4 billion for the crime of robbery, $6.8 billion for the crime of motor vehicle theft, $24.5 billion for the crime of burglary, and $53.6 billion for the crime of theft. Total losses are thus more than $438 billion!

Yet keep in mind that the largest share of these costs are in pain, suffering, and reduced quality of life rather than actual property loss. Further, a huge portion of these costs are from criminal justice system costs (expenditures on police, courts, and corrections), and crime career costs (income lost by offenders who are committing crime instead of working), two sets of costs that are not really attributable to crime itself. Keep these numbers in mind for comparison purposes with acts of elite deviance later in the chapter; you'll see how much more damage is caused by acts of elite deviance.

In-Class Activity:
Identify a behavior that is a crime that you think should not be. Then identify a behavior that is not a crime that you think should be. Then have a debate where one person argues one side, and another person argues the other side. Allow others to participate as well, providing additional justifications or evidence for their argument.

Elite Deviance

Elite deviance is a term put forth by David Simon (2005) in his book of the same name. It includes acts committed by elites—people of high social stature who tend to have great power in society. Elite deviance includes not only criminal acts but also unethical acts, civil and regulatory violations, and other harmful acts committed intentionally, recklessly, negligently, or knowingly. That is, elite deviance is made up of culpable harms, making them worthy of being legislated as crimes.

Elite deviance is a term that encompasses **white-collar crime** and **corporate crime** (Blount, 2002; Clinard & Yeager, 2005; Erman & Lundman, 2001; Frank & Lynch, 1992; Friedrichs, 2006; Michalowski & Kramer, 2006; Reiman & Leighton, 2013; Rosoff, Pontell & Tillman, 2006; Shover & Wright, 2000; Sutherland, 1977a, 1977b). These are acts that cause tremendous physical, financial, and moral harms to Americans.

Note that the term is elite *deviance* rather than elite *crime*; this is a reflection of the fact that many acts of elites, though harmful, are legal rather than illegal. Given who makes the law, votes for it, and pays for it—WORMs (discussed in Chapter 3)—it should not be surprising that many harmful acts of elites are legal. Further, considering the pro-business, conservative ideology which dominates American politics today, it makes perfect sense that we don't get tough on corporate and other elite offenders. This does not mean the behaviors are not wrong or that they should not be illegal, only that they have not been legislated as such. The fact that they are referred to as *deviance* is evidence that people tend to view them as abnormal, wrong, and bad, even though many of the acts are legal.

A Comparison of Harms Associated with Crimes and "Non-Crimes"

The label of "crime" is not a function of what is most harmful to society. If you believe that you are more likely to be victimized by street crime than by acts of elite deviance committed by wealthy individuals or corporations, you are wrong. The belief that elite deviance is less harmful than street crime is a myth—a myth created by the criminal law and reinforced by media coverage of crime. In this chapter, the harmful behaviors committed by elites against other people's property are examined. Chapter 5 examines violent behaviors of elites that kill and injure people.

There is considerable evidence that elite deviance causes more physical and property damage than all eight serious crimes combined. Estimates of course vary, considering there is no official government source on the extent and nature of elite deviance like there is on street crime.

Starting with property loss, Jeffrey Reiman & Paul Leighton (2013) estimate the costs of white-collar crimes to be in the hundreds of billions of dollars annually, far more than all street crimes combined. Even this number is an underestimate because it does not include the kinds of costs included in street crime estimates from earlier (e.g., pain and suffering, quality of life costs, etc.). A summary of governmental and nongovernmental estimates suggests that elite deviance cost Americans more than $1 trillion every year if you include the costs of defective products (Robinson & Murphy, 2009). We can see the extent of harms caused by these acts when we look at particular cases of elite deviance. For example, the Savings and Loans (S&L) scandals of the 1980s alone will cost Americans $500 billion over the next 40 years. Yet, the "average prison term for savings and loan offenders sentenced between 1988 and 1992 was 36 months, compared to 56 months for burglars and 38 months for those convicted of motor vehicle theft," even though the average loss in an S&L case was $500,000 while the loss in an average property crime during the time was $1,251 (Reiman, 1998: 128).

Most recently—in the first decade of the twenty-first century—Enron, WorldCom, and other large corporations—with assistance from the accounting firm Arthur Anderson and numerous banks—engaged in numerous forms of elite deviance that led to hundreds of billions of dollars in losses. And Wall Street and several big banks nearly collapsed the entire US economy in 2008, producing trillions of dollars in losses. Each of these events is discussed later in this chapter.

Table 4.5. Costs of Fraud in the United States

Unnecessary medical tests	$200 billion+
Consumer fraud	$190 billion
Health care fraud	$100 billion
Insurance fraud	$85 billion
Consumer fraud	$67 billion
Identify fraud	$53 billion
Securities fraud	$40 billion
Automotive fraud	$22 billion
Medicare/Medicaid fraud	$20 billion+
Telemarketing fraud	$20 billion+
Worthless medical products	$20 billion+
Credit card/check fraud	$13 billion
Cellular phone fraud	$1 billion

Sources:
Friedrichs, D. (2006). *Trusted Criminals: White Collar Crime in Contemporary Society* (3rd Ed.). Belmont, CA: Wadsworth, p. 85, 104; Reiman, J. (2006). *The Rich Get Richer and the Poor Get Prison* (8th Ed.). Boston, MA: Allyn & Bacon, p. 117; Rosoff, S., Pontell, H., & Tillman, R. (2002). *Profit Without Honor: White-Collar Crime and the Looting of America* (2nd Ed.). Upper Saddle River, NJ: Prentice Hall, p. 46, 49, 117, 120–121; Simon, D. (2006). *Elite Deviance* (8th Ed.). Boston, MA: Allyn & Bacon, p. 121.

Fraud

Fraud is a form of theft whereby a person is deprived of his or her money or property through deceit, trickery, or lies. So fraud involves two moral wrongs, theft *and* deceit. Yet, far more criminal justice resources are devoted to theft than to fraud, even though the latter is more common and more harmful. While theft requires face-to-face contact with a criminal (or direct contact with a person's property), fraud can be committed any time there is a property transaction. That is, any time someone buys, sells, or trades something, there is a potential for fraud. Fraud can also occur when a person brings any product in for service (e.g., automotive repair fraud) or when a service person is called to repair a product (e.g., appliance repair fraud). Fraud is so widespread precisely because it can occur in any exchange of money or property.

A survey by the FBI of 2,066 organizations shows how widespread fraud is — 64% reported suffering some financial loss from computer fraud in the past year. The average loss per company was more than $24,000. After extrapolating such losses to only 20% of all business in the United States, a very conservative estimate of computer fraud from the FBI suggests it costs about $67 billion per year (Evers, 2006). Based on a study by Javelin Strategy & Research, the same report suggests that identity fraud costs about $53 billion per year (Robinson & Murphy, 2009: 9).

Table 4.5 documents some estimated and established costs of fraud in the US according to various governmental and nongovernmental sources. As you can see, the costs of fraud clearly outweigh the costs of all street crime combined.

You should be sure about one thing with regard to the numbers above — they are a major underestimate. This is because the typical form of corporate fraud is mostly unknown. In fact, there are entire industries built on fraud. A few that come to mind are the corporations that make creams that "remove the appearance" of cellulite and stretch marks, "ab cruncher" machines, as well as many so-called "health foods" and weight-loss programs.

Fraud is more common than theft as well as more damaging. So, why is it not listed or treated as a serious crime? Recall who makes the law and owns the media — the very same people who are most often involved in this crime (WORMs) — the same people who tend to donate heavily to political campaigns and who own major media corporations. Also recall that the conservative political ideology is highly supportive of corporate power, even when it produces forms of fraud such as deceptive advertising.

Deceptive Advertising

Deceptive advertising is a form of fraud whereby a product is sold using false or misleading claims. That is, deceptive advertising is a form of theft whereby people willingly depart with their money because of false or misleading claims about a product that is purchased. A business can be held liable for false advertising if advertising for their products has the potential to deceive, even if the advertisement is not intended to deceive.

Since corporations are in the business of making money, logic suggests that corporations do not like to waste money on advertisements that do not work. Further, corporations employ the top marketing experts to design effective ads on sample markets and focus groups prior to using them on mass audiences. Given this, one can assume that all advertisements are intended to do exactly what they do. That is, if advertisements induce young people to try and use products (even illegal ones such as tobacco and alcohol), it is logical to assume that this is the intent of the advertisements. Further, if advertisements are deceptive, it is logical to assume they are intended to be misleading.

Even so, the government views victims of elite deviance as deserving their own victimizations: "American business has followed '**caveat emptor**' (let the buyer beware) and '**laissez faire**' **economics** (the doctrine of government noninterference in business)" (Simon & Hagan, 1999: 158). The former doctrine suggests that if you get ripped off by fraudulent salespeople it is your own fault; you should have known better. The latter doctrine suggests that the government has no legitimate role in regulating business. Of course, if your house is burglarized because you left the windows unlocked, it is not your fault; you are seen as a victim of a "serious" crime, and the government has a legitimate role intervening in this type of activity. So this is a clear contradiction in how the government responds to harmful acts based on who commits them.

The philosophy of caveat emptor and laissez-faire economics is central to the conservative political ideology introduced in Chapter 2 and puts the responsibility on consumers *not* to get swindled out of their money. Imagine if the criminal justice system followed the same philosophy. For example, imagine that you leave your house unlocked and a burglar enters and steals your computer, stereo, jewelry, and cash. You come home to find many of your valuables gone, so you call the police, only to be told, "It's your fault—you should have locked your doors," or perhaps, "Let the homeowner beware." This would be outrageous, yet, this is how most victims of fraud and deceptive advertising are treated.

According to the Federal Trade Commission (FTC), which has oversight of product advertising in the United States, the Federal Trade Commission Act states that advertising must be truthful and non-deceptive; advertisers must have evidence to back up their claims; and advertisements cannot be unfair. According to the FTC's (1983) "Deception Policy Statement," an ad is deceptive if it contains a statement (or omits information) that "is likely to mislead consumers acting reasonably" and when it is "material." It is *material* if the ad is "important to a consumer's decision to buy or use the product." For example, material claims often deal with "a product's performance, features, safety, price, or effectiveness." Finally, the FTC looks at whether advertisers can justify their claims with evidence: "The law requires that advertisers have proof before the ad runs" (FTC, 2001).

FTC's "Unfairness Policy Statement" (1980) specifies that an ad or business practice is unfair if "it causes or is likely to cause substantial consumer injury which a consumer could not reasonably avoid" and "it is not outweighed by the benefit to consumers." Further, additional laws at the federal level apply to ads for specialized products including consumer leases, credit issues, 900 telephone numbers, and other products that are sold through mail order or telephone sales. Finally, all fifty states have similar laws aimed at protecting consumers from deceptive ads (FTC, 2001).

In spite of this, many see the goal of the FTC and states to be prevention rather than punishment. That is, they are not generally interested in punishing companies for running deceptive ads. The FTC explains that when it investigates a claim of false advertising, it first "looks at the ad from the point of view of the 'reasonable consumer'—the typical person looking at the ad. Rather than focusing on certain words, the FTC looks at the ad in context—words, phrases, and pictures—to determine what it conveys to consumers." The FTC "looks at both 'express' and 'implied' claims." **Express claims** are those claims actually made in the ad, such as that a product will cure an illness. **Implied claims** are "made indirectly or by inference," such as that a product will cure an illness by killing the germs that cause that illness. According to the FTC, "advertisers must have proof to back up express *and* implied claims that consumers take from an ad" (FTC, 2001). The FTC also looks at what the ad does not say.

The typical sanction is to order the advertiser to stop its illegal acts, or to include disclosure of additional information that serves to avoid the chance of deception, but there are no fines or prison time except for the infrequent instances when an advertiser refuses to stop despite being ordered to do so. According to the FTC, its most common actions include cease and desist orders (ordering companies to stop running deceptive ads); civil penalties (fines); and corrective advertising (providing information to consumers about deceptive ads). Imagine following the same approach with burglars, thieves, or robbers! Ironically, conservative politicians—both Republican and Democrat—insist on severe criminal penalties for even relatively minor offenders at the street level (http://en.wikipedia.org/wiki/False_advertising).

The mandate of the FTC's Bureau of Consumer Protection is "to protect consumers against unfair, deceptive or fraudulent practices." According to the FTC, it focuses mostly on ads that make claims about health or safety as well as ads that make claims that consumers would have trouble evaluating for themselves. Even so, such forms of false advertising are widespread. One need only turn on the television or open up a newspaper to see numerous examples of false advertising. Given that false advertising can literally occur with any product, it is obviously widespread in the United States.

In-Class Activity
Examine ads on TV and/or in your local newspaper. Look for ads that you think are misleading. What are the express claims and implied claims in the ad? What makes them misleading?

False advertising occurs in television ads, radio ads, Internet ads, on web sites, as well as in print ads. Typically, false advertising occurs when faulty or misleading claims are made about a product. One example is a store advertising a range of household products in a given collection (e.g., furniture) that are being placed on sale. The ad specifies that "all products" in the collection are on sale, which presumably includes the table and chairs depicted in the ad. However, the table and chairs are actually *not* on sale, even though they are part of the collection and shown in the ad. Consumers who go to buy the table and chairs at the sale price become victims of false advertising when they must pay the regular price for the products.

Other examples of false advertising include inflating the original price so as to make the sale price appear more reasonable, and "near continuous sales," where items are so regularly on sale that the sale price is really the regular price. Once again, major corporations, such as the Home Shopping Network, have been found engaging in such activities.

However, a more insidious form of false advertising is referred to as "product shrinkage." **Product shrinkage** occurs when less and less of a product (e.g., potato chips, baked beans, soup, toilet paper, and virtually any other product) is packaged in the same size container over time. That is, the product is shrinking whereas the size of the package is not. Here are several real examples. One major company that produces tampons stopped offering 40 tampons in a box and began offering only 32 tampons in a box (for the same price). Women noticed, complained, and ultimately the company began offering 40 tampons again. Only, the corporation added a label to the box, saying "Now 8 more free!" Of course, women were not getting 8 free tampons, they were instead receiving the same 40 that they used to receive before the company shrank the amount of the product offered to consumers. This example of product shrinkage was noticed because it was so blatant.

Another corporation went from offering a four-pack of toilet paper that contained 400 two-ply sheets per roll to only 396 two-ply sheets per roll (meaning in a four-pack, consumers would receive 16 less two-ply sheets of toilet paper, hardly noticeable). Instead of announcing that the company was providing less product for the same price, the company said nothing and instead added an additional label to its package, saying: "Now even better!" The product was exactly the same as before, only consumers would receive less product for the same price (in essence, the product was now even better — but only for the corporation in the form of more profit). Usually, corporations say nothing about product shrinkage — they make no changes to their packaging other than the fine print on the back of the product which indicates how much of the product is included (e.g., ounces). This practice is common in virtually every product in your grocery store. It is, simply stated, accepted as legitimate business practice.

A third example is a potato chip company that advertised its popular product as "now even cheesier!" Expecting to experience a new, even better potato chip, consumers were probably disappointed to learn that the company really just included fewer chips in every bag (but for the same price). How did the chip get "even cheesier" then? The company put fewer chips in the bags but the same amount of cheese. Fewer chips and the same amount of cheese topping equals more cheese topping per chip (but still less product overall, and for the same price).

A final example of deceptive advertising is when companies promote products that simply do not work. One example is pills that are advertised as weight loss pills. Another example is diets that allow you to "eat as much food as you want and still lose weight." In fact, the only proven way to lose weight is to burn more calories than you consume, something very easy to understand but hard to do. Given this reality, any weight loss program that involves something other than consuming less calories and/or burning more calories can be considered fraudulent.

High Level Corporate Fraud

One might understand how Americans could be unaware of fraud given that it is not defined by the law as a serious crime and because it generally does not come to the attention of the media. However, there are numerous well-known corporate crimes that have involved significant, high level frauds. For this reason, it makes no sense that fraud is not treated as the most serious crime in the country. Below are three of the most recent examples.

The 1980s and 1990s gave us the Savings and Loan (S&L) scandals which cost Americans hundreds of billions of dollars in losses, and the late 1990s and early 2000s gave us the story of Enron, WorldCom, and other major corporations that defrauded Americans of additional hundreds of billions of dollars.

S&L Scandals

Starting with the Savings & Loans scandals, **S&Ls** (also known as "thrifts") were created in the 1930s to help people build homes during the Great Depression. According to Jeffrey Reiman (2006: 139): "The system had built into it important limitations on the kinds of loans that could be made and was subject to federal supervision to prevent the bank failures that came in the wake of the Depression of 1929." Yet, beginning in the 1970s, efforts were made to deregulate the S&Ls. These efforts were greatly stepped up in the 1980s under the conservative political ideology of President Reagan (see Chapter 2). The ultimate result was the collapse of scores of S&Ls, causing losses of between $200 billion to $1.4 trillion (Rosoff et al., 2006: 268)!

What led to the collapse of so many S&Ls? One significant factor was deregulation, discussed earlier (Simon, 2006). While some may see the S&L scandals resulting from individual greed and fraud, institutional and structural factors such as deregulation of financial industries were also involved (Glasberg & Skidmore, 1998). Stephen Rosoff and colleagues (2002: 269) explain:

> Although policy-makers had gradually loosened the restraints on S&L since the early 1970s, it was not until the *laissez-faire* fervor of the early Reagan administration that this approach gained widespread political acceptance as a solution to the rapidly escalating S&L crisis. In a few strokes, Washington dismantled most of the regulatory infrastructure that had kept the thrift industry together for four decades. These deregulators were convinced that the free enterprise system works best if left alone, unhampered by perhaps well-meaning but ultimately counterproductive government controls.

The context of this time was discussed in Chapter 2, and it is a good reminder of how President Reagan de-emphasized corporate crime while simultaneously ramping up the wars on street crime and drugs.

The net effect of deregulation is explained by Davita Glasberg and Dan Skidmore (1998: 111): Deregulation amounted to

> far fewer field supervisors and auditors, and thus much less oversight of the financial status and practices of the savings and loans. In the absence of adequate and regular oversight, fraud became not only possible but also standard operating procedure. Deregulation of banking ... created conditions that made widespread and regular fraudulent practices the norm.

Kitty Calavita and Henry Pontell (1990) assert that "collective embezzlement" in the S&L industry became standard operating procedure.

The laws passed by Congress and subsequent deregulation efforts that were put into place (such as raising the amount of federally guaranteed insurance on savings accounts from $40,000 to $100,000 and allowing S&Ls to pursue riskier loans) are probably better understood as "unregulation" rather than "deregulation" (Rosoff et al., 2002: 271). Francis Cullen, Gray Cavender, William Maakestad, and Michael Benson (2006: 21) conclude that, because of such changes, "S&Ls were now able to induce an infusion of money by offering high interest rates and the promise of federal insurance for deposits up to $100,000—in short, a high return on a no-risk investment. As money poured in and with little oversight by banking regulators, the S&Ls attracted many unscrupulous executives seeking to 'get rich quick.' These officials not only made irresponsibly poor investments but also engaged in criminal activities, such as arranging for kickbacks on loans and the outright theft of funds—monies often used to support lavish lifestyles."

Clearly, criminality played a major role in the failures of the S&Ls. Perhaps this is why the US Department of Justice called the scandal an "unconscionable plundering of America's financial institutions" (Cullen et al., 2006: 21). Estimates of the amount of damage caused by criminality in the S&L scandal range from 10% to 80%, but scholars agree that it is likely that more than half of the damage was caused by various forms of elite deviance (Rosoff et al., 2002: 268–269). David Simon (2006: 51) estimates that 60% of the total money lost through the S&L scandals was due to fraud, and Jeffrey Reiman (2006: 14) asserts that 70–80% of the failures resulted at least in part due to fraud.

Stephen Rosoff and colleagues (2002: 278) conclude—based on a federally funded study of the S&L scandals—that: "Crime and deliberate fraud were extensive in the thrift industry during the 1980s, thereby contributing to the collapse of hundreds of institutions and increasing the cost of the taxpayer bailout." The types of frauds involved included "desperation dealing," "collective embezzlement," and "covering up." **Desperation dealing** involves making risky investments in hopes of striking it rich. If the investments paid off, large sums of money could be earned; if they did not, taxpayers would be forced to pay back the losses. **Collective embezzlement** is simply looting, or funneling money from bank accounts into personal accounts (Friedrichs, 2006: 160). And **covering up** simply refers to hiding the nature and extent of the problem from investors, taxpayers, and the government.

Rosoff and his colleagues (2002: 273) suggest that, although collective embezzlement is a form of white-collar crime rather than corporate crime, it can also be considered "deviance by the organization." They explain: "Not only are the perpetrators themselves in management positions, but the very goals of the institution are to provide a money machine for owners and other insiders. The formal goals of the organization thus comprise a 'front' for the real goals of management, who not infrequently purchased the institution in order to loot it, then discard it after it serves its purpose."

Further, the S&L scandals occurred because of "enablers," including appraisers, accountants, and lawyers whose "services made many of the S&L scams possible. Perhaps foremost in this regard were accountants, whose audits allowed many fraudulent transactions to go unnoticed. Professional accounting firms were highly paid for their services, and thus could easily turn a blind eye when evidence of wrongdoing surfaced" (Rosoff et al., 2002: 275). One primary enabler was the US government. David Friedrichs (2006: 162) explains: "Numerous government officials helped create the circumstances that made the S&L-related crimes possible; failed to act against the thrifts as they were being mismanaged and looted, or interfered with those who should have been taking action; minimized the dimensions of the problem for a long time; and failed to take timely and effective action to respond to the crisis." Later in the scandals of Enron, WorldCom, and other large corporations involved in fraud the same enablers would encourage and/or turn a blind eye to misdeeds that would costs Americans hundreds of billions of dollars.

What Happened to the S&L Crooks?

According to Jeffrey Reiman and Paul Leighton (2013), those elites involved in the S&L scandals received relatively light punishments for their parts in the crimes. Some of the examples they provide include:

- Michael Hellerman, who defrauded two S&Ls of nearly $16 million, received 15 years in prison and a fine of $100,000. He was released after less than six years and never paid any of the fine.
- Charles Bazarian, who was convicted along with Hellerman in one of the above crimes, and who swindled $20 million from two other S&Ls, served less than two years in prison and paid $18,000 of $100,000 in fines.
- Mario Renda, who stole $16 million from a brokerage business, was sentenced to two years in prison and five years probation, along with a fine of $125,000.

He served only 21 months and paid only a small portion of the ordered $9.9 million in restitution.

- Herman Beebe, who committed loan frauds of more than $30 million, received a sentence of one year and one day but only served 10 months.
- Richard Maricucci, who stole $3.4 million while a branch manager of a bank, was sentenced to two years and three months.
- Arthur Kick, who while president of an S&L, "misappropriated" $1.2 million in loans, was sentenced to three years probation and ordered to make complete restitution.
- Edward Jolly, Jr., who while assistant regional vice president and consumer loan manager of an S&L, took $4.5 million by creating fictitious loans, was sentenced to two years and nine months.
- Ted Musacchio, who while president of an S&L stole $9.3 million, was sentenced to five years probation and to make restitution of $9.3 million; by the time of his death in 1993, he had paid only $1,000.

These cases typify what tends to happen to elite offenders in the US in spite of the enormous losses they impose on taxpayers. So elite offenders rarely receive serious punishment, even as we harshly punish street criminals who cause far less damage to society.

The Corporate Bandits

In the past ten years, corporate crime shook the United States again. Next to the terrorist attacks of September 11, 2001, and the subsequent "war on terror" launched by President George W. Bush, the story of corporate crime was the biggest story of the first decade of the twenty-first century. Jeffrey Reiman & Paul Leighton (2006) concur, writing that "2002's big crime story was a long and complicated saga of corporate financial shenanigans that caused a significant drop in stock market prices."

Dozens of corporations were accused of various kinds of corporate crimes such as fraud, including Arthur Anderson, Enron, WorldCom, Qwest, Tyco, ImClone, Global Crossing, Dynergy, CMS Energy, El Paso Corp., Halliburton, Williams Cos., AOL Time Warner, Goldman Sachs, Salomon Smith Barney, Citigroup, J.P. Morgan Chase, Schering Plough, Bristol-Myers Squibb, K-Mart, Johnson & Johnson, Adelphia, Merrill Lynch, Rite Aid, and Coca-Cola. According to *Fortune* magazine, the corporations involved were led by individuals who were "getting immensely, extraordinarily, obscenely wealthy" (Reiman, 2006: 182).

Many of these corporations were accused of the same basic fraudulent activities — essentially "cooking the books" in order to inflate profits by hiding debts so that investors would be more likely to invest money in the corporations. Many of the corporations treated debts as revenue in order to make them look more profitable. Think of it this way — imagine you wanted to get a loan from your local bank and you treated every check that you wrote in the past month not as debts against your account but as payments made to you by the companies you sent the checks to — this is what many companies in the United States did.

The cases of Enron and WorldCom have probably been the most analyzed. Enron was the seventh largest company in the United States and its stock was worth nearly

$91 per share in August 2000. By late 2001, the stock's value was less than $1 per share. Enron's collapse caused the loss of $60 billion on the stock market, more than $2 billion in pension plans, and 5,600 jobs (Cullen et al., 2006: 22). Enron ended up with debts over $31 billion and thus filed for bankruptcy protection in December 2001 (Reiman, 2006: 122).

Enron's fraudulent activities can be classified as a "disinformation campaign" because it all amounted to "hiding its degree of indebtedness from investors by treating loans as revenue, and hiding company losses by creating new firms with company capital and then attributing losses to them rather than Enron." (Reiman, 2006: 122). To make matters worse, Enron CEO Kenneth Lay sold off $103 million of his company stock while discouraging and even forbidding his employees from selling theirs, even as the value of the stock plummeted from $80 per share to only 30 cents per share. Roughly 20,000 employees thus lost their retirement accounts. Enron also intentionally manipulated California's power crisis for financial gain (Reiman, 2006: 225), something that ultimately led to the recall of the state's governor and the subsequent election of Arnold Schwarzenegger to the position of governor (Eichenwald, 2005; McLean & Peter, 2003; Schwartz & Sherron, 2004).

WorldCom's stock fell from a high of $64 per share to only nine cents per share. WorldCom's fraud was in the amount of $11 billion, and caused losses in the area of $180 billion as well as 30,000 lost jobs (Cullen et al., 2006: 121). After WorldCom was hit with a record fine for its fraud, the company changed its name to MCI and remains in business today after it was purchased by Verizon!

Just like with the S&L scandals, such corporations were assisted in their wrongdoings by various enablers, including consulting firms such as Arthur Anderson, who helped the companies hide their debts by first being their accountants and then by destroying evidence during the subsequent investigations. Interestingly, Arthur Anderson also had long ago been involved in the failing of perhaps the most infamous S&L — Charles Keating's Lincoln Savings and Loan.

The corporations were also assisted by major banks including J.P. Morgan Chase and Citigroup (Reiman, 2006: 123). The *Wall Street Journal* called the banks "Enron Enablers" and wrote: "They appear to have behaved in a guileful way and helped their corporate clients undertake unsavory practices. And they appear to have had an entire divisions that, among other things, helped corporations avoid taxes and manipulate their balance sheets through something called structured finance, which is a huge profit center for each bank" (Reiman, 2006: 122). Further, brokerage firms such as Merrill Lynch saw their employees knowingly promoting the nearly worthless stocks of these corporations.

Other major corporations also engaged in similar activity. For example, Adelphia was charged by the Security and Exchange Commission (SEC) with "fraudulently excluding $2.3 billion in debt from its earnings report. AES, AOL-Time Warner, Cedent, Halliburton, K-Mart, Lucent Technologies, MicroStrategy, Rite Aid, and Waste Management are all said to have misstated revenues in different ways at more than $100 million in each case" (Reiman, 2006: 123).

The total combined harms of the above corporate crimes are unknown, but estimates are in the hundreds of billions of dollars if not more. David Simon (2006: 126) asserts that: "Collectively, the 2002–2003 scandals helped cause a $5 trillion loss in stock market values, and cost the public at least $200 billion and one million jobs." Whatever the actual harms, there is no doubt that the financial harms exceed those caused by street crime in any year by dozens of times (and numerous people have committed suicide as a result of losing all their money and/or killed their spouses and family members as a result of the stress of losing their jobs).

What Happened to the Corporate Bandits?

Keep in mind that these corporations are not nameless, faceless entities. Each is run by Chief Executive Officers (CEO), Chief Financial Officers (CFO), and a Board of Directors—in other words, real people who made real decisions and who can be held accountable for their actions. Some were held accountable for these frauds, but most were not. ImClone's CEO, Sam Waksal, was sentenced to 87 months in prison for his role in an insider trading scandal that has shed negative light on Martha Stewart. Waksal pleaded guilty to obstruction of justice, perjury, bank fraud, and sales tax evasion. He also was sentenced to pay a fine of $3 million and more than $1.2 million in restitution. Enron founder Kenneth Lay was convicted of fraud and conspiracy but then died in July 2006 and had his convictions overturned due to being unable to appeal them. Former Enron CEO Jeffrey Skilling was sentenced to more than 24 years in prison for 19 counts of fraud, conspiracy, insider trading and lying to auditors, as well as being ordered to pay $50 million in restitution to victims. Former Enron CFO Andrew Fastow received a sentence of 6 years and was released in 2011. Interestingly, Enron paid its senior executives more than $744 million in cash and stock in the year prior to its bankruptcy filing in December 2001!

Most of the implicated companies simply paid fines to get out of trouble. For example, World Com was fined $750 million to settle the case against it, an alarmingly high figure. Yet considering that investors lost $175 billion because of World Com, we learn that the company was charged about 0.4% of the amount of financial harm they caused. Imagine going to a bank and robbing it of $100,000 and being forced only to pay back 0.4% of it (which is $400)! WorldCom changed its name and continues to do business.

The banks that were involved with illegal loans to help these corporations hide their losses and the accounting firms that oversaw them and turned a blind eye each faced their own investigations. One notable example is that federal and state regulators settled with ten Wall Street investment firms (including Citigroup, Merrill Lynch, J.P. Morgan Chase, and Credit Suisse First Boston) because of knowingly pushing bad stocks, conducting and publishing flawed research, and for conflicts of interest. They agreed to pay $1.4 billion in fines and to separate their investment banking activities and research activities. Most of these firms did not admit guilt and some changed their names to distance themselves from these scandals.

Jeffrey Reiman & Paul Leighton (2013) add the following as outcomes of the cases involving the corporate bandits:

- In the case of Adelphia, a cable company implicated in hiding $2.3 billion in debt to make itself look more profitable (which led to a stock market loss of $60 billion for investors), John and Timothy Rigas were convicted of 18 felonies each. Timothy (who had been Chief Financial Officer) was sentenced to 20 years and John (who founded the company) was sentenced to 15 years.

- In the case of the company, Arthur Andersen, which was implicated in widespread manipulation of audits for numerous huge corporations that had to restated their earnings after engaging in "creative accounting" (i.e., fraud) as well as shredding documents in the Enron case, it was convicted for obstruction of justice and thus its accounting business ended; yet, the conviction was later overturned by the US Supreme Court due to a faulty jury instruction.
- In the case of Global Crossing, which chartered its company in Bermuda to avoid taxes and allegedly inflated its stock market price by engaging in capacity swaps with Qwest Communications, no criminal charges were filed. Three executives paid civil fines of $100,000 each and admitted no wrongdoing. As for Qwest officials, its CEO Joseph Nacchio was convicted on 19 of 42 counts of insider trading and sentenced to six years in prison. The company's CFO, Robin Szeliga, was sentenced to two years probation after agreeing to testify against Nacchio. Qwest paid a penalty of $250 million, even though it caused $90 billion in losses for investors.
- In the case of Tyco, which also avoided taxes by chartering itself in Bermuda, its CEO (Dennis Kozlowski) and CFO (Mark Swartz) looted the company of about $600 million. Kozlowski and Swartz were convicted of 22 counts of larceny, conspiracy, fraud, and falsifying records, and were sentenced to between eight years, four months and 25 years in prison; both are now eligible for parole!
- In the case of WorldCom, which caused about $108 billion in losses for investors, CEO Bernard Ebbers was removed from his position but was given a severance package for $1.5 million a year for life. He received a sentence of 25 years for charges of fraud, conspiracy, and false-statement. CFO Scott Sulivan cooperated with authorities and received a sentence of only five years.

Once again, these outcomes are typical of how elite deviance is handled in the US, even as we've greatly expanded the size and scope of criminal justice agencies to deal with street crime.

The Collapse of the Housing Bubble

Although the cases of the S&Ls and the "corporate bandits" captured widespread media attention and thus are well-known to many Americans, Americans would again witness similar behaviors that nearly wrecked the entire economy, even as enormously rich people still profited from their frauds. This would happen just a few years later — one of the worst economic crises in US history. Stated simply, the main drivers or determinants of the collapse of the US economy in 2008 were greed and fraud on the part of people on Wall Street, in big banks, in the regulatory industry, and even in government. That is, this was a crime.

The General Accountability Office (GAO, 2013: 1) summarized the events this way:

The 2007–2009 financial crisis threatened the stability of the US financial system — composed of financial institutions, markets, and infrastructure — and the health of the US economy. At the peak of the crisis, the federal government introduced unprecedented support for financial markets, providing hundreds of billions of dollars of capital and over a trillion dollars of emergency loans to financial institutions. Many households suffered as a result of falling asset prices, tightening credit, and increasing unemployment.

According to the GAO, this was a *financial crisis*, and specifically a **banking crisis**:

> There is no universally accepted definition of a financial crisis. Some academic studies identify three major types of financial crises: banking crises, public debt crises, and currency crises. The most recent financial crisis in the United States is widely considered to have been a banking crisis. While researchers have defined banking crises in different ways, their definitions generally focus on indicators of severe stress on the financial system, such as runs on financial institutions or large-scale government assistance to the financial sector. The large increases in public debt that tend to follow the onset of a banking crisis can make a country more susceptible to a public debt crisis (p. 9).

This banking crisis—caused by crimes within Wall Street, the banking industry, regulatory agencies, and a basic failure of regulation by government—caused the average American household about $5,800 in income ("due to reduced economic growth during the acute stage of the financial crisis from September 2008 through the end of 2009"), plus $2,050 (due to the government's "interventions to mitigate the financial crisis"), plus about $100,000 (in "loss from declining stock and home values"). Thus, the average US household lost about $107,000 because of the economic collapse (Pew, 2010). To put this number in perspective, imagine a bank robber who successfully gets away with his or her crime, netting $107,000 in profit. Only, if this were a robber, he or she would have netted this amount from every household in the country!

The combined costs to Americans of the economic crisis are shown in Table 4.6. They total more than $12 trillion, roughly equivalent to more than 600 years of losses due to all street crimes combined! So, the harms caused by this one banking crisis are equivalent to 600 years' worth of street crime.

The Government Accountability Office (GAO) estimates that the true cost was actually higher, at about $22 trillion. This cost includes losses in Gross Domestic Product (GDP), as well as large declines in employment, household wealth, and "other economic indicators." This figure is equivalent to 1,100 years of street crime.

So, how did this happen? According to GAO (2013: 11):

> ... around mid-2007, losses in the mortgage market triggered a reassessment of financial risk in other debt instruments and sparked the financial crisis. Uncertainty about the financial condition and solvency of financial entities resulted in a liquidity and credit crunch that made the financing on which many businesses and individuals depend increasingly difficult to obtain. By late summer of 2008, the ramifications of the financial crisis ranged from the failure of financial institutions to increased losses of individual savings and corporate investments.

Sound complicated? Just wait until you consider the factors identified by scholars who have studied the crisis. Consider these identified causes of the crisis by GAO (2013: 10–11):

Table 4.6. Costs of the US Economic Crisis

- Income—The financial crisis cost the U.S. an estimated $648 billion due to slower economic growth, as measured by the difference between the Congressional Budget Office (CBO) economic forecast made in September 2008 and the actual performance of the economy from September 2008 through the end of 2009. That equates to an average of approximately $5,800 in lost income for each U.S. household.
- Government Response—Federal government spending to mitigate the financial crisis through the Troubled Asset Relief Program (TARP) will result in a net cost to taxpayers of $73 billion according to the CBO. This is approximately $2,050 per U.S. household on average.
- Home Values—The U.S. lost $3.4 trillion in real estate wealth from July 2008 to March 2009 according to the Federal Reserve. This is roughly $30,300 per U.S. household. Further, 500,000 additional foreclosures began during the acute phase of the financial crisis than were expected, based on the September 2008 CBO forecast.
- Stock Values—The U.S. lost $7.4 trillion in stock wealth from July 2008 to March 2009, according to the Federal Reserve. This is roughly $66,200 on average per U.S. household.
- Jobs—5.5 million more American jobs were lost due to slower economic growth during the financial crisis than what was predicted by the September 2008 CBO forecast.

Source: http://www.pewtrusts.org/our_work_report_detail.aspx?id=58695.

- financial innovation in the form of asset securitization, which reduced mortgage originators' incentives to be prudent in underwriting loans and made it difficult to understand the size and distribution of loss exposures throughout the system;
- imprudent business and risk management decisions based on the expectation of continued housing price appreciation;
- faulty assumptions in the models used by credit rating agencies to rate mortgage-related securities;
- gaps and weaknesses in regulatory oversight, which allowed financial institutions to take excessive risks by exploiting loopholes in capital rules and funding themselves increasingly with short-term liabilities;
- government policies to increase homeownership, including the role of Fannie Mae and Freddie Mac in supporting lending to higher-risk borrowers; and
- economic conditions, characterized by accommodative monetary policies, ample liquidity and availability of credit, and low interest rates that spurred housing investment.

GAO does not mention the actual means used by elites to cause this crisis but they are subsumed under the term "financial innovation" in the first bullet point above; they include things like subprime mortgages, residential mortgage backed securities, Alt-A mortgages, payment option adjustable rate mortgages, synthetic securities, tranches, credit enhancement, high loan-to-value lending, credit default swaps, col-lateralized debt obligations, multi-sector collateralized debt obligations, collateralized debt obligations squared, inflated home appraisals, no doc loans, yield spread premiums, and triple-A ratings (McClean & Nocera, 2010). These terms are defined at http://www.investopedia.com/dictionary/.

If you're still confused about what happened, here is a summary: The value of the housing market was inflated to levels that were not real based on numerous forms of fraud committed by people on Wall Street, in big banks and in the regulatory and government agencies that were supposed to be protecting consumers. People who were too risky to receive loans to buy homes were being given loans by banks even when it was thought and in many cases known that they would default on their loans; the US government played a role here by encouraging homeownership even among people who could not afford it. Wall Street agencies then sold these bad loans in numerous forms, dividing them up into new financial products guaranteed by the US government due to their high ratings even though it was in many cases known that people would default on the loans; thus some investors bet against the loans (thinking they would fail and therefore create enormous profit for those betting against repayment). The whole thing was like a giant **pyramid scheme** whereby people were profiting in the banks (as they made too many loans) and on Wall Street (as they sold and invested in the loans and newly created financial products based on these loans) even though the original products on which they were profiting were worthless.

That is, the housing market rose to record levels in the form of an enormous housing bubble, and that bubble would inevitably pop and create the massive economic collapse in the United States. Record numbers of home foreclosures — even those that had been obtained with Triple-A ratings by people who were victims of predatory lending practices and subprime mortgages — caused the collapse of the entire US economy after the securities based on these mortgages proved worthless. Companies that had invested in these securities who had taken on much greater risk that was reasonable based on the amount of cash they had on hand lost hundreds of billions of dollars; many of them were bailed out by the US government (i.e., tax payers), thereby driving up national debt.

Two independent groups, one part of the US government and the other appointed by it, investigated the 2008 financial crisis. First, the **US Senate's Permanent Subcommittee on Investigations** was tasked with conducting a bi-partisan investigation into the origins of the 2008 financial crisis. According to the Subcommittee: "The goals of this investigation were to construct a public record of the facts in order to deepen the understanding of what happened; identify some of the root causes of the crisis; and provide a factual foundation for the ongoing effort to fortify the country against the recurrence of a similar crisis in the future" (p. 1).

Senate Subcommittee Investigation

The Subcommittee identified "four root causes" of the crisis: "high risk lending by U.S. financial institutions; regulatory failures; inflated credit ratings; and high risk, poor quality financial products designed and sold by some investment banks" (p. 2). Thus, banks, regulatory agencies, credit rating agencies, and Wall Street agents were responsible for the economic collapse. So it makes sense to attribute the harms of the economic collapse to acts of elite deviance.

First, the crisis began when banks pursued higher and higher risk loans, backed by mortgage securities. When the loans failed, so too did the securities and financial instruments based on them. The Subcommittee reports that, during this process, large banks knowingly engaged in fraudulent loan practices, pushing loans that they knew would lead to default. Such behavior makes them culpable for the outcomes produced by this practice.

Why did large banks pursue this practice? The Subcommittee writes that they did so "because higher risk loans and mortgage backed securities could be sold for higher prices on Wall Street." Such loans and securities "garnered higher prices because higher risk meant the securities paid a higher coupon rate than other comparably rated securities, and investors paid a higher price to buy them. Selling or securitizing the loans also removed them from [the banks'] books and appeared to insulate [them] from risk" (p. 4).

The Subcommittee investigation indicates that "unacceptable lending and securitization practices were … present at a host of financial institutions that originated, sold, and securitized billions of dollars in high risk, poor quality home loans that inundated U.S. financial markets." Ultimately, since the securities were generally investments on worthless loans, they "plummeted in value, leaving banks and investors with huge losses that helped send the economy into a downward spiral. These lenders were not the victims of the financial crisis; the high risk loans they issued were the fuel that ignited the financial crisis" (p. 4). That is, the banks started the crisis — it was elite deviance.

Among their wrongful behaviors, the banks "engaged in a host of shoddy lending practices that produced billions of dollars in high risk, poor quality mortgages and mortgage backed securities" (p. 3). This includes

> qualifying high risk borrowers for larger loans than they could afford; steering borrowers from conventional mortgages to higher risk loan products; accepting loan applications without verifying the borrower's income; using loans with low, short term "teaser" rates that could lead to payment shock when higher interest rates took effect later on; promoting negatively amortizing loans in which many borrowers increased rather than paid down their debt; and authorizing loans with multiple layers of risk (p. 3).

Major banks also "failed to enforce compliance with their own lending standards; allowed excessive loan error and exception rates; exercised weak oversight over the third party mortgage brokers who supplied half or more of their loans; and tolerated the issuance of loans with fraudulent or erroneous borrower information." Finally, they "designed compensation incentives that rewarded loan personnel for issuing a large volume of higher risk loans, valuing speed and volume over loan quality" (p. 3). That is, employees were rewarded for reckless behavior, one possible explanation for the widespread deviance there.

Second, the Subcommittee finds that regulators knew of deficiencies in banks and did not take steps to stop them, requested corrective action but did not demand it, and continued to rate them as financially sound even when they knew they were not. Instead of "policing the banks" to protect the US economy and the American people, regulators deferred to the managers of banks and counted on them to police themselves. The Subcommittee calls this "a regulatory approach with disastrous results" (p. 5), sort of like allowing burglars and bank robbers to police themselves.

The lack of effective regulation "allowed high risk loans at the bank to proliferate, negatively impacting investors across the United States and around the world ... The result was a mortgage market saturated with risky loans, and financial institutions that were supposed to hold predominantly safe investments but instead held portfolios rife with high risk, poor quality mortgages." The inevitable result of such practices was that as people started to default on loans "in record numbers and mortgage related securities plummeted in value, financial institutions around the globe suffered hundreds of billions of dollars in losses, triggering an economic disaster." According to the Subcommittee: "The regulatory failures that set the stage for those losses were a proximate cause of the financial crisis" (p. 5). Thus, allowing criminal companies to police themselves was a second cause of the crisis.

Third, the largest credit rating agencies — Moody's Investors Service, Inc. (Moody's) and Standard & Poor's Financial Services LLC (S&P) — charged with rating loans and financial instruments based on those loans, failed by rating even the most speculative and risk loans at their highest possible levels. These agencies were thus clearly negligent in their duties.

According to the Subcommittee, multiple problems were "responsible for the inaccurate ratings, including conflicts of interest that placed achieving market share and increased revenues ahead of ensuring accurate ratings." What role did Moody's and S&P play in the crisis? The Subcommittee writes: "Between 2004 and 2007, Moody's and S&P issued credit ratings for tens of thousands of US residential mortgage backed securities (RMBS) and collateralized debt obligations (CDO). Taking in increasing revenue from Wall Street firms, Moody's and S&P issued AAA and other investment grade credit ratings for the vast majority of those RMBS and CDO securities, deeming them safe investments even though many relied on high risk home loans" (p. 6).

Once these high risk mortgages "began incurring delinquencies and defaults at an alarming rate ... Moody's and S&P continued for six months to issue investment grade ratings for numerous RMBS and CDO securities" (p. 6). That is, even after knowing that high risk RMBS's and CDO's were failing, these rating agencies knowingly gave highly risky and speculative products high ratings, making them also responsible for the subsequent economic collapse. Such behavior meets the standard of recklessness and thus makes credit ratings agencies a third cause of the crisis.

Starting in July 2007, "as mortgage delinquencies intensified and RMBS and CDO securities began incurring losses, both companies abruptly reversed course and began downgrading at record numbers hundreds and then thousands of their RMBS and CDO ratings, some less than a year old." When this happened, "banks, pension funds, and insurance companies, who are by rule barred from owning low rated securities, were forced to sell off their downgraded RMBS and CDO holdings, because they had lost their investment grade status." This caused major losses because RMBS and CDO securities lost their value (p. 6).

According to the Subcommittee: "The subprime RMBS market initially froze and then collapsed, leaving investors and financial firms around the world holding unmarketable subprime RMBS securities that were plummeting in value. A few months later, the CDO market collapsed as well" (p. 6).

The problem with rating risky loan products with the AAA rating is that, normally, such products have less than a 1% probability of failing. This sends a message to investors that such products are excellent investments even though, because of the dishonesty of banks, regulators, and credit rating agencies, "the vast majority of RMBS and CDO securities with AAA ratings" were in actually just junk: "Analysts have determined that over 90% of the AAA ratings given to subprime RMBS securities originated in 2006 and 2007 were later downgraded by the credit rating agencies to junk status" (p. 6).

The result? Not only did a lot of people lose a lot of money, but "widespread losses led, in turn, to a loss of investor confidence in the value of the AAA rating, in the holdings of major U.S. financial institutions, and even in the viability of U.S. financial markets." The Subcommittee thus concludes: "Inaccurate AAA credit ratings introduced risk into the U.S. financial system and constituted a key cause of the financial crisis. In addition, the July mass downgrades, which were unprecedented in number and scope, precipitated the collapse of the RMBS and CDO secondary markets, and perhaps more than any other single event triggered the beginning of the financial crisis" (p. 6).

The "inherent conflict of interest arising from the system used to pay for credit ratings" was also problematic because Wall Street firms paid credit rating agencies and then used the ratings to promote their products. This amounts to paying someone to help you sell a product, like a salesperson, but in this case the salesperson is supposed to be a neutral actor meant to protect the consumer rather than represent the seller. According to the Subcommittee: "The rating agencies weakened their standards as each competed to provide the most favorable rating to win business and greater market share. The result was a race to the bottom" (p. 7).

Within the rating agencies, other problems contributed to the ultimate collapse, including:

> rating models that failed to include relevant mortgage performance data; unclear and subjective criteria used to produce ratings; a failure to apply updated rating models to existing rated transactions; and a failure to provide adequate staffing to perform rating and surveillance services, despite record revenues. Compounding these problems were federal regulations that required the purchase of investment grade securities by banks and others, which created pressure on the credit rating agencies to issue investment grade ratings. While these federal regulations were intended to help investors stay away from unsafe securities, they had the opposite effect when the AAA ratings proved inaccurate (p. 7).

What makes the credit rating agencies culpable? The Subcommittee concludes that they "were aware of problems in the mortgage market, including an unsustainable rise in housing prices, the high risk nature of the loans being issued, lax lending standards, and rampant mortgage fraud. Instead of using this information to temper their ratings, the firms continued to issue a high volume of investment grade ratings for mortgage backed securities." The Subcommittee concludes that investors would have been discouraged from making such risk investments had the credit rating agencies just done their jobs (p. 7). Yet, since "the credit rating agencies' profits became increasingly reliant on the fees generated by issuing a large volume of structured finance ratings," Moody's and S&P had a financial incentive to provide AAA ratings to tens of thousands of high risk RMBS and CDO securities. As with the banks and investors, ratings agencies engaged in high-level deviance for monetary reward.

And fourth, there is Wall Street itself. The Subcommittee rightly notes that the "complex financial instruments" designed and promoted by Wall Street agents—including RMBS and CDO securities, as well credit default swaps (CDS), and CDS contracts linked to the ABX Index (a measure of the overall value of mortgages made to borrowers with subprime or weak credit)—gave them the opportunity to create enormous wealth from financial products not even understood by the average person (p. 8).

The products work this way: A family gets a loan from a bank to buy a house. That loan is protected by a federal agency in case of default. Similar loans from across the country are then packaged and sold as securities so that investors can bet for or against these products. According to the Subcommittee: "From 2004 to 2008, U.S. financial institutions issued nearly $2.5 trillion in RMBS and over $1.4 trillion in CDO securities, backed primarily by mortgage related products" (p. 8). If the loans themselves are bad, then so too are the securities on which they are based.

Yet, since investment banks charged fees of anywhere from $1 to $8 million to underwrite an RMBS securitization, and $5 to $10 million to be the placement agent for a CDO securitization, investment banks were generating enormous revenues by handle mortgage related securitizations. According to the Subcommittee:

> Investment banks sold RMBS and CDO securities to investors around the world, and helped develop a secondary market where RMBS and CDO securities could be traded. The investment banks' trading desks participated in those secondary markets, buying and selling RMBS and CDO securities either on behalf of their clients or in connection with their own proprietary transactions. The financial products developed by investment banks allowed investors to profit, not only from the success of an RMBS or CDO securitization, but also from its failure. CDS contracts, for example, allowed counterparties to wager on the rise or fall in the value of a specific RMBS security or on a collection of RMBS and other assets contained or referenced in a CDO. Major investment banks developed standardized CDS contracts that could also be traded on a secondary market. In addition, they established the ABX Index which allowed counterparties to wager on the rise or fall in the value of a basket of subprime RMBS securities, which could be used to reflect the status of the subprime mortgage market as a whole. The investment banks sometimes matched up parties who wanted to take opposite sides in a transaction and other times took one or the other side of the transaction to accommodate a client. At still other times, investment banks used these financial instruments to make their own proprietary wagers. In extreme cases, some investment banks set up structured finance transactions which enabled them to profit at the expense of their clients (p. 8).

Incredibly, major banks began quickly selling off and writing down their subprime RMBS and CDO inventory, and began building short positions that would allow them "to profit from the decline of the mortgage market." Large banks made hundreds of billions of dollars in profits betting against products that they knew to be worthless while simultaneously selling and promoting the products to their clients and without telling them that they were themselves betting against the products (p. 9)! Thus, these actors knowingly sold bad loans to clients in order to profit from them; of course, the only way they'd profit is if the loans failed, which means they'd only gain if their own clients lost. Talk about deviance!

According to the Subcommittee, investment banks "were the driving force behind the structured finance products that provided a steady stream of funding for lenders originating high risk, poor quality loans and that magnified risk throughout the U.S. financial system. The investment banks that engineered, sold, traded, and profited from mortgage related structured finance products were a major cause of the financial crisis" (p. 11).

The kinds of fraud that occurred in this case could not have occurred under previous US laws that were meant to reduce the risks associated with such behaviors. For example, the **Banking Act of 1933** (aka, Glass-Steagall) prevented large banks from operating both commercial bank activities and security firms. Banks were forbidden, for example, to purchase securities for customers or invest in securities for the bank, issue or underwrite securities, and so forth. Beginning in the 1960s, the law was interpreted by legislators (under pressure from lobbyists) allow banks to participate in more and more securities investing and the law was finally overturned by the **Financial Services Modernization Act of 1999**. Once large banks were allowed to engage in the securities business, the money held in commercial banks was could be lost through speculative Wall Street activity.

The Subcommittee concludes by providing an excellent summary of the four identified causes of the collapse and how they impacted each other to produce the crisis:

> The four causative factors examined in this Report are interconnected. Lenders introduced new levels of risk into the US financial system by selling and securitizing complex home loans with high risk features and poor underwriting. The credit rating agencies labeled the resulting securities as safe investments, facilitating their purchase by institutional investors around the world. Federal banking regulators failed to ensure safe and sound lending practices and risk management, and stood on the sidelines as large financial institutions active in US financial markets purchased billions of dollars in mortgage related securities containing high risk, poor quality mortgages. Investment banks magnified the risk to the system by engineering and promoting risky mortgage related structured finance products, and enabling investors to use naked credit default swaps and synthetic instruments to bet on the failure rather than the success of US financial instruments. Some investment banks also ignored the conflicts of interest created by their products, placed their financial interests before those of their clients, and even bet against the very securities they were recommending and marketing to their clients. Together these factors produced a mortgage market saturated with high risk, poor quality mortgages and securities that, when they began incurring losses, caused financial institutions around the world to lose billions of dollars, produced rampant unemployment and foreclosures, and ruptured faith in US capital markets (p. 12).

Financial Crisis Inquiry Commission Investigation

A second investigation was conducted by "**The Financial Crisis Inquiry Commission**"—a group created to "examine the causes of the current financial and economic crisis in the United States" and report back to the President of the United States, the US Congress, and the American people. According to the Commission: "Our task was first to determine what happened and how it happened so that we could understand why it happened" (p. xv). They conclude:

> While the vulnerabilities that created the potential for crisis were years in the making, it was the collapse of the housing bubble—fueled by low interest rates, easy and available credit, scant regulation, and toxic mortgages—that was the spark that ignited a string of events, which led to a full-blown crisis in the fall of 2008. Trillions of dollars in risky mortgages had become embedded throughout the financial system, as mortgage-related securities were packaged, repackaged, and sold to investors around the world. When the bubble burst, hundreds of billions of dollars in losses in mortgages and mortgage-related securities shook markets as well as financial institutions that had significant exposures to those mortgages and had borrowed heavily against them. This happened not just in the United States but around the world. The losses were magnified by derivatives such as synthetic securities (p. xvi).

The major findings of the Commission are reported in the appendix for Chapter 4.

The Inquiry then goes on to identify and discuss the role that mortgage-lending standards, the mortgage securitization process, over-the-counter derivatives (e.g., credit default swaps, collateralized debt obligations, and other derivatives), and failures of credit rating agencies played in the crisis. According to the Inquiry, it was elite deviance that caused the economic collapse.

What Happened to the People Who Caused the Crisis?

Incredibly, even though the names and agencies involved in the financial or banking crisis have been identified, not a single person has been arrested or incarcerated for their crimes. As noted by Matt Taibbi:

> Nobody goes to jail. This is the mantra of the financial-crisis era, one that saw virtually every major bank and financial company on Wall Street embroiled in obscene criminal scandals that impoverished millions and collectively destroyed hundreds of billions, in fact, trillions of dollars of the world's wealth—and nobody went to jail. Nobody, that is, except Bernie Madoff, a flamboyant and pathological celebrity con artist, whose victims happened to be other rich and famous people.
>
> The rest of them, all of them, got off. Not a single executive who ran the companies that cooked up and cashed in on the phony financial boom—an industrywide scam that involved the mass sale of mismarked, fraudulent mortgage-backed securities—has ever been convicted. Their names by now are familiar to even the most casual Middle American news consumer: companies like AIG, Goldman Sachs, Lehman Brothers, JP Morgan Chase, Bank of America and Morgan Stanley. Most of these firms were directly involved in elaborate fraud

and theft. Lehman Brothers hid billions in loans from its investors. Bank of America lied about billions in bonuses. Goldman Sachs failed to tell clients how it put together the born-to-lose toxic mortgage deals it was selling. What's more, many of these companies had corporate chieftains whose actions cost investors billions—from AIG derivatives chief Joe Cassano, who assured investors they would not lose even "one dollar" just months before his unit imploded, to the $263 million in compensation that former Lehman chief Dick "The Gorilla" Fuld conveniently failed to disclose. Yet not one of them has faced time behind bars.

Instead of prison time, the companies pay fines—tiny in comparison to the damages they inflicted—and always paid off using shareholder money rather than that of the CEOs, CFOs, and corporate managers responsible for the crimes.

In-Class Activity:
Read Matt Taibbi's article, "Why Isn't Wall Street in Jail?" at: http://www.rolling stone.com/politics/news/why-isnt-wall-street-in-jail-20110216.
Explain why the US government has not gone after the executives who caused the financial collapse.

According to Taibbi's analysis, and that of many others (e.g., Arnold, 2013), lax enforcement by the US government and federal agencies responsible for enforcing laws about corporate crime caused the crisis of 2008. Taibbi offers these examples:

> Over and over, even the most obvious cases of fraud and insider dealing got gummed up in the works, and high-ranking executives were almost never prosecuted for their crimes. In 2003, Freddie Mac coughed up $125 million after it was caught misreporting its earnings by $5 billion; nobody went to jail. In 2006, Fannie Mae was fined $400 million, but executives who had overseen phony accounting techniques to jack up their bonuses faced no criminal charges. That same year, AIG paid $1.6 billion after it was caught in a major accounting scandal that would indirectly lead to its collapse two years later, but no executives at the insurance giant were prosecuted.

And this approach continues to this day. Taibbi offers the following examples to prove the point:

- Goldman Sachs paid $550 million [in 2010] when it was caught defrauding investors with crappy mortgages, but no executive has been fined or jailed.
- Bank of America was caught hiding $5.8 billion in bonuses from shareholders as part of its takeover of Merrill Lynch. The SEC tried to let the bank off with a settlement of only $33 million, but Judge Jed Rakoff rejected the action as a "facade of enforcement." So the SEC quintupled the settlement—but it didn't require either Merrill or Bank of America to admit to wrongdoing.
- Citigroup was nailed for hiding some $40 billion in liabilities from investors. [In 2010] the SEC settled with Citi for $75 million. In a rare move, it also fined two Citi executives, former CFO Gary Crittenden and investor-relations chief Arthur Tildesley Jr. Their penalties, combined, came to a whopping $180,000.

Incredibly, Taibbi shares the story of a financial crimes conference that was attended both by top law enforcement officials (e.g., with the Security and Exchange Commission) as well as top Wall Street attorneys—the very people who would defend corporate criminals if they were ever to be arrested for such crimes. Imagine bank robbers and FBI officers attending a conference together, eating together, hanging out together, etc.! Why would such people associate in such a way? Because of a revolving door between enforcement officials and Wall Street investors: "The Revolving Door isn't just a footnote in financial law enforcement; over the past decade, more than a dozen high-ranking SEC officials have gone on to lucrative jobs at Wall Street banks or white-shoe law firms, where partnerships are worth millions."

Who is another party to this type of cozy relationship? It goes all the way to the President of the United States, a good reminder of the relationship between lobbying, law, and law enforcement (as discussed in Chapter 2). According to Taibbi, Goldman Sachs was the "number-one private campaign contributor" to President Obama. Further, a Citigroup executive was put in charge of Obama's economic transition team, and Obama "just named an executive of JP Morgan Chase, the proud owner of $7.7 million in Chase stock, his new chief of staff."

Chris Arnold (2013) adds that the government actually has few investigators responsible for pursuing such cases, that the cases are extremely complex, and that the government does not view the actions of Wall Street firms and large banks as crimes. Of course, the cases are complex, but many of them involved clear violations of the criminal law. As for the number of investigators, who is responsible for that? Policy-makers—lawmakers—who as shown in Chapter 2, tend to be pro-business conservatives.

Summary

The law fails to define the acts that pose the greatest threat to Americans as crimes and especially as serious crimes. In this chapter, you learned that Americans are far more likely to suffer property victimization from white-collar and corporate crime, especially through acts of fraud. Fraud causes far more property loss than all street crimes combined, yet it remains a "less serious" crime in the United States, meaning relative to street crimes, people are rarely arrested, convicted, and punished for their crimes.

In fact, the high level frauds outlined in this chapter led to enormous enrichment for those who committed them, and in some cases, literally no one was held accountable. In other cases, US taxpayers were forced by lawmakers to bail out companies implicated in the collapse of the US economy.

Why does this occur? It is not because the acts are committed without culpability. The acts summarized in this chapter were committed intentionally, others knowingly. Still others involved clear example of negligence and recklessness, meaning the people who committed them are morally responsible for their behaviors. So, why weren't these elite criminals held responsible for their crimes?

Recall who makes the law and who owns the media. WORMs—white, older, rich men—largely decide what acts are crimes (and which are not) as well as which are serious crimes (and which are not). It is in their interest, as well as the interests of those who donate to their political campaigns and fund their operations, to keep status quo approaches to crime control in place.

The law does not define such acts as crime and the media generally fail to despite the actions that cause such widespread damage as crimes or serious crimes. While decisions to define crimes as serious or not in the FBI's Uniform Crime Reports (UCR) were made in the 1930s, it is conservative politicians (both Republicans and Democrats) since the 1980s through today who made the decisions to deregulate large businesses, thereby making it easier to commit massive and widespread fraud. Further, it is conservative politicians (both Republicans and Democrats) who decided to continue to ignore white-collar and corporate crime while simultaneously vigorously pursuing street criminals (even as the harms caused by the former so clearly dwarf the latter).

To a large degree, President Ronald Reagan's explicit focus on street crime and simultaneous promotion of policies that deregulated big business helps explain not only why we as a nation largely ignore white-collar and corporate crime but also why it is more common today that before the massive deregulation that so enables it (Hagan, 2010). And since both Republicans and Democrats have embraced this conservative ideology, thereby assuring it will continue into the future.

It is thus politics and ideology that explain the outcome identified in this chapter. Whereas Americans ideally value crime control and due process goals found in the Declaration of Independence and the US Constitution—equality, rights, life, liberty, the pursuit of happiness, justice, domestic tranquility, common defence, general welfare— the real criminal justice system is unequally applied, does not equally protect our rights and liberty, does not assure our happiness, tranquility, common defence, or welfare, and therefore is in some ways unjust or biased. Recall that this type of bias is called *innocent bias*.

Innocent bias occurs because criminal justice pursues only street crimes committed by certain people under certain circumstances while simultaneously ignoring the acts that actually cause the most harm to society. In this way, the criminal justice system is ineffective at reducing crime and highly unfair to those groups to whom the law is more commonly applied.

Key Terms

- **Banking Act of 1933**: The Banking Act of 1933 established the Federal Deposit Insurance Corporation (FDIC), which provides deposit insurance to protect individual bank accounts, as well as prevented large banks from engaging in its commercial activities and engaging in securities investments.
- **Banking Crisis**: A banking crisis is when major stress is placed on large banks that requires taxpayer assistance and that can be caused by greed and speculative investments on Wall Street.
- **Caveat Emptor**: Caveat emptor means "let the buyer beware," and this phrase captures the approach of law enforcement toward cases such as deceptive advertising.
- **Collective Embezzlement**: Collective embezzlement is stealing money that you have legal access to, such as when you are holding an investment but then loot or steal it.

- **Corporate Crime:** Corporate crime is made up of acts committed by corporations that are illegal and tend to harm consumers.
- **Covering Up:** Covering up is when efforts are made to hide criminal activity from investors, taxpayers, and the government.
- **Crime:** A crime is an act or behavior that violates the criminal law.
- **Culpability:** Culpability means a responsibility or blameworthiness. It includes acts committed intentionally, recklessly, negligently, or knowingly.
- **Deceptive Advertising:** Deceptive advertising is a form of fraud where a product is sold using false or misleading claims.
- **Desperation Dealing:** Desperation dealing is making risky investments in hopes of striking it rich where taxpayers are on the hook to repay bets that do not pay off.
- **Elite Deviance:** Elite deviance is made up of harmful acts committed by elites, including white-collar and corporate crime.
- **Express Claims:** Express claims are claims made by sellers of products that are actually made.
- **Financial Crisis Inquiry Commission:** The Financial Crisis Inquiry Commission was a ten-member group created by Congress to study the causes of the banking crisis of 2008.
- **Financial Services Modernization Act of 1999:** The Financial Services Modernization Act of 1999 overturned provisions of the Banking Act of 1933, thereby allowing the consolidation of commercial and investment banks.
- **Fraud:** Fraud is a form of theft that is accomplished through deceit or lies.
- **Implied Claims:** Implied claims are claims that are made indirectly by manufacturers of products or that are inferred by consumers.
- **Intentionality:** Intentionality refers to an act that is done on purpose.
- **Knowingly:** Knowingly means an act is done with the knowledge that a particular outcome is likely.
- **Laissez-faire Economics:** Laissez-faire economics refers to the idea that government should not interfere with business.
- **Negligence:** Negligence refers to failing to do something legally required of you.
- **Part 1 Index Offenses:** Part 1 Index Offenses include the violent crimes of murder and nonnegligent manslaughter, forcible rape, robbery, and aggravated assault, and the property crimes of burglary, theft, motor vehicle theft, and arson.
- **Product Shrinkage:** Product shrinkage is when manufacturers offer less and less of a product in the same size package over time.
- **Pyramid Scheme:** A pyramid scheme is a phony investment scheme whereby the money to earlier investors can only be sustained as long as new investors are constantly added.
- **Recklessness:** Recklessness refers to acting without regard to human life or property.
- **S&Ls:** Savings & Loans (S&Ls) are banks created in the 1930s to help people build homes during the Great Depression.
- **Serious Crime:** Serious crime refers to the crimes that are thought by the Federal Bureau of Investigation to occur with the most frequency, to be the most widespread, and to do the most harm.
- **Street Crime:** Street crime is those forms of crimes committed on the streets of America, which are synonymous with serious crime.

- **US Senate's Permanent Subcommittee on Investigations:** The US Senate's Permanent Subcommittee on Investigations is the primary investigative subcommittee of the Committee on Homeland Security and Government Affairs; its main responsibilities are to study and investigate the efficiency and economy of operations of all branches of the government, and to study and investigate the compliance or noncompliance with rules, regulations and laws for those acts that impact the national health, welfare, and safety.
- **White-Collar Crime:** White-collar crime is made up of acts committed by people in the course of their jobs, which are illegal and produce harm, usually against the company where they work.

Discussion Questions

1) What is crime?
2) Can any behavior really be considered a crime? Explain.
3) What is culpability?
4) Compare and contrast intentionally, negligently, recklessly, and knowingly.
5) What is street crime?
6) What makes a crime serious?
7) List and define the Part 1 Index Offenses.
8) What are the most common and least common street crimes?
9) Which groups in society are most and least likely to be victimized by street crime?
10) What is elite deviance?
11) Compare and contrast white-collar crime and corporate crime.
12) What is fraud? How much damage does fraud cause in the US?
13) What is deceptive advertising? What are express claims and implied claims?
14) What are caveat emptor laissez-faire economics? How do these doctrines encourage elite deviance?
15) What is product shrinkage?
16) What is an S&L? Explain why the S&L crisis happened.
17) What roles did desperation dealing, collective embezzlement, and covering up play in the S&L scandals?
18) What was the typical punishment faced by the S&L criminals?
19) Who were the "corporate bandits?" How much damage did they cause?
20) What was the typical punishment faced by the corporate bandits?
21) What caused the banking crisis in 2008? Summarize the findings of the US Senate's Permanent Subcommittee on Investigations and the Financial Crisis Inquiry Commission. What role did the following play in the crisis: securitization, subprime mortgages, no doc loans, credit enhancement, synthetic securities, credit default swaps, collateralized debt obligations?
22) How much damage did the banking crisis cost? How many years worth of street crime were these damages equated with?
23) What is a pyramid scheme?
24) What role did the Financial Services Modernization Act of 1999 and its revision of the Banking Act of 1933 play in the crisis?
25) What happened to the people who caused the banking crisis?

Appendix for Chapter 4

Findings of The Financial Crisis Inquiry Commission

We conclude this financial crisis was avoidable. The crisis was the result of human action and inaction, not of Mother Nature or computer models gone haywire. The captains of finance and the public stewards of our financial system ignored warnings and failed to question, understand, and manage evolving risks within a system essential to the well-being of the American public. Theirs was a big miss, not a stumble. While the business cycle cannot be repealed, a crisis of this magnitude need not have occurred.

Despite the expressed view of many on Wall Street and in Washington that the crisis could not have been foreseen or avoided, there were warning signs. The tragedy was that they were ignored or discounted. There was an explosion in risky subprime lending and securitization, an unsustainable rise in housing prices, widespread reports of egregious and predatory lending practices, dramatic increases in household mortgage debt, and exponential growth in financial firms' trading activities, unregulated derivatives, and short-term "repo" lending markets, among many other red flags. Yet there was pervasive permissiveness; little meaningful action was taken to quell the threats in a timely manner.

The prime example is the Federal Reserve's pivotal failure to stem the flow of toxic mortgages, which it could have done by setting prudent mortgage-lending standards. The Federal Reserve was the one entity empowered to do so and it did not. The record of our examination is replete with evidence of other failures: financial institutions made, bought, and sold mortgage securities they never examined, did not care to examine, or knew to be defective; firms depended on tens of billions of dollars of borrowing that had to be renewed each and every night, secured by subprime mortgage securities; and major firms and investors blindly relied on credit rating agencies as their arbiters of risk.

We conclude widespread failures in financial regulation and supervision proved devastating to the stability of the nation's financial markets. The sentries were not at their posts, in no small part due to the widely accepted faith in the self-correcting nature of the markets and the ability of financial institutions to effectively police themselves. More than 30 years of deregulation and reliance on self-regulation by financial institutions, championed by former Federal Reserve chairman Alan Greenspan and others, supported by successive administrations and Congresses, and actively pushed by the powerful financial industry at every turn, had stripped away key safeguards, which could have helped avoid catastrophe. This approach had opened up gaps in oversight of critical areas with trillions of dollars at risk, such as the shadow banking system and over-the-counter derivatives markets. In addition, the government permitted financial firms to pick their preferred regulators in what became a race to the weakest supervisor.

Yet we do not accept the view that regulators lacked the power to protect the financial system. They had ample power in many arenas and they chose not to use it ... In case after case after case, regulators continued to rate the institutions they oversaw as safe and sound even in the face of mounting troubles, often downgrading them just before their collapse. And where regulators lacked authority, they could have sought it. Too often, they lacked the political will—in a political and ideological environment that constrained it—as well as the fortitude to critically challenge the institutions and the entire system they were entrusted to oversee.

Changes in the regulatory system occurred in many instances as financial markets evolved … But as the report will show, the financial industry itself played a key role in weakening regulatory constraints on institutions, markets, and products. It did not surprise the Commission that an industry of such wealth and power would exert pressure on policy makers and regulators. From 1999 to 2008, the financial sector expended $2.7 billion in reported federal lobbying expenses; individuals and political action committees in the sector made more than $1 billion in campaign contributions. What troubled us was the extent to which the nation was deprived of the necessary strength and independence of the oversight necessary to safeguard financial stability.

We conclude dramatic failures of corporate governance and risk management at many systemically important financial institutions were a key cause of this crisis. There was a view that instincts for self-preservation inside major financial firms would shield them from fatal risk-taking without the need for a steady regulatory hand, which, the firms argued, would stifle innovation. Too many of these institutions acted recklessly, taking on too much risk, with too little capital, and with too much dependence on short-term funding. In many respects, this reflected a fundamental change in these institutions, particularly the large investment banks and bank holding companies, which focused their activities increasingly on risky trading activities that produced hefty profits. They took on enormous exposures in acquiring and supporting subprime lenders and creating, packaging, repackaging, and selling trillions of dollars in mortgage-related securities, including synthetic financial products. …

Financial institutions and credit rating agencies embraced mathematical models as reliable predictors of risks, replacing judgment in too many instances. Too often, risk management became risk justification.

Compensation systems — designed in an environment of cheap money, intense competition, and light regulation — too often rewarded the quick deal, the short-term gain — without proper consideration of long-term consequences. Often, those systems encouraged the big bet — where the payoff on the upside could be huge and the downside limited. This was the case up and down the line — from the corporate boardroom to the mortgage broker on the street.

We conclude a combination of excessive borrowing, risky investments, and lack of transparency put the financial system on a collision course with crisis. Clearly, this vulnerability was related to failures of corporate governance and regulation, but it is significant enough by itself to warrant our attention here.

In the years leading up to the crisis, too many financial institutions, as well as too many households, borrowed to the hilt, leaving them vulnerable to financial distress or ruin if the value of their investments declined even modestly. For example, as of 2007, the five major investment banks — Bear Stearns, Goldman Sachs, Lehman Brothers, Merrill Lynch, and Morgan Stanley — were operating with extraordinarily thin capital. By one measure, their leverage ratios were as high as 40 to 1, meaning for every $40 in assets, there was only $1 in capital to cover losses. Less than a 3% drop in asset values could wipe out a firm. To make matters worse, much of their borrowing was short-term, in the overnight market — meaning the borrowing had to be renewed each and every day …

And the leverage was often hidden — in derivatives positions, in off-balance-sheet entities, and through "window dressing" of financial reports available to the investing public …

[F]rom 2001 to 2007, national mortgage debt almost doubled, and the amount of mortgage debt per household rose more than 63% from $91,500 to $149,500, even while wages were essentially stagnant. When the housing downturn hit, heavily indebted financial firms and families alike were walloped.

The heavy debt taken on by some financial institutions was exacerbated by the risky assets they were acquiring with that debt. As the mortgage and real estate markets churned out riskier and riskier loans and securities, many financial institutions loaded up on them.... And again, the risk wasn't being taken on just by the big financial firms, but by families, too. Nearly one in 10 mortgage borrowers in 2005 and 2006 took out "option ARM" loans, which meant they could choose to make payments so low that their mortgage balances rose every month.

Within the financial system, the dangers of this debt were magnified because transparency was not required or desired. Massive, short-term borrowing, combined with obligations unseen by others in the market, heightened the chances the system could rapidly unravel. In the early part of the 20th century, we erected a series of protections—the Federal Reserve as a lender of last resort, federal deposit insurance, ample regulations—to provide a bulwark against the panics that had regularly plagued America's banking system in the 19th century. Yet, over the past 30-plus years, we permitted the growth of a shadow banking system—opaque and laden with short-term debt—that rivaled the size of the traditional banking system. Key components of the market—for example, the multitrillion-dollar repo lending market, off-balance-sheet entities, and the use of over-the-counter derivatives—were hidden from view, without the protections we had constructed to prevent financial meltdowns. We had a 21st-century financial system with 19th-century safeguards.

When the housing and mortgage markets cratered, the lack of transparency, the extraordinary debt loads, the short-term loans, and the risky assets all came home to roost. What resulted was panic. We had reaped what we had sown.

We conclude the government was ill prepared for the crisis, and its inconsistent response added to the uncertainty and panic in the financial markets. As part of our charge, it was appropriate to review government actions taken in response to the developing crisis, not just those policies or actions that preceded it, to determine if any of those responses contributed to or exacerbated the crisis.

As our report shows, key policy makers—the Treasury Department, the Federal Reserve Board, and the Federal Reserve Bank of New York—who were best positioned to watch over our markets were ill prepared for the events of 2007 and 2008.

Other agencies were also behind the curve. They were hampered because they did not have a clear grasp of the financial system they were charged with overseeing, particularly as it had evolved in the years leading up to the crisis. This was in no small measure due to the lack of transparency in key markets. They thought risk had been diversified when, in fact, it had been concentrated. Time and again, from the spring of 2007 on, policy makers and regulators were caught off guard as the contagion spread, responding on an ad hoc basis with specific programs to put fingers in the dike. There was no comprehensive and strategic plan for containment, because they lacked a full understanding of the risks and interconnections in the financial markets. Some regulators have conceded this error. We had allowed the system to race ahead of our ability to protect it.

While there was some awareness of, or at least a debate about, the housing bubble, the record reflects that senior public officials did not recognize that a bursting of the bubble could threaten the entire financial system. Throughout the summer of 2007, both Federal Reserve Chairman Ben Bernanke and Treasury Secretary Henry Paulson offered public assurances that the turmoil in the subprime mortgage markets would be contained ...

We conclude there was a systemic breakdown in accountability and ethics. The integrity of our financial markets and the public's trust in those markets are essential to the economic well-being of our nation. The soundness and the sustained prosperity of the financial system and our economy rely on the notions of fair dealing, responsibility, and transparency. In our economy, we expect businesses and individuals to pursue profits, at the same time that they produce products and services of quality and conduct themselves well.

Unfortunately — as has been the case in past speculative booms and busts — we witnessed an erosion of standards of responsibility and ethics that exacerbated the financial crisis. This was not universal, but these breaches stretched from the ground level to the corporate suites. They resulted not only in significant financial consequences but also in damage to the trust of investors, businesses, and the public in the financial system.

For example, our examination found, according to one measure, that the percentage of borrowers who defaulted on their mortgages within just a matter of months after taking a loan nearly doubled from the summer of 2006 to late 2007. This data indicates they likely took out mortgages that they never had the capacity or intention to pay … mortgage brokers … were paid "yield spread premiums" by lenders to put borrowers into higher-cost loans so they would get bigger fees, often never disclosed to borrowers. [There was a] rising incidence of mortgage fraud, which flourished in an environment of collapsing lending standards and lax regulation. The number of suspicious activity reports — reports of possible financial crimes filed by depository banks and their affiliates — related to mortgage fraud grew 20-fold between 1996 and 2005 and then more than doubled again between 2005 and 2009. One study places the losses resulting from fraud on mortgage loans made between 2005 and 2007 at $112 billion.

Lenders made loans that they knew borrowers could not afford and that could cause massive losses to investors in mortgage securities. … But they did not stop.

… [M]ajor financial institutions ineffectively sampled loans they were purchasing to package and sell to investors. They knew a significant percentage of the sampled loans did not meet their own underwriting standards or those of the originators. Nonetheless, they sold those securities to investors … this critical information was not disclosed.

THESE CONCLUSIONS must be viewed in the context of human nature and individual and societal responsibility. First, to pin this crisis on mortal flaws like greed and hubris would be simplistic. It was the failure to account for human weakness that is relevant to this crisis.

Second, we clearly believe the crisis was a result of human mistakes, misjudgments, and misdeeds that resulted in systemic failures for which our nation has paid dearly. … [S]pecific firms and individuals acted irresponsibly. Yet a crisis of this magnitude cannot be the work of a few bad actors, and such was not the case here. At the same time, the breadth of this crisis does not mean that "everyone is at fault"; many firms and individuals did not participate in the excesses that spawned disaster.

We do place special responsibility with the public leaders charged with protecting our financial system, those entrusted to run our regulatory agencies, and the chief executives of companies whose failures drove us to crisis. These individuals sought and accepted positions of significant responsibility and obligation. Tone at the top does matter and, in this instance, we were let down. No one said "no."

But as a nation, we must also accept responsibility for what we permitted to occur. Collectively, but certainly not unanimously, we acquiesced to or embraced a system, a set of policies and actions, that gave rise to our present predicament.

Available at: http://www.gpo.gov/fdsys/pkg/GPO-FCIC/pdf/GPO-FCIC.pdf.

Chapter 5

Violent Street Crime versus Elite Deviance

"Ultimately, the responsibility for the explosion at the Upper Big Branch mine lies with the management of Massey Energy. The company broke faith with its workers by frequently and knowingly violating the law and blatantly disregarding known safety practices while creating a public perception that its operations exceeded industry safety standards ... The April 5, 2010, explosion was not something that happened out of the blue, an event that could not have been anticipated or prevented. It was, to the contrary, a completely predictable result for a company that ignored basic safety standards and put too much faith in its own mythology."

—Government's Independent Investigation Panel, West Virginia

Violent Corporate Crime?

In the last chapter, I showed that acts of elites (e.g., white-collar and corporate crime) cause far more damage or property loss than all street crimes combined. Yet, these acts are largely ignored by the criminal justice system. And I suggested we do not vigorously pursue such acts because of the law and the media.

First, the law tends not to define these acts as crimes or serious crimes. This means that police will not arrest people who commit these acts, courts will not convict them, and correctional agencies will not punish them. Second, the media tend not to focus their attention on these acts, instead focusing on acts of "serious" street crime. This means people will not be concerned about them, view them as serious social problems, or call on legislators to do something about them.

It is thus fair to conclude that US crime fighting is characterized by an institutionalized bias because these societal institutions are biased against street crime and the people who commit them. Stated differently, the law and media are biased in favor of the people who commit white-collar and corporate crimes—the very people who make the law, own the media, and contribute to both financially. For this reason, white, older, rich men—WORMs—rarely come to the attention of the criminal justice system.

Recall that *innocent bias* refers to unfairness in criminal justice that exists because of unfair criminal laws. It is called "innocent" because it does not emerge from intentional discrimination on the part of individual police officers, prosecutors, or other agents of criminal justice. Instead, innocent bias occurs when criminal justice agents innocently enforce biased criminal laws. As you saw in the last chapter, the law (and thus the system) tends to ignore property crimes committed by the powerful.

As bad as it is that states and the US government tend to ignore elite deviance that harms people's property, it is even worse that they also tend to ignore or downplay extremely harmful violent acts committed by elites. As shown in this chapter, elite deviance is also more deadly than street crime, harming and killing more Americans than all street crimes combined. To be sure, there are differences between murder and the acts discussed in this chapter; these differences are identified and discussed. Yet, as will be shown throughout, acts of violence by elites tend to be committed with *culpability*, meaning that the people who engage in them are legally and morally responsible for the harms that result.

Elite Violence

Not only does elite deviance so clearly lead to more property loss than street crime, but it is also far more deadly than street crime. Table 5.1 shows the estimated number of deaths caused by various forms of behaviors (some illegal and some not). As you see, acts of elite deviance and far more damaging than street crime. Some of these behaviors are discussed below.

In-Class Activity:
Pull up the website "Preventable Medical Errors" from the American Association for Justice at: http://www.justice.org/cps/rde/justice/hs.xsl/8677.htm. Read the main findings. Then discuss why you think medical errors are so common in the US and what can be done to prevent them. Then pull up the report by NPR titled, "How Many People Die from Medical Errors in Hospitals" at: http://www.npr.org/blogs/health/2013/09/20/224507654/how-many-die-from-medical-mistakes-in-u-s-hospitals. Do you believe the number of people who die from medical mistakes is really this high?

According to Jeffrey Reiman & Paul Leighton (2013), who painstakingly analyze available data on workplace violence, 50,000 people die each year due to occupational diseases, and another 250,000 contract job-related serious illnesses. Another 4,000 or so die each year at work, and about 2.8 million people are seriously injured enough at work to have to miss work days. This means at least 54,000 people die each year from occupational disease and injury and more than 3 million become seriously ill or are seriously injured at work. Others claim that 100,000 people die every year due to exposure to toxic substances at work (Jamieson, 2000; Simon, 2006).

Reiman & Leighton convincingly argue that the majority of these injuries and deaths are as much beyond the control of the workers as being murdered is beyond the control of the murder victim. The fact that many of these deaths and injuries result from the negligence or recklessness of people who work for corporations demands our attention.

Table 5.1. Death Caused by Elite Deviance

Tobacco	443,000
Medical treatment & infection	325,000
Poverty & income inequality	291,000
Adverse reactions to prescriptions	100,000
Hospital error	98,000
Air pollution	55,000
Occupational disease & injury	54,000
Lack of health insurance	45,000
Defective products	20,000

Sources: Harvard University. http://news.harvard.edu/gazette/story/2009/09/harvard-medical-study-links-lack-of-insurance-to-45000-u-s-deaths-a-year; Reiman, J., & Leighton, P. (2013). *The Rich Get Richer and the Poor Get Prison: Ideology, Class, and Criminal Justice.* Upper Saddle River, NJ: Pearson; Robinson, M., & Murphy, D. (2009). *Greed is Good: Elite Deviance and Maximization in America.* Lanham, MD: Rowman & Littlefield.

Consider the explosion at a fertilizer factory in Waco, Texas. At the time of this writing, it is thought that as many as 35 people died in a massive explosion at the West Chemical and Fertilizer Company in April 2013. Although the cause of the explosion is as of now unknown, what we do know is that the plant had not been fully inspected by the Occupational Safety and Health Administration (OSHA) since 1985. Further, the company's owners did not tell the Department of Homeland Security about the enormous amount of fertilizer stored on site, even though this is required by federal regulations. In fact, company executives had reported that the only possible bad outcome at the plant was a small fire and release of smoke that might last ten minutes.

The plant did not get a full safety review again largely because it was such a low priority to OSHA (which is vastly understaffed due to budget cuts by conservative politicians who believe regulation of business is unnecessary because it interferes with profit) because the company told OSHA the risk of fire was low. This is true even though an earlier explosion at a plant in Sergeant Bluff, Iowa, which also manufactured ammonium nitrate fertilizer (the same kind used at the West Chemical and Fertilizer Company), killed four people and injured 18. In other words, company executives lied to federal officials and lots of people died as a result. If the company were an individual, it would be considered a mass murder, clearly worthy of criminal justice intervention. And even though there was probably no intent to kill multiple people, an investigation into the explosion will probably reveal clear evidence of *negligent* and *reckless* behavior on part of employees of the company, making it morally and legally responsible for the deaths and thus legally culpable.

Although some of the injuries, deaths, and illnesses due to hazardous workplaces in the US could be blamed on the workers themselves, "a substantial portion of workers' deaths, injuries, and diseases are caused by the violation of prevailing laws and regulations" (Cullen et al., 2006: 26). Given all the specific cases described in the literature, scholars are confident that as many as half of all injuries and deaths of workers are caused by corporate negligence and recklessness, and in some cases "laws are broken intentionally" (p. 28). The case of Harry McShane, whose picture is featured in Figure 5.1, is typical

Figure 5.1. Workplace injury

Courtesy of Library of Congress Prints and Photographs Division

of workplace injury cases. He was pulled into a piece of equipment at a factory and lost an arm and broke a leg.

Jeffrey Reiman (2006: 79) dismisses the criticism that people who die at work are to blame, writing:

> To say that some of these workers died from accidents due to their own carelessness is about as helpful as saying that some of those who died at the hands of murderers deserved it. It overlooks the fact that, when workers are careless, it is not because they love to live dangerously. They have production quotas to meet, quotas that they themselves do not set. If quotas were set with an eye to keeping work at a safe pace rather than keeping the production-to-wages ratio as high as possible, it might be more reasonable to expect workers to take the time to be careful.

According to Stephen Rosoff, Henry Pontell, & Robert Tillman (2002: 168), "in tough economic times, management is more apt to tolerate hazardous equipment, neglect safety precautions, ignore dangerous conditions, and disregard the welfare of workers. Safety, it seems, does not necessarily pay. After all, workers' compensation benefits are relatively inexpensive, and fines for fatal accidents are insignificant for big corporations." Recall the conservative political ideology introduced in Chapter 2; it puts corporate profits above all else, including effective regulation of industry meant to save lives. Both Republicans and Democrats have embraced this ideology.

Defective Products

Defective products include any good or service that is unreasonably dangerous to those who purchase the good or service. Tens of millions of defective products are likely being used by consumers in the United States alone (Consumer Products Safety Commission, 2013). These products are considered defective because they have the potential to seriously injure or kill the users. The word "defective" is generally understood to mean imperfect or faulty.

According to the US **Consumer Product Safety Commission (CPSC)** the total cost associated with defective products in the United States is $700 billion every year! This cost includes "deaths, injuries and property damage from consumer product incidents."

When you compare the damages caused by defective products with those losses caused by all "serious" property crimes discussed in the last chapter, it is clear that costs of defective products are far worse. Yet the costs of defective products identified by CPSC include not only *direct costs* but also *indirect costs* — things such as pain and suffering and lost wages due to injury. Thus, the two numbers are not entirely comparable, although there is simply no doubt that defective products are more damaging than all street crime combined, especially when you consider injuries and death caused by these products (these are discussed later in the chapter).

The CPSC employs less than 500 employees which were responsible for monitoring the safety of more than 15,000 kinds of consumer products. Like most regulatory agencies (including OSHA), the CPSC has fewer employees and less money than in the past, because of deregulation of businesses by Congress starting in the 1980s under the conservative political ideology (discussed in Chapter 3). So, not only does deregulation of business assures massive and widespread fraud, it literally kills and injures people, too.

According to its web site, the CPSC "is committed to protecting consumers and families from products that pose a fire, electrical, chemical, or mechanical hazard or can injure children." It aims to "ensure the safety of consumer products — such as toys, cribs, power tools, cigarette lighters, and household chemicals."

Although the true extent of injuries and deaths that can be attributed to defective products cannot be reliably known, experts agree that more people are injured and killed from defective products each year than from all street crimes combined. Recall that murder kills approximately 15,000 people per year and violent street crimes cause physical injuries to less than 1 million people. Further, the most common violent street crime is assault, which typically does not lead to any serious injury requiring hospital treatment.

Out-of-Class Activity:

Go to the website of the Consumer Product Safety Commission and examine their statistics on injuries associated with various products at: http://www.cpsc.gov/en/Research—Statistics/Injury-Statistics/. Choose a type of product and examine how many injuries and/or deaths are caused by those products according to this organization.

Figure 5.2. Children's lunchboxes

Part of Wikimedia Commons. Originally posted to Flickr by _nickd. Available at: http://en.wikipedia.org/wiki/File:Lunch_boxes.jpg.

It is known that even though more than 1,000 products are recalled each year, more than 20,000 people in the United States are killed annually by defective products. This number is understood to represent the minimum killed by defective products, for it excludes the approximately 440,000 who die each year from tobacco-related illnesses, the approximately 300,000 who die from eating high fat diets (including large amounts of fast food products) and not exercising enough, the more than 100,000 who die from adverse reactions to legal and approved drugs, and the 60,000 who die each year due to toxic chemicals (Robinson, 2006).

An estimated 30 million Americans are injured each year by defective products, as well. For example, nearly 200,000 children require emergency room care for toy-related injuries, and more than 2 million people suffer from serious reactions related to approved drugs. The Centers for Disease Control and Prevention (CDC) estimates that food-borne diseases, caused by pathogens such as Listeria, Salmonella, and Toxoplasma, lead to more than 75 million illnesses, 325,000 hospitalizations, and 5,000 deaths every year in the United States (Robinson, 2006).

The dangers of defective products cannot be understated. Often, even after a recall, products end up back in the hands of additional consumers because they are resold to unknowing customers rather than being destroyed. Here is a recent example: The Cable News Network (CNN) reported that in 2005, government scientists tested 60 soft, vinyl lunchboxes and found that one in five contained "amounts of lead that medical experts consider unsafe—and several had more than 10 times hazardous levels." Figure 5.2 illustrates some "classic" lunchboxes, which are clearly designed for use by children.

However, the Consumer Product Safety Commission (CPSC) did not tell the public! Instead, it released a statement saying they found "no instances of hazardous levels." Further, the CPSC "refused to release their actual test results, citing regulations that protect manufacturers from having their information released to the public." Only after the Associated Press issued a Freedom of Information Act request did the CPSC send along documents that led to the discovery of the test results. According to CNN: "The results of the first type of test, looking for the actual lead content of the vinyl, showed that 20 percent of the bags had more than 600 parts per million of lead—the federal safe level for paint and other products. The highest level was 9,600 ppm, more than 16 times the federal standard. But the CPSC did not use those results."

Amazingly, a CPSC spokesperson said: "When it comes to a lunchbox, it's carried. The food that you put in the lunch box may have an outer wrapping, a baggie, so there isn't direct exposure. The direct exposure would be if kids were putting their lunchboxes in their mouth, which isn't a common way for children to interact with their lunchbox."

Alexa Engelman, a researcher at the Oakland, California-based Center for Environmental Health, reacted: "They found levels that we consider very high … They knew this all along and they didn't take action on it. It's upsetting to me. Why are we, as a country, protecting the companies? We should be protecting the kids. I don't think in this instance they did their job."

Since the Food and Drug Administration (FDA) reviewed the test results and sent a letter to lunch box manufacturers telling them that the lunchboxes may be dangerous, it appears the action of the CPSC was negligent in nature. Wal-Mart stopped selling such lunchboxes due to safety concerns.

High levels of lead in blood can lead to learning problems, reduced intelligence, hyperactivity and attention deficit disorder (Nigg, Knottnerus, Martel, Nikolas, Cavanagh, Karmaus & Rappley, 2008; Nigg, Nikolas, Knottnerus, Cavanagh & Friderichi, 2010). Further, no level of lead in the blood is considered safe. This led Dr. Bruce Lamphear, a lead poisoning specialist at the Children's Hospital Medical Center in Cincinnati, Ohio, to say: "I don't think the Consumer Product Safety Commission has lived up to its role to protect kids from lead … As a public agency, their work should be transparent. And if one is to err on the side of protecting children rather than protecting lunch box makers, then certainly you would want to lower the levels."

Here is another recent example: In 2013, a civil jury ruled against Exxon to the tune of $236 million for adding a chemical, methyl tertiary butyl ether (MTBE), to its gasoline. MTBE was added by Exxon to reduce smog, but the chemical was found to rapidly find its way into groundwater, leading to contamination. The jury found that Exxon created a defective product and was negligent in failing to warn distributors and consumers about hazards posed by MTBE. Of course, Exxon is also widely known for the huge oil spill in 1989 off the coast of Alaska when its large tanker, the Valdez, ran aground. This is shown in Figure 5.3.

Defects occur in all kinds of products, ranging from food products, drugs, medical devices, automobiles, household products, toys, and even cosmetics. David Friedrichs (2006: 75) acknowledges that some products are just inherently dangerous, but then asserts "much evidence suggests that corporations, in their almost single-minded pursuit

Figure 5.3. Oil spill emanating from the *Exxon Valdez*

Photo courtesy of the *Exxon Valdez* Oil Spill Trustee Council.

of profit, have been negligent—sometimes criminally negligent—in their disregard for consumer safety."

Consumer protection agencies such as *Consumer Reports* provide information on recently recalled products. The frequency with which products are recalled is simply stunning, and includes hundreds of cars, sports utility vehicles (SUVs), trucks and vans; children's toys; dozens of appliances; lawn products; car seats; electronic devices; home improvement and home furnishing products; as well as several types of foods and beverages; drugs and health products; some household products such as automatic garage door openers; and ironically, some safety products such as gun trigger locks, carbon-monoxide, and smoke detectors. Some defective products even involve those aimed at protecting police such as some bullet-proof vests, as well as some devices meant to protect society from criminals, such as electronic monitoring bracelets.

It has been alleged that other products, including some intended for the most vulnerable consumers (such as child safety seats) are defectively designed, shoddily manufactured, and inadequately tested by regulatory agencies. Similar claims have been made against some baby cribs. Such products produce thousands of deaths and hundreds of thousands of injuries annually in the United States.

Some specific kinds of foods have been addressed in the realm of defective product legislation and regulation. For example, beef was considered very unsafe before the 1970s despite several federal laws requiring safety and inspection standards. Even today, meat inspectors are understaffed and meat plants are rarely inspected. In the late 1990s, the federal government declared that E. coli bacteria (Escherichia coli O157:H7) was an epidemic because it was so widespread in the nation's meat. Part of the reason bacterial infections of meat are so common is because of how the meat is processed. Meat packing plants run at a very fast and unsafe speed, increasing the risk of disease spreading from fecal matter and stomach contents of the animals to the carcasses (Schlosser, 2002). The speed of the assembly line also contributes to thousands of injuries of employees every year, making the meat-packing industry among the most dangerous jobs in America (Human Rights Watch, 2004; Schlosser, 2001).

Automobiles are frequently found to be defective in one of two ways: first, there are design defects that are discovered by corporations and not fixed; second, corporations routinely resist safety devices until forced to adopt them by public demand (Robinson, 2006). Examples of the latter include resisting putting in safety windshields and air bags. Yet, the most well-known case of a defective product involved a car that was known by its manufacturer to be defective but was not recalled for the purpose of saving the company money.

Ford Pinto and Explorer

The most well-known case of a defective product is the Ford Pinto. This automobile was manufactured in the 1970s despite the findings of pre-crash tests which showed that Ford knew of ruptured fuel lines being caused by rear-end collisions. Ford learned that it would cost $11 per car to fix the automobiles but calculated that it could save $87.5 million by not fixing the cars (Robinson, 2006). This was based on the assumption that hundreds of people would be killed and injured and thousands of cars burned at minimal costs to the company. Unfortunately for the company and its customers, Ford underestimated the prevalence of the crashes and the size of the civil judgments against it.

In this case, the company simply reasoned that fixing a known product defect would cost more than letting people die in fiery crashes. David Simon explains: "Although the company calculated that it would cost only $11 to make each car safe, it decided that this was too costly. Ford reasoned that 180 burn deaths, 180 serious burn injuries, and 2,100 burned vehicles would costs $49.5 million (each death was calculated at $200,000)." The $200,000 figure was created by the National Highway Traffic Safety Administration (NHTSA) "under pressure from the auto industry" (Mother Jones, 1977). But doing a recall of all Pintos and making each $11 repair would amount to $137 million. Thus, to save money, Ford chose not to fix the cars and instead to market them and sell them to would-be victims. Ford literally calculated that it would be cheaper to let people burn and die in their car than to fix the car and save lives. This is reckless and thus makes Ford culpable for the injuries and deaths caused by the defect.

In this case, Ford engineer Dennis Gioia (1992) explained his failures to recognize the defect in the Pinto and the company to recall the car. His main argument is that the corporate scripts that guided thinking and activity about models such as the Pinto precluded consideration of morality and ethics because they simply did not include them.

Ford had a more recent run-in with allegations of defective products, when Firestone tires on its Ford Explorer models were rupturing during driving and causing drivers to flip and crash their cars, often being seriously injured or killed. When evidence began to mount that there was a problem, Ford was slow to recall its product in the United States even though it had already recalled products in more than a dozen countries a year earlier. Further, Ford did not alert the **National Highway Transportation Safety Administration (NHTSA)**, as required by federal law, when employees in other countries found defects in Firestone tires on their cars (19 months prior to the US recall) (Rosoff et al., 2002: 99).

Although the CEOs of Ford and Firestone blamed each other for the problems, evidence suggests it was the unique combination of Firestone tires on Ford Explorers that was the problem. The tires were subject to likely rupture (and so many customers were told to drive with underinflated tires), but the Ford Explorer had a high center of gravity and thus was subject to likely rollovers after tire rupture. Ford denied responsibility but subsequently redesigned the Ford Explorer for "a smoother ride." Ford widened the wheel base and lowered the car (both having the effect of lowering the center of gravity), which reduced the risk of rollover accidents.

What Happened to Ford and Firestone?

Amazingly, this is not the first time there has been a serious problem with Firestone tires. In the 1970s a problem of tread separation was noted in Firestone tires. After the problem was discovered by Firestone and NHTSA, the company continued to make, advertise, and sell the product. Under intense pressure to do something about the tire, Firestone decided to sell off the tires at clearance prices! Even though the tires causes thousands of accidents, hundreds of injuries and 34 known deaths, the company was fined a mere $50,000! (Simon, 2006: 135).

Documents internal to these companies show that they were aware of the problems and kept them secret, and that it took years for the problems to finally come to light. This is typical in defective products cases, including other automobiles such as General Motors (GM) approved conversion vans that become deadly when steel roofs are removed; defective seat belts and seat belt buckles in some GM and Ford cars; faulty back-door latches in Chrysler minivans that open when struck from the rear or side and cause passengers to be thrown out on to the street; and GM sidebag and sidesaddle gas tanks located on the side of trucks outside of the protective frame that easily rupture when struck from the side. This latter product has caused more fatalities than any other defective vehicle (Robinson, 2006).

In 1992, NHTSA asked GM to voluntarily recall pickup trucks with such gas tanks. GM refused and the Department of Transportation Secretary found in 1994 that GM knew about the defect since the 1970s. GM entered into a deal with the Department of Justice to avoid a recall and has paid hundreds of millions of dollars in settlements to victims instead. Thousands of these vehicles are still on the road (Robinson, 2006).

With the exception of Ford, who was acquitted at trial in the Pinto case, the makers of each of the above products were ordered by courts to pay millions of dollars to compensate victims. Not one corporate executive went to jail or prison. And each company continues to sell its cars, although redesigned as noted earlier. Such is life under the conservative political ideology when it comes to crime and criminal justice.

Unhealthy Foods and Dangerous Drugs

Injuries and deaths caused by defective products do not include those attributable to poor health care, pollution, and food additives (Reiman, 2006). Nor do they include deaths caused by the chemical additives in food or adulterated food products (Simon, 2006). Nor do they include deaths and illnesses attributed to consumption of too much fast food, high-fat foods, sugary foods, high-salt foods, and so forth, each of which is heavily marketed to consumers, especially children (Friedrichs, 2006). Studies show that nearly all (90–100%) of advertisements for food on television during shows intended for kids (e.g., Saturday morning cartoons) promote sugar-coated cereals, candies, and other unhealthy snacks, and literally none advertise fruits and vegetables and other healthy foods (Simon, 2006).

David Simon (2006: 142) indicates that advertising aimed at kids is

> effective because the advertisers have done their research. Social science techniques have been used by motivation researchers in laboratory situations to determine how children of various ages react to different visual and auditory stimuli. Children are watched through two-way mirrors, their behavior is photographed, and their autonomic responses (for example, eye pupil dilation) are recorded to see what sustains their interest, their subconscious involvement, and the degree of pleasure that they experience. Thus, advertisers have found that if one can associate fun, power, or a fascinating animated character with a product, children will want that product.

McDonald's "Happy Meal" is a great example.

Some would likely claim that many of the foods Americans consume can be considered defective, in that they are extremely dangerous due to high fat and saturated fat content, high levels of cholesterol, high calories, and deficiencies in important vitamins and minerals. Eric Schlosser (2002) documents the harmful nature of most types of fast food, with a focus on McDonald's. Further, he shows how the McDonald's corporation has received numerous perks and incentives from Congress in order to succeed within, and ultimately come to dominate the fast food industry; the numerous additives (including chemicals) used to flavor popular foods; how likely it is that consumers are consuming fecal matter in their hamburgers; as well as the highly dangerous work in the nation's meat packing industry.

Greg Critser (2004) shows how more than 60% of Americans became overweight and more than 20% became obese, as well as the various illnesses and costs this imposes on society. More importantly, he discovers that much of the blame lies with corporations, particularly producers and marketers of unhealthy products and product sweeteners such as high fructose corn syrup.

Even school lunches are unhealthy. Marion Nestle (2007) puts much of the blame on the food industry. Its lobbying activities, public relations, advertising (including to children in schools), soft-drink vending in schools, and promotion of heavy portions of high-fat foods produces all kinds of bad outcomes for children. She also points out that food companies promote overeating, even knowing the risk this poses. Michelle Simon (2006) demonstrates that the motivation for the nation's major food companies is greed—fast profit without regard for the health consequences of their actions. Table 5.2 illustrates some outcomes of the American diet.

Pharmaceutical corporations also have promoted their own drugs even after determining that the drugs were dangerous. David Friedrichs (2006: 77) suggests that, at times, the "corporations put the pursuit of profits ahead of scrupulous concern for the health and safety of the users of their products." Today, one can see dozens of pharmaceutical ads every day on television and in magazines that promote the use of drugs

Table 5.2. Outcomes of the American Diet

Low energy/poor cognitive performance
Weight gain/obesity
Arthritis
High cholesterol
Heart disease/heart attack
Hypertension/high blood pressure
Kidney disease/renal failure
Cancer
Type II Diabetes

for a wide variety of ailments. The companies encourage consumers to talk to their doctors about the drugs (rather than having the doctors suggest drugs and other forms of treatment based on the nature of conditions actually suffered by their patients). Sometimes the drugs' side effects sound worse (and may be worse) than the conditions they are meant to treat. At other times, the drugs are promoted for use by children even though they have not been tested on children (e.g., drugs to treat "mental illnesses" in kids).

Out-of-Class Activity
Visit the website of Drug War Facts at: http://www.drugwarfacts.org/cms/Causes_ of_Death#sthash.aKxwJBeI.dpbs.
Read their data on deaths caused by illicit drugs. Which types of drugs are the most dangerous? Why? And do we have a war on these types of drugs? Why or why not?

Testing results are not reported to the public, nor are they required to even be reported to the Food and Drug Administration (FDA). And the pharmaceutical industry often conducts its own tests and/or pays doctors and medical researchers to conduct the tests for them, raising the obvious potential for conflicts of interest (Angell, 2005; Brody, 2007; Crista, 2007; Law, 2006; Moynihan & Cassels, 2006; Weber, 2006).

Incredibly, a 2013 study found that more than half of all recalls of pharmaceuticals between 2004 and 2012 were for different forms of "dietary supplements." This amounts to more than 450 "Class I" recalls of supplements used for dietary reasons, including supplements marketed to consumers for purposes of weight loss, bodybuilding, and sexual enhancement. Unlike, say, crime, such products are subjected to very little government regulation. In the case of dietary supplements, the Food and Drug Administration (FDA) does not screen them prior to their public distribution. Thus, the products often make claims but include the statement, "This statement has not been evaluated by the FDA. This product is not intended to diagnose, treat, cure, or prevent any disease." Products that do not work are not recalled; products are only recalled when they are found to be dangerous.

According to the website of the FDA:

> [T]he manufacturer is responsible for ensuring that its dietary supplement products are safe before they are marketed. Unlike drug products that must be proven safe and effective for their intended use before marketing, there are no provisions in the law for FDA to "approve" dietary supplements for safety or effectiveness before they reach the consumer. Under [the law], once the product is marketed, FDA has the responsibility for showing that a dietary supplement is "unsafe," before it can take action to restrict the product's use or removal from the marketplace. However, manufacturers and distributors of dietary supplements must record, investigate and forward to FDA any reports they receive of serious adverse events associated with the use of their products that are reported to them directly. FDA is able to evaluate these reports and any other adverse event information reported directly to us by healthcare providers or consumers to identify early signals that a product may present safety risks to consumers.

So, the FDA has the burden of proof to demonstrate danger (like the criminal justice system has the burden to prove guilt in a criminal trial), but in the case of unsafe drugs and other products, the FDA relies on the manufacturers of products to assure their safety (unlike in the case of the crimes when we don't count on criminals to *not* commit crimes). This is one serious contradiction of criminal justice under the conservative political ideology.

Hazardous Toys

A recent example of defective products involved the most vulnerable of all consumers — children. Literally millions of toys have been recalled recently by major corporations such as Mattel, Fisher-Price, and Toys "R" Us, among others, due to excessive lead levels, especially in toys produced in China.

David Barboza (2007) asks: "Why is lead paint — or lead, for that matter — turning up in so many recalls involving Chinese-made goods? The simplest answer, experts and toy companies in China say, is price. Paint with higher levels of lead often sells for a third of the cost of paint with low levels. So Chinese factory owners, trying to eke out profits in an intensely competitive and poorly regulated market, sometimes cut corners and use the cheaper leaded paint." That is, the company values profit over human safety and life.

As a result of the vast recalls, studies have been undertaken to examine toys for hazardous materials, including but not limited to lead. One study found high lead levels common in hundreds of toys, and the vast majority of toys have not been recalled. Further, there are dangerous levels of other kinds of chemicals in children's toys besides lead. Healthytoys.org has a list of toys by type with results from product tests.

The organization tested more than 1,200 children's products as well as more than 3,000 product components. They found that "[l]ead in products is widespread." Specifically, lead was detected in 35% of tested products, including 38% of the jewelry samples. Whereas the maximum recommended exposure to lead is 40 parts per million (ppm), the tests showed that 17% of products tested were at levels above 600 ppm.

Further, some of the most highly advertised and popular toys were found to be unsafe (Healthytoys, 2008).

Additionally, the tests revealed other dangerous chemicals in children's toys. Dangerous chemicals found in high levels included cadmium, arsenic, and mercury. Further, many of the toys were even made from dangerous materials such as polyvinyl chloride (PVC) plastic. The organization says: "PVC is the worst plastic from an environmental health perspective because it creates major hazards in its manufacture, product life and disposal and contains additives that are dangerous to human health. PVC plastic without additives is a very brittle plastic. In order to make it flexible and to give it other properties, additional chemicals must be added. Phthalates are very commonly added to PVC to make it soft and flexible; however, they can leach out of the plastic. Phthalates have been implicated in some health problems in laboratory tests. Lead, cadmium and other heavy metals are also commonly added to PVC products" (Healthytoys, 2008).

What Happens to Companies That Manufacture These Products?

Manufacturing defective products is not a crime, and companies that do it are not subjected to criminal punishment. This is a form of bias in favor of elites—predominantly white, older, rich men (WORMs)—the very people who make the law and own the media. Even though defective products cause more damage than literally all street crime combined, police, courts, and corrections are directed to focus their resources on the latter. As noted earlier, politicians who hold the conservative political ideology aim to protect big business, even as they vigorously pursue less damaging street crimes.

Incredibly, even as we are aware of the dangers posed by products such as high fat foods, sugary foods, and prescription drugs, the companies that manufacture these products are still in business promoting their products to consumers. They use ads that make the products appear more healthy than they are, better for you than they actually are, or that simply ignore the widespread damage that they cause.

Tobacco

Earlier, it was noted that tobacco is excluded from data on defective products, even though products made with tobacco are clearly defective—in that they can and *will* injure and kill you when used. According to the Centers for Disease and Prevention (CDC), smoking tobacco leads to approximately 443,000 deaths every year in the US, including 49,000 second-hand smoke deaths, through cancer, heart disease, stroke, and lung diseases. On average, smokers die between 13 and 14 years earlier than nonsmokers. Further, for every person who dies from smoking, another 20 will suffer some serious illness. Further, the costs of smoking to society are at least $193 billion annually including $97 billion in lost productivity and $96 billion in health care expenditures, and the cost of secondhand smoke is more than $10 billion every year including health care expenditures, morbidity, and mortality (CDC, 2013).

Given these numbers, this means tobacco use kills more people than murder and causes more financial loss than all street crimes combined! Whereas murder by definition is intentional, manufacturing and promoting the use of tobacco for the specific purpose of killing people is not intentional. Yet, lawsuits against the tobacco industry and the release of internal documents have shown that the tobacco industry's recklessness and negligence have produced hundreds of thousands of deaths in the United States each year. According to Matthew Robinson & Daniel Murphy (2009: 107), major tobacco corporations

> purposely misled the public and Congress for more than 40 years with regard to the dangers of smoking cigarettes; that they intentionally marketed to children and adolescents through cartoon characters such as "Joe Camel" as well as through product advertisements in magazines, movies, and popular hang-outs; that they increased the addictiveness of their products through adding nicotine and chemicals that heightened the effects of nicotine; that they attacked and attempted to discredit anti-smoking advocates and whistle-blowers; that they lied under oath to Congress when asked about the addictiveness of their products; that they financially coerced companies making smoking-cessation products; and even intentionally funded and produced faulty science through their own Tobacco Institute to cloud the significant issues.

Yet manufacturing tobacco and tobacco use are legal, in spite of the harms they cause. There are numerous reasons why tobacco is legal; among them is the amount of money they spend each year lobbying Congress as well as advertising their products. With regard to the former cost, the Center for Responsive Politics (2013) reports that tobacco companies spent $16.8 million on lobbying at the federal level in 2012. According to the Center: "The contributions to federal candidates and political committees from the tobacco industry, which includes makers of cigarettes, cigars and smokeless tobacco, as well as their trade groups, have drastically decreased since 2002." Specifically, the tobacco industry spent more than $65 million in 1998, employing 242 lobbyists, but by 2009, total lobbying expenditures declined to just about $25 million and the industry employed only 175 lobbyists (LaRussa, 2010).

The reason for the decline? According to Cassandra LaRussa (2010): "The tobacco industry, once a lobbying juggernaut, has watched its political influence wane as its cancer-causing products became increasingly toxic—politically speaking." With regard to the latter costs, the CDC (2013) reports that tobacco companies spent more than $8 billion advertising their products in 2010, or $22 million every single day.

Consider how tobacco companies have used their power in the past to defeat proposals in Congress aimed at even reducing smoking. According to the Center for Responsive Politics, major tobacco companies gave $57.6 million in political contributions to national parties between 1990 and 2006, including $23.2 million in PAC money and $29 million in **soft money** (money paid to political parties rather than individual candidates). During this time, about 75% of tobacco money went to Republicans.

That is significant because, in June 1998, Senate Republicans defeated legislation that would have raised over $500 billion over 25 years through a $1.10 tax increase on a pack of cigarettes (Common Cause, 1999; Salant, 1999). The bill was aimed at reducing smoking among children, which has been shown to save lives. According to Common Cause, on June 17, 1998, Senators who voted against the bill "received on average more than four times the tobacco industry ... PAC contributions during the three most recent election cycles as those voting to move the bill forward."

Common Cause reports that, between January 1993 through March 1998, the 43 Senators who voted against the bill received an average of $20,761 from tobacco PACs, versus $4,970 received on average by the 57 Senators voting for the bill. Given that more than 80% of tobacco money went to Republicans, it is not surprising that 40 of the 42 Senators voting against the bill were Republicans.

Is this bribery? No. Tobacco lobbyists are not buying votes, which is illegal. Tobacco companies and federal legislators alike insist that the money does not buy votes; instead it buys them access. That is, large companies—like big tobacco—can afford greater access to lawmakers that normal, everyday citizens and the groups that represent them. In the case of big tobacco, the result is that the most addictive drug on the planet continues to be abused by more than 20% of the American population.

Most significant is that both sides of the aisle regularly accept money from the same lobbying groups. This is one way to assure that the drug remains legal. Meanwhile, the public (about 80% of whom are not smokers) suffers tremendous harms as a result of tobacco use. Given the harmfulness of this drug, its legal status does not make sense considering that some far less deadly drugs are illegal. Politicians routinely justify the illicit nature of many drugs on the grounds that they are dangerous or deadly. Yet, according to the federal government, deaths from all illicit drugs combined (including abuse of prescription drugs) are about 38,000, versus more than 440,000 for tobacco. That's right, according to our own government, tobacco kills about 12 times more people than all illicit drugs, including prescription drugs! Historically, it has been the leading cause of preventable death and illness in the United States every year!

Tobacco executives have avoided criminal convictions for their negligent and reckless behaviors in part because of the tobacco lobby's historical stranglehold on Congress. Incredibly, tobacco executives even said, under oath, that they did not believe tobacco was addictive. At the same time, people continue to smoke and die because of big tobacco's seemingly bottomless advertising budget and willingness to target even children to ensure the sale of its products.

The industry and its executives operate with criminal impunity even as more than 3,800 children smoke their first cigarette every day, about 1,000 children become daily smokers, and about 70% of smokers want to quit but cannot due to their physical addiction (CDC, 2013). Rather than facing jail or prison time for producing products that harm so many people, major tobacco companies entered into a financial agreement in the 1990s with the states to pay hundreds of billions of dollars in compensatory damages to states over decades. The money was to be used for various purposes, including preventing youth smoking; in reality, the money has been used by states for various costs completely unrelated to smoking as they struggled with large deficits (Robinson & Murphy, 2009). According to the CDC (2013), states will collect about $26 billion in 2013 from tobacco taxes and legal settlements, but they will spend less than 2% on tobacco control programs.

Tobacco companies subsequently raised the prices of their products and passed the costs on to their customers. Imagine a drug dealer getting you hooked on its product as a child, then getting busted for lying about the product to make it look sexy, cool, and consistent with independence and strength, and then being forced to pay for their behavior but then being allowed to raise their prices in order to cover the costs—that's the tobacco industry! Imagine the same drug dealer being allowed to lobby Congress to make or keep their drugs legal—that's the tobacco industry! Civil juries in some states have found tobacco companies liable for reckless disregard for human life, outrageous conduct, negligence, misrepresentation of the facts, fraud, and even selling a defective product, but no one is being criminally punished for their conduct (Robinson & Murphy, 2009). Perhaps an editorial in the *Journal of the American Medical Association* (JAMA) said it best, when it concluded that "the evidence is unequivocal—the US public has been duped by the tobacco industry."

Out-of-Class Activity:
Do some research into the actions of the tobacco industry. What specific actions did they take that could be defined as crimes? Specifically, what makes them culpable for the harms associated with smoking?

Some scholars thus claim that the criminal law should recognize any act that causes harm to others, as long as the act is done intentionally, negligently, recklessly, or knowingly, as discussed earlier. The problem is that corporations are rarely held criminally responsible for the harms they inflict on Americans. Why not? Because the "most powerful organization in our society is the corporation. Corporations have become more powerful than governments, or religious institutions, or labor unions" (Mokhiber & Weissman, 1999: 96). One way they assure their harmful stay legal is lobbyists, discussed in Chapter 3.

Hazardous Workplaces

Many Americans work in **hazardous workplaces**, meaning their places of work are dangerous—not just inherently dangerous based on the nature of the work, but more so because of the negligence and recklessness of employers. The most common sources of death of workers are illnesses contracted at work. One example is brown lung (**byssinosis**), which is often caused by particles found in cotton dust within textile factories (Rosoff et al., 2002). Other examples include **silicosis, pneumoconiosis** ("black lung disease"), and **asbestosis** (Cullen et al., 2006).

Workers also regularly die at businesses who are even recently cited for safety regulation violations (Rosoff et al., 2002). An example is the twenty-six miners who died in an explosion in Letcher County, Kentucky. The company (Scotia Coal Company) they worked for had been cited 652 times for violations, including 60 for inadequate ventilation (which caused methane to build up in the mine allowing the explosion to occur). A similar case in West Virginia in 2006 led to the deaths of 12 miners, this time due to a lack of oxygen after a collapse. The company these men worked for (Massey Energy) had been cited more than 200 times for safety violations and even had to suspend operations 16 times for not following safety rules (Cullen et al., 2006).

And consider the case of 29 workers who died in 2010 in West Virginia in a mine, also operated by Massey Energy. According to Source Watch (2013), Massey Energy company is the 4th largest provider of coal in the United States and the largest producer of Central Appalachian coal. It is the largest company operating in places like West Virginia where coal mining operations (including mountaintop removal projects) are common.

The company has a long history of legal problems, including lawsuits filed against them for allegedly pumping waste coal slurry into empty mines reportedly known to be cracked and thus defective, thereby contaminating local drinking water (in more than one location and over more than a decade!). The company settled these cases out of court, admitting no guilt and receiving no punishment.

The company has also been sued for allegedly exposing young children to harmful coal dust from a silo built less than 300 feet from an elementary school; yet the company won this suit after plaintiffs were unable to show they were harmed. Another suit alleging that safety officials knowingly exposed miners to levels of coal dust higher than what are permitted by federal regulations is, at the time of this writing, still in the courts.

In addition, the company has settled other lawsuits for knowingly violating the **Clean Water Act** thousands of times over numerous years. These lawsuits alleged that Massey did not properly dispose of waste, thereby polluting waterways and drinking water and that the company violated limits on metal and other pollutant levels at more than a dozen plants, which also threatened clean water.

The breadth and depth of wrongdoing by this company is hard to grasp. Consider a specific example. In 2000, a coal sludge impoundment in Martin County, Kentucky broke into an abandoned underground mine. More than 300 million gallons of waste flowed into the Tug Fork River. The yards of many neighbors were filled with this toxic material, and hundreds of miles of rivers were polluted. In this event, nearly 30,000 residents had to deal with contaminated water and all aquatic life in various waterways was killed.

Most notably, the company has made a history of killing its own employees. According to records from Source Watch (2013), Massey (along with Consol Energy) had the worst fatality record for miners of any US coal company. Both companies allowed 23 of their employees to die at the worksite between 2000 and 2009. During this same time, Massey also had 62,000 workplace safety violations, more than 25,000 of which were deemed "significant and substantial." The company paid nearly $45 million in fines as a result.

Then, in 2010, a major disaster occurred at the Massey Energy's Upper Big Branch mine in West Virginia where 29 of its employees died, making Massey Energy the largest killer of employees of any coal company in the country. There was little surprise among those following the company and knowing its history when the company was found responsible for the conditions that led to the deaths of these employees.

The mine had been cited for at least six violations related to ventilation during the year of the deadly disaster as well as 50 "unwarrantable failure citations"—a serious finding of negligence (e.g., one citation was for failing to properly mark escape routes for miners in case of an accident). The mine had a total of 458 total safety violations in the year prior to the disaster and there had been an additional three fatalities at the mine in 12 years prior to this one.

According to Jeffrey Reiman & Paul Leighton (2013: 67), Massey was found to have systematically, intentionally, and aggressively "avoided compliance with safety and health standards, and to thwart detection of that non-compliance by federal and state regulators." This makes their actions negligent and reckless. For example, the Governor's Independent

Investigation Panel (2011)—who carefully reviewed the disaster in order to determine what caused it and who is responsible—found that the company engaged in negligent, reckless, and knowing behaviors that make it culpable for the deaths of the workers. Specifically, the company knowingly maintained and operated defective machinery which caused the fire, allowed a water-spray system meant to suppress coal dust to malfunction, failed to properly ventilate the mine or clean out excessive coal dust, and failed to take corrective action when federal regulators identified potentially dangerous conditions. The company also knowingly interfered with workers who actually tried to make the mine safer and maintained "a culture in which wrongdoing became acceptable." Beyond this, the company—which had a policy on paper that forbade security guards from giving advance notice to workers of a federal inspection, consistently violated the policy in order to try to trick federal regulators working with the Mine Safety and Health Administration (MSHA), the agency responsible for mine safety.

According to Democracy Now (2011), the independent probe of the West Virginia mining disaster concluded "that mining giant, Massey Energy, was responsible for the April 2010 explosion that killed 29 underground coal mining workers." The report matches "preliminary findings by federal investigators earlier this year that Massey repeatedly violated federal rules on ventilation and minimizing coal dust to reduce the risk of explosion, and rejects Massey's claim that a burst of gas from a hole in the mine floor was at fault."

The report identifies system failures that specifically caused the explosion which killed the workers, noted specific regulatory failures that assured the disaster would occur, and also identified a culture at the Massey company which normalized deviance. The report even went so far as to state that the company simply put profit before people, using its power in the region to recklessly run to failure, thereby assuring the deaths of its own workers: "The story of Upper Big Branch is a cautionary tale of hubris. A company that was a towering presence in the Appalachian coalfields operated its mines in a profoundly reckless manner, and 29 coal miners paid with their lives for the corporate risk-taking." As noted in the report: "In addition to inattention to basic safety standards, Massey exhibited a corporate mentality that placed the drive to produce above worker safety."

With the report, investigators note that the company had previously been found to operate with "reckless disregard" for safety rules in connection with the deaths of workers in an earlier "accident." And, although the CEO of the company instituted a plan called "S-1" (referring to safety is the number one priority of the company) it "in fact appeared to be just a slogan" since the company continued to operate in an unsafe way even when it was known to the CEO.

As if dying in a fire or explosion or due to a lack of oxygen resulting from a collapse is not bad enough, the report also stated that most of the miners killed had coal workers' pneumoconiosis, also known as "black lung disease." Specifically, 17 of the 24 victims (71%) who had enough lung tissue remaining for a determination (or 71 percent) had CWP. The national prevalence rate for CWP among active underground miners in the US is 3% and in West Virginia is about 8%.

Another form of recklessness of the corporation was fabrication of safety reports, aimed at misleading inspectors. The company even maintained duplicate books on daily mine operations, one containing the honest account on hazards and another indicating no serious safety issues. This proves that managers at the mine knew of the hazards but ignored them, making them culpable for negligent and reckless criminality.

Importantly, the independent report also discusses Massey's incredible influence on politics in the state and region, which Massey uses "to attempt to control West Virginia's political system" as well as its regulatory bodies. Massey, through its lobbying activities in the state, is able to resist meaningful regulations. Further, it turns out that regulatory agencies such as the MSHA, are largely staffed and thus controlled by industry insiders. This is a great example of how the law is used to serve powerful interests, as predicted by the *conflict school of the* law introduced in Chapter 2. Imagine if we policed street criminals this way, allowing them to lobby lawmakers as well as regulate their own behaviors!

Another report, this time by the **Mine Safety and Health Administration (MSHA)**, also found that the deaths at the Upper Big Branch mine were "entirely preventable" because they were caused by serious and correctable safety violations that occurred because of "a pervasive culture that valued production over safety" (US Department of Labor, 2012).

One dozen specific violations by Massey contributed to the explosion; these included "the company's 'unwarrantable failure' to follow federal rules governing mine ventilation, roof control, and the cleanup of highly explosive coal dust" as well as "a 'reckless disregard' for requirements to perform periodic safety examinations and fix the problems identified, a systematic effort to warn underground workers of impending inspections and intimidate miners so they wouldn't complain about hazardous conditions."

This investigation found "multiple examples of systematic, intentional, and aggressive efforts by PCC/Massey to avoid compliance with safety and health standards, and to thwart detection of that non-compliance by federal and state regulators." Specific findings from the investigation are found in the appendix to Chapter 5.

What Happened to Massey?

On October 26, 2011, Hughie Elbert Stover, PCC's former head of security for UBB, was found guilty in the United States District Court for the Southern District of West Virginia of a felony count of making false, fictitious and fraudulent statements to MSHA regarding company policy on advance notice. In an interview with the MSHA accident investigation team, Stover testified that Massey had a policy prohibiting security guards from providing advance notice of MSHA inspections; however, the evidence indicated that he had personally directed guards to provide advance notice.

Massey agreed to pay $10.8 million in civil penalties as part a larger, $209.5 million settlement. The company was subsequently purchased by another company. Yet, Massey's CEO denied the findings of the report, saying: "We don't feel like that we contributed in any way to the accident. We do not believe that coal dust was a meaningful factor." Instead, he blamed the explosion on a buildup of methane gas.

In spite of this claim, Massey's record at the mine, as well as others, speaks for itself. The company has had hundreds of safety violations at numerous mines, and the US Department of Labor even filed a preliminary injunction in US District Court for persistent dangerous conditions a mine in Pike County, Kentucky. That mine had almost 2,000 safety violations as well as another deadly mine explosion in 2010.

Incredibly, this is not the first time the company witnessed mining disasters that led to the deaths of employees. In 2006, a fire at another mine in West Virginia killed two employees. Widows of the miners filed suit alleging Massey CEO Don Blankenship of "personally engendering a corporate attitude of indifference and hostility towards safety measures which stood in the way of profit." This lawsuit was settled but the outcome has not been reported. A Massey subsidiary—Aracoma Coal Company—pleaded guilty to 10 criminal charges in this case and was fined $2.5 million as well as an additional $1.7 million for federal safety violations.

And even after the 2010 Big Branch mine disaster, another coal mine was evacuated by federal regulators after they found two dozen serious safety violations that could have produced another fire or explosion. This included excessive coal dust, weak water sprayers, improper ventilation, and illegal use of mining machines (the same conditions that led to the deaths at Upper Big Branch). Assistant Secretary of Labor Joe Main stated: "The conduct and behavior exhibited when we caught the mine operator by surprise is nothing short of outrageous. The conditions observed at Randolph Mine place miners at serious risk to the threat of fire, explosion and black lung." And he suggested that mining companies "still aren't getting it ... despite the tragedy at Upper Big Branch ..."

Some executives in the company have been convicted of crimes related to the Upper Big Branch mine. One—head of security—was sentenced to three years in a federal prison and another—a mine foreman—received a ten-month sentence, both for crimes related to destroying documents related to safety inspections. The CEO and no other senior executives have been charged criminally (Pavlo, 2012). This, in spite of the finding of the United Mine Workers Association that this was a case of "industrial homicide" (Berkes, 2011). The President of a subsidiary coal company pleaded guilty to conspiracy and implicated the CEO of Massey; he faces up to six years in prison. Another employee of that company was sentenced to 21 months in prison (Associated Press, 2013).

Meanwhile, the budget for mining inspections has been increased and additional regulations have been passed. Yet, in spite of regulators recently discovering hundreds of violations at West Virginia mines, no citations have been issued and no one has been held accountable. This includes for serious violations related to the build-up of too much coal dust, which can produce massive explosions like the one that killed 29 workers in Upper Big Branch (Berkes, 2013). Consider this further evidence of the double standard of justice in the US, the result of innocent bias produced by the criminal law and media coverage of crime.

British Petroleum

Another example is the explosion on the Deepwater Horizon oil well in the Gulf of Mexico in April 2010, which resulted in the deaths of 11 drilling employees and the largest oil spill in US history, BP underestimated risks of leaks in its drilling equipment; failed to follow required safety regulations and lobbied against additional regulations; was allowed to self-regulate through the Minerals Management Services (MMS) (now known as the **Bureau of Ocean Energy Management, Regulation and Enforcement**), an indicator of poor social controls; stopped all internal inspections before the leak in the Gulf occurred; used non-trained, non-certified inspectors; manipulated inspection reports to hide its culpability; lied to the Environmental Protection Agency (EPA);

Figure 5.5. BP disaster protestors

Albert H. Teich / Shutterstock.com

disabled warning sensors; skipped routine maintenance and used outdated equipment; deemphasized safety and demoted safety officers; ignored clear warnings of impending disaster; and even followed the approach of "run to failure" since failure was perceived as less costly than abiding by safety regulations (Lustgarten, 2012). A protest of the company is depicted in Figure 5.5.

The final report of the National Commission on the BP Deepwater Horizon Oil Spill and Offshore Drilling found that the disaster "well could have been prevented." Further, the Commission identified "a series of identifiable mistakes made by BP, Halliburton [who was contracted to cement the well], and Transocean [who ran the drilling operation]" that caused the disaster, and claim they "reveal such systematic failures in risk management that they place in doubt the safety culture of the entire industry." Got that? The culture of the entire drilling industry does not adequately stress safety.

Because of this, as well as the serious problems with oversight and regulation, the Commission recommends that: "Fundamental reform will be needed in both the structure of those in charge of regulatory oversight and their internal decisionmaking process to ensure their political autonomy, technical expertise, and their full consideration of environmental protection concerns." Further, "the oil and gas industry will need to take its own, unilateral steps to increase dramatically safety throughout the industry, including self-policing mechanisms that supplement governmental enforcement" (National Commission, 2011: vii). In essence, a review of the disaster led to the conclusion that poor regulation is a significant cause of the crime.

The National Commission (2011: 115) also assigned blame, accepted by BP itself, saying the explosion and subsequent loss of life as well as the disastrous oil spill "was the product of several individual missteps and oversights by BP, Halliburton, and Transocean, which government regulators lacked the authority, the necessary resources, and the technical expertise to prevent." That is, regulations alone could not have stopped the disaster. Specifically, "(1) each of the mistakes made on the rig and onshore by industry and government increased the risk of a well blowout; (2) the cumulative risk that resulted from these decisions and actions was both unreasonably large and avoidable; and (3) the risk of a catastrophic blowout was ultimately realized on April 20 and several of the mistakes were contributing causes of the blowout."

Decisions made by BP, Halliburton, and Transocean had "less risky alternatives" and yet those less risky decisions were not made. Why were risky decisions—such as ignoring clear signs of a potential major disaster—made? The National Commission (2011) speculates that cutting corners was perceived to save time and thus money. In other words, greed explains the failures. And greed that costs the lives of innocent people and leads to billions of dollars in losses only makes sense in the context of the deregulation and promotion of big business by politicians of bother political parties who have embraced the conservative political ideology.

The Commission notes:

> Corporations understandably encourage cost-saving and efficiency. But given the dangers of deepwater drilling, companies involved must have in place strict policies requiring rigorous analysis and proof that less-costly alternatives are in fact equally safe. If BP had any such policies in place, it does not appear that its Macondo team adhered to them. Unless companies create and enforce such policies, there is simply too great a risk that *financial pressures* will systematically bias decisionmaking in favor of time- and cost-savings (p. 126, emphasis added).

This is as close to a statement we can expect out of a government-funded organization of the role that unfettered capitalism plays in corporate malfeasance that we can likely expect.

Interestingly, these companies have long histories of these kinds of actions. Consider BP, who, according to Jeff Bone (2012: 17) had a "safety, ethics and environmental record [that] was abysmal" even prior to the Deepwater Horizon disaster. This includes:

- A 2005 explosion at a BP Texas City Refinery operation that killed 15 workers and injured 170 more (BP was fined for this by the Occupational Health and Safety Board, and the fine was ultimately increased after BP failed to make necessary safety improvements).
- A 2006 oil spill on Alaska's North Slope that occurred to due faulty pipelines (BP paid more fines because of this spill).
- A 2008 leak of oil on the Oil Platform Atlantis in the Gulf of Mexico.

Internal documents from BP show the company was aware of the problems that led to these disasters, making it hard to call them "accidents" (Bone, 2012).

So while some define the BP corporate culture as corrupt, the truth is BP operates much like numerous large corporations around the world today, doing whatever it takes—legal and illegal—to maximize wealth for its executives and shareholders. When caught in even massive and deadly wrongful behaviors, they simply pay huge fines and then just treat the fines as the costs of doing business, passing them on to consumers as a form of externalized cost.

In-Class Activity:
Is the company BP a criminal? Are they murderers? Have a debate where someone on one side makes one argument while another person makes the case for the other side. Allow others to participate and offer evidence or justifications for their viewpoints.

What Happened to British Petroleum?

In this case, BP has pleaded guilty to 14 criminal counts, including manslaughter, and will pay a $4.5 billion fine over five years, including $1.256 billion in criminal fines as part of its settlement with the US Justice Department (Rampton & Gardner, 2012). Although this is the "largest criminal payment in U.S. history" and BP still faces additional penalties that stem from violations of civil laws such as the Clean Water Act, the company is still financially viable and drilling around the world, and is still the leading supplier of fuel to the US military (Muffson, 2012).

However, BP has been banned from new federal contracts with the US government due to its "lack of business integrity." This means BP cannot receive any further federal contracts until "they demonstrate they can meet federal business standards" (Rampton & Gardner, 2012). Many believe this is just an effort to have leverage to force BP to pay future penalties as part of the civil case.

Amazingly (because it is so rare in such cases), some company executives are also facing criminal charges, including two rig operators who face manslaughter charges. Robert Kaluza and Donald Vidrine, who were the top two ranking BP supervisors on the Deepwater Horizon drilling rig, have been indicted on 23 criminal counts, including manslaughter, for negligence related to ignoring warning signs of the potential disaster. Further, another employee — David Rainey, a former BP vice president — was indicted for "hiding information from Congress and lying to law enforcement officials by understating the rate at which oil was gushing into the Gulf of Mexico" (Rampton & Gardner, 2012).

Still, no "higher ups" in the company are imperiled. That is, those that set the standards of malfeasance and dishonesty — as well as expect it from their employees and reward it — are not facing criminal charges and will not be incarcerated for the deaths of eleven employees who were killed due to the gross negligence and recklessness identified by investigators. Further, no government agents are implicated, in spite of their apparent involvement in a cover-up to keep the full extent of the damage secret (Bradshaw, 2012). This is just more evidence of the double standard of justice that is part of the criminal justice system today and is a good example of innocent bias — bias in the law that will be found in all branches of criminal justice (e.g., in arrests, convictions, and correctional punishment).

How Corporate Violence Is Different

Of course, corporate violence is different in some key ways than violence on the streets of America. Matthew Robinson & Daniel Murphy (2009) note that violent street crime is direct and immediate, corporate violence is indirect and often delayed. That is, the latter does not involve one person directly hurting another but instead "results from policies and actions, undertaken on behalf of the corporation, that result in the exposure of people to harmful conditions, products, or substances" (Friedrichs, 1995: 70). Whereas violent street crime results in an immediate harm, harms from corporate violence occur days, weeks, months, and even years after the corporate decisions are made which put people at risk.

Second, whereas violent street crime is typically committed by one person acting alone or in conjunction with a small group of closely-knit people, corporate violence involves "a large number of individuals acting collectively" (Friedrichs, 1995: 70). For example, murder involves the "killing of *one human being by another.*" Other forms of killing can be perpetrated by numerous individuals (e.g., boards of directors of corporations) on large numbers of other individuals.

Third, whereas street violence *can be* motivated by financial gain, corporate violence is, "virtually by definition ... motivated by the desire to maximize corporate profit (or survival) and minimize corporate overhead...." (Friedrichs, 1995: 71). Street violence is often impulsive and motivated by intense emotions such as anger and jealousy. Given this, you could thus argue that corporate violence is worse than street violence since the former is normal and planned whereas the latter is generally viewed as abnormal and unplanned. That is, it could be argued that street criminals are "situationally" criminal whereas corporate criminals are "regularly" criminals. Yet, the former are pursued by police, courts, and corrections to the turn of more than $200 billion a year, whereas the latter are generally ignored and allowed to continue to harm us to the tune of about $1 trillion annually.

Finally, whereas street violence typically results from *intentional* acts, corporate violence results from other kinds of culpable behaviors and "is a consequence rather than a specifically intended outcome" (Friedrichs, 1995: 71). For example, tobacco companies obviously do not intend to kill any particular person, nor do fast food companies that make, market, and sell foods high in calories and saturated fat. Similarly, doctors and hospital staff, employers, and manufacturers of defective products typically do not kill people on purpose. That is, people do not die from cigarettes, conditions related to obesity, hospital error, occupational disease and injury, or unsafe products because of the *intentional* acts of corporations. Yet, deaths produced by these acts are still the result of culpable acts (Robinson & Murphy, 2009).

 The primary difference between murder and the other forms of killing in Table 5.3 is that murder is intentional. The Federal Bureau of Investigation (FBI, 2007) defines murder as "the *willful* (nonnegligent) killing of one human being by another." When an act is done willfully or intentionally, it is committed with "a guilty mind" (*mens rea*) and on purpose. An example of a murder is when a man kills his wife with a gun after an argument or for insurance money.

Table 5.3. Murder versus Other Forms of Killings

	Murder	Other forms of killing
Timeframe	Immediate	Delayed
Motivation	Numerous	Financial; greed
Offender	Individual	Group
Culpability	Intentional	Reckless, negligent, knowing

As you've seen, many of the deaths discussed in this chapter result from the negligent, reckless, and knowing behaviors of elites—corporate executives, food companies, doctors, employers, and manufacturers; therefore, they are good examples of culpable killings. Although it is true that acts committed with intent are generally considered more serious than those committed negligently, recklessly, or knowingly, people killed by big tobacco, food companies, as well as reckless and negligent doctors, employers, and product manufacturers are just as dead as those murdered. This is why many view those killed by such behaviors as victims (Karmen, 2006).

Further, American citizens are strongly influenced by the actions of elites (including corporations) through their advertising campaigns for products such as cigarettes, fast food, and other products. Although victims of elite deviance sometimes play a role in their own victimizations (e.g., smokers choose to smoke, people choose to eat too much fast food), they do so under heavy influence from the efforts of the corporations who make a killing (literally) by selling their products. Interestingly, criminologists have shown that many victims of street crime also play a role in their own victimization (Felson, 2002). Yet, when a man kills his girlfriend after years of abuse after the victim chooses to remain in the relationship, society does not excuse the killer's behavior. Similarly, when a person is murdered after leaving the windows in his home unlocked, the police still pursue the murderer. Thus, you might question the logic of ignoring the killer in cases of elite deviance just because he or she is a corporate executive and commits his or her killings indirectly and from afar.

Keep in mind a lesson learned from Chapter 3. The criminal law may inherently biased against the poor because the criminal law is written by the wealthy, lobbied for (and against) by the wealthy, and disproportionately voted for by the wealthy. This means that the label of "crime" is applied to only a small portion of acts that are harmful to Americans and the label of "serious crime" is reserved for those acts that the government perceives to be committed primarily by the poor. The result? Far greater focus in the United States on street crime rather than on elite deviance, even though the latter is far more dangerous. This is a bias in the criminal law that will be enforced by police, courts, and corrections as they carry out the law (i.e., innocent bias).

Why Aren't the Most Serious Harms Legislated as Crimes?

Why does our own government fail to define the acts that are most dangerous to us as the most serious crimes? In this book, it is argued that this occurs because lawmakers are not representative of the US population and thus do not serve their interests but instead serve the interests of those kinds of people who make the law, fund the law, and also own the mainstream media.

Here, Richard Quinney's (2000) theory of the *social reality of crime* is useful. His theory offers several, related propositions, which are paraphrased below:

- Crime is a definition of human conduct created by those political agents authorized to do so in a society.
- Crimes are those behaviors that conflict with those interests in society that are in power, especially those that make the criminal law and set criminal justice policy.
- Those people who are least likely to be involved in legislating behaviors as crimes are most likely to have their behaviors legislated as crimes.
- Those people who are most likely to be involved in legislating behaviors as crimes are least likely to have their behaviors legislated as crimes.
- Conceptions of crime emerge from the powerful and are reinforced by means of mass communication including the media (pp. 15–23).

It is these institutions—the law and the media—that determine first what is illegal (and what is not) and second those behaviors we fear (and those we do not). Recall the lesson from earlier that the media, like lawmakers, tend to be wealthy and white, so these are the powerful people in society.

The negligent and reckless acts that produce harms associated with elite deviance are undeniably disproportionately committed by wealthier Caucasians. This is illustrated in Table 5.4, which compares the typical offender and victim of street crime and elite deviance.

Whereas poor people and people of color are rounded up for street crimes, particularly drug crimes, white-collar and corporate criminals typically walk away unscathed or with a slap on the wrist. Studies show that prosecution of white-collar and corporate criminals represents the "road not taken" (Shapiro, 1995) and that most white-collar

Table 5.4. Elite and Street Offenders

	Street crime	Elite deviance
Gender	Male	Male
Social class	Lower to middle	Middle to upper
Race/Ethnicity	Black/Hispanic*	White

* Police, courts, and correctional statistics show that people of color are disproportionately involved in some acts of street crimes, but self-report studies do not show large differences in offending by race or ethnicity.

criminals are repeat offenders who are nonetheless punished only with administrative sanctions or simple warnings (Weisburd, Chayet, & Waring, 1990). Jeffrey Reiman & Paul Leighton (2013: 121) write that when we are talking about

> the kinds of crimes poor people almost never have the opportunity to commit, such as antitrust violations, industrial safety violations, embezzlement, and serious tax evasion, the criminal justice system shows an increasingly benign and merciful face. The more likely that a crime is the type committed by middle- and upper-class people, the less likely it will be treated as a criminal offense. When it comes to crime in the streets, where the perpetrator is apt to be poor, he or she is even more likely to be arrested and formally charged. When it comes to crime in the suites, where the offender is apt to be affluent, the system is most likely to deal with the crime noncriminally, that is, by civil litigation or informal settlement.

As noted earlier, arrests of white-collar and corporate offenders are made unlikely by deregulation efforts of politicians. In the 1980s, budgets of the Consumer Product Safety Commission (defined earlier), **Occupational Safety and Health Administration**, and **Federal Trade Commission** were slashed, and requirements relating to pharmaceutical and automotive safety were lifted or softened (Kappeler et al., 2000: 135). Most of these changes in policy were attached as "riders" to large bills in Congress. Others were passed in plain sight based on the conservative argument that too much government is bad for the economy. The result of these actions is the kind of crimes discussed in this and the last chapter.

In fact, the history of government regulation has been one of businesses regulating themselves for their own benefit and gain. Many regulators are former corporate executives or go to work for corporations after their regulating days are over (Hagan, 1998). Also recall the close connections between lobbyists and legislators demonstrated in Chapter 3. Thus, there is a double standard of justice in the United States. While we spend more than one hundred billion dollars each year fighting street crimes that produce relatively minor harms, we allow businesses to police themselves, and we give "little effort to enforce the law against [white-collar and corporate] criminals. When we do catch them at their nefarious deeds, we tap them on the wrist, make them say they are sorry, and send them about their criminal business" (Kappeler et al., 2000: 134).

Richard Quinney (2000: 41) concludes that "the content of the law, including the substantive regulations and the procedural rules, represents the interests of the segments of society that have the power to shape public policy." Thus: "Formulation of law allows some segments of society to protect and perpetuate their own interests. By formulating law, some segments are able to control others to their own advantage" (p. 42). As such, his argument is thus consistent with that of Jeffrey Reiman & Paul Leighton (2013), introduced in Chapter 1, who suggested criminal justice serve limited interests by controlling some segments of the population.

Quinney's theory is a good reminder of the role of politics in criminal justice. He explains that

> criminal laws ... are formulated by those segments of society which have the power to shape public policy. The formulation of criminal law is thus an act

of politics: Public policy is established by some for governing the lives and affairs of all inhabitants of a society. Crime, them is a definition of human conduct that is created in the course of the political life of the community (Quinney, 2000: 43).

And clearly, the decisions of politicians are motivated by their own ideology, one that aims to protect the powerful (e.g., corporations) even at the expense of the people.

Victor Kappeler and his colleagues (2000) concur about the law failing to expand definitions of crime to recognized harmful acts of the powerful. They state:

> The government has a vested interest in maintaining the existing social definition of crime and extending this definition to groups and behaviors that are perceived to be a threat to the existing social order.... Similarly, the government has an interest in seeing that the existing criminal justice system's response to crime is not significantly altered in purpose or function.

According to these authors, the government's interests are served by promoting myths about crime and criminal justice. These myths are not only false but dangerous— dangerous because they allow harmful acts to be committed against innocent people by others with virtual impunity, even when done so intentionally or with culpability. And they are promoted by the mass media, which are owned by powerful US corporations. In essence, the definition of crime is a threat to justice in the United States, because people who intentionally, recklessly, negligently, and knowingly kill and injure Americans do so without being held accountable for their actions.

Why Does All This Matter? Myths of Crime

While we all walk around with images of crime and serious crime in our heads— images informed both by the criminal law as well as media coverage of crime which tell us what and who are dangerous and what and who are not—mostly what we see is **myth**.

Myths of crime are created when acts are defined as crimes by the criminal law, and these myths are reinforced as the mass media broadcast stories about crime as well as when police, courts, and corrections enforce the criminal law (Barkan & Bryjak, 2008; Bohm & Walker, 2012; Kappeler & Potter, 2012). That is, every time a street criminal is arrested or punished and the cased makes the news, false conceptions of crime are created and reinforced. Based on the way crime is framed by the criminal law and the media, the following myths are created and reinforced:

• Crime is an act committed by one person against one person

If you re-examine the list of serious crimes from the last chapter, you'll notice that each is generally an act committed by one person against another (e.g., one person kills another person, one person robs another person, one person assaults another person, one person steals from another person, etc.). For this reason, when we think of crime, we tend to think of acts committed by a single person against another.

There are clearly exceptions to this rule in the case of high profile cases that received national media attention (e.g., terrorist attacks such as the bombing of a federal building in Oklahoma City, 9/11, and the Boston Marathon bombing). Yet white-collar and corporate crimes almost always involve more than one offender and always involve a large number of victims, as shown in this chapter. These offenders and victims are rarely recognized in the media and the offenders are rarely identified as criminals by the law or the media. This creates misconceptions in consumers of information about who is dangerous and who is not. We tend to fear and perceive risks from individuals rather than groups of people or corporations.

- Most crime is violent in nature

Although violent crime is the crime that most Americans fear, the fact is that the great bulk of crime is committed against people's property. Since the law tends to treat violent crime more seriously than property crime, and because the media focuses more attention on it, we tend to conflate crime with violence.

In fact, the majority of crime is committed against people's property. When you include acts of white-collar and corporate crime discussed in the last chapter, property crime makes up about 99% of all crime. Lives are ideally more important than money, so our focus on deadly acts is understandable and even commendable. Yet, as shown in this chapter, we do not tend to focus on the acts that do the most physical damage to people but instead on violent street crime.

- Street crime is the most serious crime in America

Since serious crime is literally synonymous with street crime, it makes sense that people tend to think street crime is the most serious crime in America. But if you consider the acts that *actually* do the most harm and are the most frequently occurring and geographically widespread, serious crimes are not street crimes but instead are made up of acts of elite deviance.

Stated simply, it is acts of white-collar and corporate crime that are most common in America, as well as the most harmful. People are unaware of this for they are not constantly bombarded with images of deviant and dangerous elites as they are of common street criminals. For this reason, we perceive greater risk from street crimes than from white-collar and corporate criminals, and we fear them far more than is justified based on the degree of threat they actually pose. Meanwhile, we do not perceive risk from or feel fear of the people most likely to harm us.

Jeffrey Reiman & Paul Leighton (2013: 66) state the reality of crime in America: "The fact is the label 'crime' is not used in America to name all or the worst of the actions that cause misery and suffering to Americans. It is reserved primarily for the dangerous actions of the poor." This is why "[t]he criminal justice system does not protect us from the gravest threats to life, limb, or possessions. Its definitions of crime are not simply a reflection of the objective dangers that threaten us" (p. 105). In fact, the most dangerous acts of the wealthy, many identified in this chapter, are called "accidents" or "tragedies" even though they often result from culpable acts of elites.

Recall the metaphor of a spotlight introduced earlier. The law focuses our attention on the acts of the powerless by defining those acts as crimes (like shining a spotlight of attention on them), and the media covers them so much more broadly and intently (like shining a spotlight of attention on them). Because of these spotlights, people see street crime as the most serious, even while the harms of elite deviance are far worse.

- Poor people are more dangerous than rich people

Street crime is committed by everyone but is disproportionately committed by people without resources. For example, rich people tend not to rob banks (because they own them). Yet this does not mean that poor people are more dangerous than rich people, for it is rich people who disproportionately tend to commit acts of white-collar and corporate crime. Consider the harmful acts committed by banks discussed in the last chapter that led to the economic collapse in the US.

Since white-collar and corporate crime lead to far more damage and harm than street crime, this means the people who commit them (rich people) are actually more dangerous. Sure, a rich person is unlikely to stick a gun in your face and demand your money, or to rob a bank with a weapon, but you are actually more likely to die at the hands of a wealthy person than a poor person. Harms committed by poor people are more visible and thus we are more aware of them, but they are not, in fact, more dangerous. As noted by Jeffrey Reiman & Paul Leighton (2013: 102): "Based on the knowledge we have, there can be no doubt that air pollution, tobacco, and food additives amount to a chemical war that makes the crime wave look like a football scrimmage" (not to mention all the other harms identified in this chapter). Again, it is the spotlight of the law and the media that create this myth.

• People of color are more dangerous than white people

As noted above, street crime is committed by everyone but some forms of it are disproportionately committed by people of color. For example, in Chapter 1, you learned that blacks tend to commit a very large share of murder and robbery. Yet this does not mean that black people are more dangerous than white people, for it is white people who disproportionately tend to commit acts of white-collar and corporate crime.

It is a myth that black people and other people of color are more dangerous than white people. According to Michelle Alexander (2012: 28), whose argument about criminal justice was reviewed in Chapter 1, "current stereotypes of black men as aggressive, unruly predators" can be traced back at least as far back as Reconstruction "when whites feared that an angry mass of black men might rise up and attack them or rape their women," if not slavery (when after all, blacks were viewed as less than human). This notion was heightened during the civil rights movement by conservative politicians, then subsequently reinforced in the 1980s and later by other conservative politicians, as shown in Chapter 2.

The mainstream media today are largely responsible for the maintenance of stereotypes about race and crime. According to Michael Tonry (2011: 7), not only do the news and entertainment media tend to focus on blacks as offenders and whites as victims, but they also reinforce the notion that "blacks with a dark skin tone are more likely to be criminals than blacks with a moderate or light skin tone" and that certain "black facial features—dark skin, wide nose, full lips—are associated with criminality." This is consistent with studies reviewed in Chapter 3.

• Corporate crime is just property crime

There is a common conception that corporate crime only hurts out property. People even use this as a reason *not* to focus on it, even though the great bulk of street crime (which we do focus on and zealously pursue) is committed against property. Yet, as shown in this chapter, more people are physically injured and killed by acts of corporate crime than all street crimes combined; in fact, it's not even close! Given this, it is time to recognize once and for all that elites are dangerous; their crimes injure and kill more people every year than all street crimes combined.

Summary

The law fails to define the acts that pose the greatest threat to Americans as crimes and especially as serious crimes. In this chapter, you saw that Americans are far more likely to suffer violent victimization from corporate crime, including at hazardous workplaces, at the hands of tobacco companies, and because of defective products. Each of these cause more death and injury than all street crimes combined, including murder. Yet, as with the property crimes discussed in the last chapter, relative to street crimes, people are rarely arrested, convicted, and punished for their crimes.

Why does this occur? Just as with the property crimes discussed in Chapter 4, it is not because the acts are committed without culpability. Acts summarized in this chapter are committed intentionally, knowingly, negligently, and recklessly, meaning the people who committed them are morally responsible for their behaviors.

Once again, recall who makes the law and who owns the media. WORMs — white, older, rich men — largely decide what acts are crimes (and which are not) as well as which are serious crimes (and which are not). It is in their interest, as well as the interests of those who donate to their political campaigns and fund their operations, to keep status quo approaches to crime control in place.

The conservative political ideology mandates that we ignore the kinds of acts seen in this chapter; they are just the cost of doing business. The widespread deregulation that enables it will assure these acts will continue into the future. The result of the policies we pursue to fight street crime as well as the ones we don't enact to combat elite deviance amount to a bias in criminal justice called innocent bias.

Thus again, it is politics and ideology that explain the outcome identified in this chapter. Whereas Americans ideally value crime control and due process goals found in the Declaration of Independence and the US Constitution — equality, rights, life, liberty, the pursuit of happiness, justice, domestic tranquility, common defence, general welfare — the real criminal justice system is unequally applied, does not equally protect our rights and liberty, does not assure our happiness, tranquility, common defence, or welfare, and therefore is in some ways unjust or biased.

Key Terms

- **Asbestosis**: Asbestosis is a health condition caused by inhaling asbestos.
- **Bureau of Ocean Energy Management, Regulation and Enforcement**: The Bureau of Ocean Energy Management, Regulation and Enforcement is responsible for the safety and environmental oversight of offshore oil and gas operations, including permitting and inspections.
- **Byssinosis**: Byssinosis, aka brown lung, is a health condition resulting from exposure to cotton dust in poorly vented work spaces.

- **Clean Water Act:** The Clean Water Act became law in 1972 and regulates the discharge of pollutants into US waterways.
- **Consumer Product Safety Commission (CPSC):** The Consumer Product Safety Commission is charged with protecting the public from unreasonable risks of serious injury or death from more than 15,000 types of consumer products.
- **Defective Products:** Defective products are goods sold that contain a serious problem of imperfection of fault which leads them to be dangerous to consumers.
- **Federal Trade Commission:** The Federal Trade Commission is aimed at preventing business practices that are anticompetitive, deceptive, or unfair to consumers.
- **Hazardous Workplaces:** A hazardous workplace is a dangerous workplace that is known to be dangerous yet is not corrected by management.
- **Mine Safety and Health Administration (MSHA):** The Mine Safety and Health Administration (MSHA) was formed in 1978 to enforce compliance with mandatory safety and health standards, to reduce the frequency and severity of accidents, to minimize health hazards, and to promote improved safety and health conditions in mines.
- **Myth:** A myth is a popular belief about something or someone that is unfounded or false, something that people believe to be true but that is not.
- **National Highway Transportation Safety Administration (NHTSA):** The National Highway Transportation Safety Administration is the lead federal agency responsible for assuring safety of roads and motor vehicles.
- **Occupational Safety and Health Administration:** The Occupational Safety and Health Administration attempts to assure the healthy environments of workplaces across the nation.
- **Pneumoconiosis:** Pneumoconiosis is a health condition caused by exposure to coal dust.
- **Silicosis:** Silicosis is a health condition caused by exposure to silica dust as found in blasting operations and glass factories.
- **Soft Money:** Soft money is a donation to a political party rather than a particular candidate.

Discussion Questions

1) Identify and discuss some forms of elite violence.
2) How much damage does elite violence cause?
3) How many people die from workplace injuries and hazards?
4) What are defective products? How many people die from them?
5) What is the Consumer Product Safety Commission?
6) What caused the Exxon Valdez oil spill?
7) Outline alleged misconduct by Ford and Firestone in the Pinto and tire cases.
8) What happened to Ford and Firestone executives in these cases?
9) What is the National Highway Transportation Safety Administration?
10) Identify and discuss damages caused by unhealthy foods and dangerous drugs.
11) What happened to producers of defective products including hazardous toys?
12) What damages are caused by tobacco smoking?
13) How are tobacco companies culpable for harms suffered by smokers?

14) What is soft money and what role has it played in keeping tobacco legal?
15) What is a hazardous workplace? What are byssinosis, silicosis, pneumoconiosis, and asbestosis?
16) What is the Clean Water Act?
17) What is the Mine Safety and Health Administration?
18) What caused the mining disaster of the "Upper Big Branch" mine run by Massey Energy?
19) What happened to Massey executives?
20) What caused the BP gulf oil spill?
21) What is the Bureau of Ocean Energy Management, Regulation and Enforcement?
22) What happened to BP executives?
23) How is corporate violence difference from street violence?
24) Use Richard Quinney's "social reality of crime" to explain why corporate violence is not considered serious crime.
25) What is the Occupational Safety and Health Administration?
26) What is the Federal Trade Commission?
27) What is a myth? Outline the major myths of crime created by the law and media coverage of crime.

Appendix for Chapter 5

Findings of the Mine Safety and Health Administration (MSHA)

Specific Accident Investigation Conclusions—
Physical Causes of the Explosion
   • A small amount of methane, likely liberated from the mine floor, accumulated in the longwall area due to poor ventilation and roof control practices

Based on physical evidence, the investigation concluded that methane was likely liberated from floor fractures into the mine atmosphere on April 5, the day of the explosion. The investigation team subsequently identified floor fractures with methane liberation at longwall shields (a system of hydraulic jacks that supports the roof as coal is being mined) near the tailgate, the end of the longwall where the explosion began.

This methane liberation occurred because PCC/Massey mined into a fault zone that was a reservoir and conduit for methane. MSHA believes that this is the same fault zone associated with methane inundations at UBB in 2003 and 2004, and a 1997 methane explosion.

PCC/Massey's failure to comply with its roof control plan allowed methane to accumulate in the tailgate area. UBB's roof control plan required placement of supplemental supports, in the form of two rows of 8-foot cable bolts or posts, between the primary supports in the longwall tailgate. PCC/Massey installed only one row of these supplemental supports. This lack of roof support contributed to the fall of the tailgate roof, which in turn restricted the airflow leaving the longwall face. The reduced air flow allowed methane to accumulate in the tailgate without being diluted or ventilated from the mine. As a result, an explosive mixture of methane was present in this area.
   • PCC/Massey failed to maintain the UBB longwall shearer, creating an ignition source for accumulated methane

MSHA has identified the longwall shearer as the likely source of the ignition of the methane accumulated in the tailgate area. PCC/Massey was using the longwall shearer to mine in the area near the tailgate. Evidence showed that methane likely migrated from behind the longwall shields to the longwall shearer, and that an accumulation of methane developed near the tailgate. Evidence also revealed that the longwall shearer was not properly maintained by PCC/Massey. Two of the cutting bits on the tail drum were worn flat and lost their carbide tips. The dull, worn shearer bits likely created an ignition source by creating hot streaks while cutting sandstone.

Well-maintained longwall shearers, which include sharp bits and effective water spray systems, protect against these kinds of ignitions and also control the dust during the mining process. The water sprays create air pressure to move methane away from the area where the shearer is cutting and prevents ignitions by spraying water to suppress hot streaks on the longwall face. At the time of the accident, PCC/Massey's longwall shearer was cutting through both coal and sandstone with seven water-spray nozzles missing. As a result, the shearer did not have the minimum required water pressure.

The ineffective sprays failed to move the methane away from the shearer bits and cool the hot streaks created during the mining process. As a result, methane ignited.

The evidence indicated that the flame from the initial methane ignition then ignited a larger accumulation of methane. However, the ignition of the larger body of methane did not happen immediately. Approximately two minutes elapsed between the ignition and the explosion. The electronically recorded event log indicates the shearer was shut off with the remote control just before 3:00 p.m. MSHA has concluded that the tail shearer operator stopped the shearer shortly after the initial ignition, which continued to burn near the longwall tailgate. Realizing that the ignition could not be controlled, the miners in the tailgate area began evacuating. At approximately 3:02 p.m., the flame encountered a larger methane accumulation in the tailgate area, triggering a localized explosion.

- PCC/Massey allowed coal dust to accumulate throughout UBB, providing a fuel source for a massive explosion

The small methane explosion near the tailgate immediately encountered fuel in the form of dangerous accumulations of float coal dust and coal dust, which propagated the explosion beginning in the tailgate entry. The resulting coal dust explosion killed the 29 miners. PCC/Massey records demonstrate that examiners allowed these and other accumulations in the mine to build up over days, weeks, and months. Loose coal, coal dust and float coal dust were abundant in all areas of the mine, including the area affected by the explosion. Many of these accumulations were left from the initial development of this area of the mine, indicating a long-established policy of ignoring basic safety practices.

- PCC/Massey failed to rock dust the mine adequately to prevent a coal dust explosion and its propagation through the mine

If the mine had been rock dusted so that the coal dust had contained sufficient quantities of incombustible content, the localized methane explosion would not have propagated, or expanded, any further. According to testimony and other evidence, PCC/Massey applied grossly inadequate quantities of rock dust. Miners stated that areas were not well dusted, that the walls, roof and floor in areas of the mine were dark colored—which indicates a lack of rock dust. There is no evidence that during the mining of the longwall, PCC/Massey ever applied rock dust in the tailgate entry—the entry where the mine's ventilation system carried coal dust from the mining process.

The mine's rock dusting equipment frequently failed As a result of a systematic failure to properly apply rock dust, the coal dust explosion continued to propagate through the mine, killing miners as far as approximately 5,000 feet from the point of ignition.

Specific Accident Investigation Conclusions—
PCC/Massey's Management Practices that Led to the Explosion

- PCC/Massey failed to perform required mine examinations adequately and remedy known hazards and violations of law

MSHA regulations require mine operators to examine certain areas of the mine on a weekly basis, as well as before and during each shift, to identify hazardous conditions. MSHA's accident investigation found that PCC/Massey regularly failed to examine the mine properly for hazards putting miners at risk and directly contributing to the April 5 explosion. At UBB, PCC/Massey examiners often did not travel to areas they were required to inspect or, in some cases, travelled to the areas but did not perform the required inspections and measurements. For example, PCC/Massey conducted no methane examinations on the longwall tailgate, the area of the longwall where the explosion began, in the weeks prior to the explosion. Even when PCC/Massey performed inspections and identified hazards, it frequently did not correct them. Because of these practices, loose coal, coal dust, and float coal dust accumulated to dangerous levels over days, weeks, and months and provided the fuel for the April 5 explosion.

- PCC/Massey kept two sets of books, thus concealing hazardous conditions

During the course of the investigation, MSHA discovered that PCC/Massey kept two sets of books at UBB: one set of production and maintenance books for internal use only, and the required examination books that, under the Mine Act, are open to review by MSHA and miners. MSHA regulations mandate that the required examination books contain a record of all hazards. Enforcement personnel must rely on their accuracy and completeness to guide them in conducting their physical inspections.

PCC/Massey often recorded hazards in its internal production and maintenance books, but failed to record the same hazards in the required examination book provided to enforcement personnel to review. Some of the hazards described in the hidden "second set of books" were consistent with conditions that existed at the time of the explosion, including the practice of removing sprays on the longwall shearer. Testimony from miners at UBB revealed they felt pressured by management not to record hazards in the required examination books. Furthermore, even when PCC/Massey recorded hazards in the required examination books — such as belts that needed to be cleaned or rock dusted — it often failed to correct the identified hazards.

In addition to undocumented hazards in the required examination books, PCC/Massey failed to report accident data accurately. MSHA's post-accident audit revealed that, in 2009, UBB had twice as many accidents as the operator reported to MSHA.

- PCC/Massey intimidated miners to prevent MSHA from receiving evidence of safety and health violations and hazards

The Mine Act protects miners if they are fired or subjected to other adverse employment actions because they reported a safety or health hazard. These whistleblower protections give miners a voice in the workplace and allow them to protect themselves when mine operators engage in illegal and dangerous practices. Testimony revealed that UBB's miners were intimidated to prevent them from exercising their whistleblower rights. Production delays to resolve safety-related issues often were met by UBB officials with threats of retaliation and disciplinary actions. On one occasion when a foreman stopped production to fix ventilation problems, Chris Blanchard, PCC's president, was overheard saying: "If you don't start running coal up there, I'm going to bring the whole crew outside and get rid of every one of you."

Witness interviews also revealed that a top company official suspended a section foreman who delayed production for one or two hours to make needed safety corrections. MSHA did not receive a single safety or health complaint relating to underground conditions at UBB for approximately four years preceding the explosion even though MSHA offers a toll-free hotline for miners to make anonymous safety and health complaints. PCC/Massey also had a toll-free number for safety and health complaints, but miners testified that they were reluctant to use it for fear of retaliation.

- PCC/Massey failed to provide adequate training for workers

Records and testimony indicate that PCC/Massey inadequately trained their examiners, foremen and miners in mine health and safety. It failed to provide experienced miner training, especially in the area of hazard recognition; failed to provide task training to those performing new job tasks; and failed to provide required annual refresher training. This lack of training left miners unequipped to identify and correct hazards at UBB.

- PCC/Massey established a regular practice of giving advance notice of inspections to hide violations and hazards from enforcement personnel

Under the Mine Act, it is illegal for mine operators' employees to give advance notice of an inspection by MSHA enforcement personnel. Despite this statutory prohibition, UBB miners testified that PCC/Massey mine personnel on the surface routinely notified them prior to the arrival of enforcement personnel. Miners and others testified they were instructed by upper management to alert miners underground of the arrival of enforcement personnel so hazardous conditions could be concealed. UBB dispatchers testified they were told to notify miners underground when MSHA inspectors arrived on the property, and if they did not, there would be consequences.

Advance notice gave those underground the opportunity to alter conditions and fix or hide hazards immediately prior to enforcement personnel's arrival on the working section. PCC/Massey also made ventilation changes in the areas where MSHA inspectors planned to travel, concealing actual production conditions from enforcement personnel.

Available at http://www.msha.gov/Fatals/2010/UBB/FTL10c0331noappx.pdf.

Chapter 6

Innocent Bias in Criminal Justice

"The reality is that we live in a two-tier criminal justice system in America, with one level for corporations and one for living, breathing humans. It's a system that undermines deterrence and allows corporate criminals to inflict their damage—pollution, corruption, fraud, worker and consumer injury and death—unchecked."

—Russell Mokhiber

Innocent Bias Revisited

A criminal justice system that vigorously pursues some crimes committed by some people while simultaneously ignoring other harmful behaviors committed by other people is guaranteed to fail to achieve its goals of reducing crime and doing justice, and it is certain to fail to live up to the American ideals of crime control and due process found in the Declaration of Independence and US Constitution. Yet, this is the criminal justice system we have.

As shown in this book, our criminal justice system is plagued by this problem largely because of failures of the law and the media. First, the law—written by white, older, rich men (WORMs)—fails to define the harmful acts of the powerful as crimes and serious crimes. Second, the media—owned and operated by WORMs—fails to focus widespread American attention on these acts, in spite of how commonly they occur and how much damage they cause. The result is a criminal justice system that vigorously pursues some types of crimes (i.e., street crime) while ignoring others (e.g., corporate crime), even as the latter impose far more costs on society than the former.

A criminal justice system plagued by this problem will be characterized by *innocent bias*, a form of bias defined earlier in the book as unfairness in criminal justice that exists because of unfair criminal laws. Recall that it is called "innocent" because it does not emerge from intentional discrimination on the part of individual police officers, prosecutors, or other agents of criminal justice. Instead, innocent bias occurs when criminal justice agents innocently enforce biased criminal laws. So this type of bias does not occur because of the actions of individual (bad) actors such as a racist police officer or a classist prosecutor or a sexist judge; instead it exists because of biases that are now part of Americans institutions; American criminal justice is characterized by institutionalized discrimination, created by biased laws made by politicians pursuing their conservative ideology and reinforced by corporate media aimed at achieving profit above all else.

Once innocent bias is established by the law and media, what does it look like in criminal justice practice? One must only examine the incredible disparities in policing, courts, and corrections in order to see it. In this chapter, innocent bias in these criminal justice agencies is examined, demonstrating that each is characterized by alarming disparities pertaining to race and ethnicity, class, and gender. The data will show that the people most likely to be arrested, convicted, and sentenced to serious criminal sanctions (e.g., prison, death penalty) are young, poor men of color (i.e., poor, young black males). When you consider that these are *not* the most dangerous people the United States—because these are *not* the people who commit acts of white-collar and corporate crime—you see a serious problem with American criminal justice: it does *not* hold accountable the worst offenders in the nation, and instead catches and punishes people in part because of whom they are and where they are situated in life.

Policing and Race, Class, and Gender

An examination of policing statistics reveals the typical "client" in criminal justice. Beginning with arrests, Table 6.1 illustrates that most people arrested for crime in the US are young people. Specifically, about 12% are under the age of 18 years, and about 76% are under the age of 40 years; only about 24% are over the age of 40 years, and less than 10% are in their 50s or 60s (recall that most lawmakers are in their 50s and 60s).

Table 6.2 shows that whites make up the majority of **arrests** for crimes of all kinds but that African Americans are overrepresented among arrestees for all types of crimes. That is, African Americans—who made up about 12.6% of the US population in 2010 (US Census, 2011)—comprised more than 28% of people arrested for street crimes, including 38% of those arrested for violent crime, 30% for property crime, and 32% for drug crime (recall that most lawmakers are white).

According to data depicted in Table 6.3, the great bulk of arrestees for crime are also men. Women, who are the majority of the US population, are thus vastly underrepresented among arrestees (recall that most lawmakers are men).

Unfortunately, it is not possible to create a figure on arrests by social class because there are no widespread data on social class when it comes to criminal justice practice (Reiman & Leighton, 2013). But, it is clear that nearly everyone arrested for street crimes is poor or middle class (and certainly not wealthy). According to many estimates, about 80% of people arrested in any year are poor (Butler, 2013; Reiman & Leighton, 2013; Shelden, 2007). Recall that most lawmakers are wealthy.

Indeed, studies regularly find evidence that police officers most often stop, question, search, and arrest the poor (Desmond & Valdez, 2013; Donoghue, 2002; Walsh, 2008). This is likely because police are generally found to most heavily focus their resources on poor areas, especially those inhabited by large numbers of African Americans (Desmond & Valdez, 2013).

Table 6.1. Arrests by Age (2011)

	Under 18	18–19	20–29	30–39	40–49	50–59	60+
Violent crime	12.7%	8.8%	35.4%	20.4%	14%	6.8%	1.8%
Property crime	20.4%	11.9%	31.7%	16.6%	12.3%	5.7%	1.4%
Drug crime	9.6%	11.9%	11%	19.4%	12.3%	5.6%	1%
Total	11.8%	9.2%	35.1%	20.2%	14.6%	7.6%	2%

Source: Sourcebook of Criminal Justice Statistics (2011). Table 4.7.2011. Arrests by offense charged and age, United States, 2011. Retrieved June 4, 2013 from: http://www.albany.edu/sourcebook/pdf/t472011.pdf.

Table 6.2. Arrests by Race (2011)

	White	Black	Other
Violent crime	59.4%	38.3%	2.2%
Property crime	68.1%	29.5%	2.4%
Drug crime	66.9%	31.7%	1.4%
Total	69.2%	28.4%	2.4%

Source: Sourcebook of Criminal Justice Statistics (2011). Table 4.10.2011. Arrests by offense charged, age group, and race, United States, 2011. Retrieved June 4, 2013 from: http://www.albany.edu/sourcebook/pdf/t4102011.pdf.

Table 6.3. Arrests by Sex (2011)

	Male	Female
Violent crime	80.4%	19.6%
Property crime	62.9%	37.1%
Drug crime	80.2%	19.8%
Total	74.1%	25.9%

Source: Sourcebook of Criminal Justice Statistics (2011). Table 4.8.2011. Arrests by offense charged and sex, United States, 2011. Retrieved June 4, 2013 from: http://www.albany.edu/sourcebook/pdf/t482011.pdf.

Whether intended or not, many suggest that the whole "law and order" movement has had its most dramatic and negative impacts on poor people (Walsh, 2008). As one example, the domestic aspects of the drug war are fought almost exclusively in poor areas, having little to no impact on drug abuse rates while simultaneously leading to the arrests of millions of people every year and stigmatizing the urban poor (Donoghue, 2002).

Why Do the Police Arrest
Young, Poor Men of Color?

One could create a conspiracy theory asserting that the reason we arrest so many young, poor men of color is because they are the enemy of those who make the law and own the media in the United States—white, older, rich males (WORMs). This would be at best a simplistic argument, and at worst, an incorrect argument, for there are valid reasons that police tend to arrest young, poor men of color at higher rates than other groups in society.

Starting with age, criminologists have long posited that street crime is most common during the time when a person is between the ages of 15 to 25 years. The relationship between age and street crime can be depicted in an image commonly referred to as the **age-crime curve** (Sweeten, Piquero, & Steinberg, 2013). Figure 6.1 illustrates trends in arrests for various types of serious street crimes, as reported by the US Department of Justice. What you clearly see in the figure is that the risk of offending (as measured here in arrests by police) tends to peak between the ages of 15 and 25 years, then generally declines afterward.

The tail end of the figures captures what is often called the **aging out phenomenon**, when people supposedly "age out of crime," meaning they grow up, mature, and generally stop committing crimes. Longitudinal research shows that various reasons account for why people stop committing serious street crimes; generally people get into fulfilling marriages, find meaningful employment, make new friends that conform to the law, and develop reasons to conform to the law, which are often called a **stake in conformity** (Robinson & Beaver, 2009; Sampson & Laub, 2003).

Given these realities, it is not surprising that most people arrested for crimes tend to be younger—you should actually expect police to be arresting more young people than elderly people since young people commit more street crime. However, you must remember that the people on tail end of the age-crime figures (middle-age to older folks) are actually the ones who are the most dangerous, for they are the ones engaged in acts of elite deviance.

That police don't focus their attention on elite deviance explains why there are not more middle-aged and older people arrested; that they focus on street crime explains why so many young people are arrested. Given who makes the law (which determines that is illegal and what is serious, as well as what is not) and given who owns the media (which determines what we view as dangerous and what we fear), it makes sense that our focus is on the crimes of the young. Recall the metaphor of the spotlight introduced earlier in the book; the law and media focus a spotlight of attention on street crime and thus our attention (and that of the police is focused squarely on it). If the law and media focused their attention on corporate crime and other acts of elite deviance, more older people would be getting arrested and the age-crime curve would be turned on its head.

Figure 6.1. Age and Crime

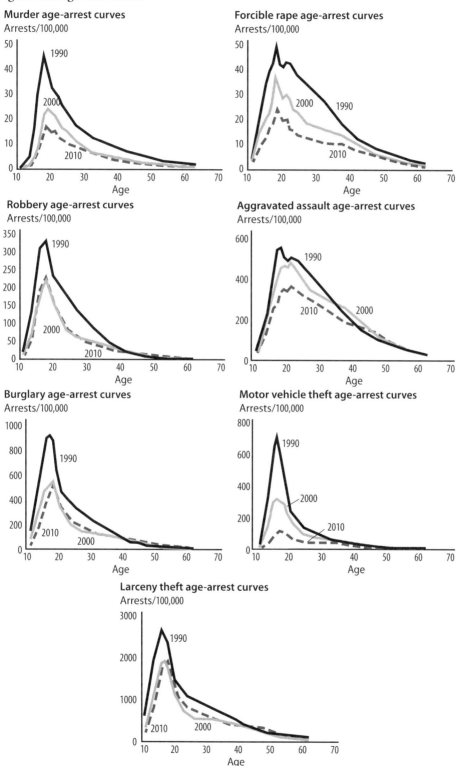

Source: http://www.bjs.gov/content/pub/pdf/aus9010.pdf.

In-Class Activity:

If criminologists examined relationships between age and all types of crimes, including elite deviance, what would the age-crime curve look like? Try to create a new chart that more accurately depicts relationships between age and all types of crime.

As for race, since African Americans are overrepresented among arrestees, a logical question is, do African Americans commit more crime? The answer is, yes (for some crimes) and no (as a general rule). Or, to be more specific, it depends on the type of crime you are talking about (Lynch, 2000; Warren, 2010). Clearly, African Americans do not commit more acts of elite deviance than whites, as whites commit the great bulk of such behaviors—so they are not more dangerous than white people. Yet, there are some street crimes for which African Americans are overrepresented. Two examples from Chapter 2 include murder and robbery, two of the most serious crimes in America. Recall that, in any given year, African Americans commit about 50% of these crimes, even though they account for only about 12% of the US population.

Yet also recall from Chapters 4 and 5 that there are numerous other ways to kill people and take people's money or property that are not considered murder or robbery. If these acts were included in arrest statistics (and if we actually arrested people for them), then whites would make up a much higher portion of people arrested for such crimes and would likely even be overrepresented among offenders.

That we don't consider such offenses murder or robbery is evidence of the institutional bias in the criminal law, and the fact that people are not arrested for them is evidence that this bias innocently continues into law enforcement. Stated differently, that police don't focus their attention on elite deviance explains why there are not more white people arrested; that they focus on street crime explains why so many people of color are arrested. Given who makes the law (which determines that is illegal and what is serious, as well as what is not) and given who owns the media (which determines what we view as dangerous and what we fear), it makes sense that our focus is on the crimes committed by people of color. If the law and media focused their attention on corporate crimes and other forms of elite deviance, more whites would be getting arrested and our understanding of race and crime would be greatly changed.

In-Class Activity:

If criminologists examined relationships between race and all types of crimes, including elite deviance, what arrests for crime look like by race? Estimate the percentage of arrests by race for all types of crime.

Policing and Contextual Bias

In addition to the presence of innocent bias, an exhaustive review of criminal justice processes (including the courts) finds evidence of *contextual bias* including among the police (Walker, Spohn, & DeLone, 2013). Recall from Chapter 1 that this term refers to discrimination found in particular contexts or circumstances, as in when police in some jurisdiction use race and ethnicity to profile people. This might explain why African Americans and Hispanics are more likely to be stopped, questioned, searched, and arrested by the police than whites; they are also more likely to have force used against them, including excessive force and lethal force.

Sure enough, studies routinely find that police most commonly stop, question, search, and arrest people of color, especially African Americans (Britton, 2000). In fact, a meta-analysis of more than two dozen data sets that produced 40 separate research reports found "with strong consistency that minority suspects are more likely to be arrested than White suspects" (Kochel, Wilson, & Mastrofski, 2011: 473). This is because police are looking for the types of crimes that people of color are most likely to be involved with, and because there are more police in the places where they live.

Even for relatively minor offenses such as marijuana possession, it is young, poor African American males who are most likely to be arrested. This is especially true since the early 1990s when the drug war continued to pick up steam as part of the conservative wars on crime and drugs (Nguyen & Reuter, 2012). In fact, national evidence now exists to show that arrests for drug crimes among people of color increased while arrests for whites did not increase, even as rates of drug use for people of color did not go up; scholars suggest that as economic conditions worsened, police were utilized to step up enforcement of drug offenses (Parker & Maggard, 2005).

A study of drug enforcement in the city of Seattle is particularly revealing. The authors examined drug arrests and police enforcement practices there and found that African Americans were vastly overrepresented among arrests for drug crimes in the city. Specifically, 64% of the people arrested for selling methamphetamine, ecstasy, powder cocaine, crack cocaine, and heroin were African Americans even though the majority of people who sell these drugs are white (Beckett, Nyrop & Pfingst, 2006).

According to the authors, there were three reasons that explained the fact that blacks made up a majority of those arrested even though most drug dealers are white: 1) the police focused heavily on crack cocaine (the one drug where African Americans were most involved in selling); 2) the police put more emphasis on outdoor drug venues (where African Americans were more likely to be selling); and 3) the police devoted more resources to racially heterogeneous areas (meaning far less attention to predominantly white drug dealing areas) (Beckett, Nyrop & Pfingst, 2006). The authors suggest that race plays either an implicit or explicit role in each of these disparity-producing factors. That is, race helps account for why police targeted certain drugs, places, or people (Beckett, Nyrop & Pfingst, 2006).

Yet it is not *just* race that explains the greater crack or outdoor markets. First, crack cocaine is perceived as a dangerous drug, yet it is no more dangerous than powder cocaine, as noted in Chapter 1. It is perceived to be more associated with street-level violence associated with the marketplace than powder; hence, police will devote more resources to it. Second, outdoor markets are more visible and thus are more likely to generate citizen complaints; hence, police will devote more resources to them. Finally, that police devote more resources to racially heterogeneous areas may be explained by the fact that they are more likely to be found in lower-class areas whereas predominantly white outdoor markets are more likely to be found in middle-class areas.

So even though race is *not* the exclusive reason racial disparities exist in Seattle drug arrests (as well as in other large cities and for other crimes), it remains a fact that race has a good deal to do with it. Recall the arguments from Chapters 1, 2, and 3 that race and racial stereotypes are so clearly intertwined with perceptions of dangerousness and criminality. That is, "blackness" is now strongly correlated with criminal and it is people of color — especially poor young men of color — whom we fear. So, even with racially neutral police officers operating in a "colorblind" society, we'll see disparities in arrests by police.

When New York City recently released data on the people it stops and questions using its controversial **stop and frisk** policy meant to reduce crime by identifying people with guns *before* they commit crimes, the data merely served to continue if not intensify a controversy associated with disparities in arrests. According to the police data, all from 2011, almost 90% of those targeted by the police department through its stop and frisk policy were either African American or Hispanic; together, African Americans and Hispanics make up less than 53% of the city's population (Velez, 2013). Precinct by precinct data showed similar results, including:

- The precinct with the most stops was Brooklyn's 75th (including East New York and Cypress Hills). There, more than 31,000 people were stopped and frisked, and 97% were either African American or Hispanic.
- The precinct with the second highest number of stops was Brooklyn's 73rd Precinct (including Brownsville). There, 25,167 people were stopped and frisked, and about 98% were either African American or Hispanic.
- The precinct with the third highest number of stops was the 115th precinct (including East Elmhurst, Corona and Jackson Heights in Queens). There, 18,156 were stopped and frisked, and about 93% were either African American or Hispanic.
- The precinct with the fourth highest number of stops was the 40th Precinct in the Bronx (covering Mott Haven and Melrose). There, 17,690 were stopped and frisked, and almost 99% were either African American or Hispanic.
- The precinct with the fifth highest number of stops was the 90th precinct in Williamsburg, Brooklyn. There, 17,566 people were stopped and frisked, and about 89% were either African American or Hispanic (Velez, 2013).

A large majority of people stopped and frisked did not have a weapon and were not arrested. Thus, an official with the New York Civil Liberties Union suggested the data proved racial profiling by the police, saying: "While it appears at first blush to be a slick, fact-filled response, nothing in the report can dispute the reality that stop and frisk NYPD-style is targeted overwhelmingly at people of color, so innocent of any criminal wrongdoing, that all but 12% walk away without so much as a ticket." A judge in New York City found the practice unconstitutional, finding it to be a violation of the Fourth Amendment's ban on unreasonable searches and the 14th Amendment's guarantee of equal protection. However, a three judge panel of the federal circuit court with jurisdiction over this region blocked this ruling over fears that the judge was not acting impartially in the case.

Police officials denied they were profiling people based on race and instead insisted they were targeting the people and places were crime risks were highest. Yet, just as with the example of drug arrests in Seattle, race has much to do with why police target certain people and places. Ultimately the federal courts will determine if the city's stop and frisk policy is constitutional.

As long as police have **discretion**, we will find racial disparities in police statistics (Jones, 2012). We should especially expect such outcomes given the stereotypical image of the offender produced by the criminal law and media coverage of crime discussed in Chapter 3. As noted earlier, it is young, poor, minority men who are perceived to be the most threatening to society, and so as the police (including lawmakers, city and county officials, and so forth) perceive a greater social threat—often referred to as the **minority threat** or **racial threat** or **social threat hypothesis**—we can expect arrests and other negative outcomes including police brutality to rise (Smith & Holmes, 2003). According to this hypothesis, police direct more resources to areas where larger portions of the population are made up of people perceived to be dangerous (e.g., people of color).

> **Out-of-Class Activity:**
> Find an article on the minority threat or racial threat or social threat hypothesis. What did the authors do and what did they find? Share the findings of the research with the class.

Contrast those who make the law—white, older, rich men (WORMs)—with those we arrest—non-white, younger, poor men—and you see the only common demographic characteristic between those who make the law and those who suffer most from it is maleness. Hence you might better understand the arguments presented in Chapter 1 that the criminal justice has its most detrimental effects on people of color, the poor, and young people, whether intended or not (Alexander, 2012; Reiman & Leighton, 2013; Shelden, 2007; Tonry, 2012; Walker, Spohn & DeLone, 2013).

Courts and Race, Class, and Gender

Table 6.4 illustrates that the great bulk of court "clients" in **state courts** are also young people, as would be expected given who is arrested. Specifically, 73% are under the age

Table 6.4. Convictions in State Courts by Age (2006)

	Under 20	20–29	30–39	40–49	50–59	60+
Violent crime	11%	42%	24%	16%	5%	2%
Property crime	9%	40%	26%	19%	5%	1%
Drug crime	4%	41%	26%	21%	7%	1%
Total	7%	40%	26%	20%	6%	1%

Source: Sourcebook of Criminal Justice Statistics (2006). Table 5.45.2006. Percent distribution of characteristics of felony offenders convicted in State courts. Retrieved June 4, 2013 from: http://www.albany.edu/sourcebook/pdf/t5452006.pdf.

of 40 years; only about 27% are over the age of 40 years, and less than 10% are in their 50s or 60s (recall that most lawmakers are in their 50s and 60s).

Table 6.5 shows that whites make up the majority of those convicted of all kinds in state courts but that African Americans were also overrepresented among convicts for all types of crimes. Recall that African Americans comprise less than 13% of the US population, yet they comprised 38% of people convicted for crimes, including 44% of those convicted for drug crime, 39% for violent crime, and 33% for property crime (recall that most lawmakers are white).

According to data depicted in Table 6.6, the great bulk of those convicted for crimes in state courts are men. Women, who are the majority of the US population, are thus also vastly underrepresented among convicts (recall that most lawmakers are men).

Data from the federal level show a similar picture, although Table 6.7 illustrates that those convicted of crimes in **federal courts** tend be a bit older than those convicted in state courts. Still, about 75% of those convicted in federal courts are below the age of 40 years while only 25% are over the age of 40 years. Again, people in the same age range as lawmakers are rarely clients in criminal courts.

Like in state courts, the majority of those convicted in federal courts are white, although again African Americans are overrepresented among federal convicts. This reality is shown in Table 6.8.

Like in state courts, a large majority of those convicted of federal crimes are men. This is depicted in Table 6.9.

Just as with police data, there are limited data with regard to social class and courts, especially with regard to the portion of people handled in courts that are poor. Estimates are pretty consistent that about 80% of people charged in courts are poor or **indigent** (Robinson, 2009). Thus, we can be confident that the courts primarily process poor people through the system. And let's not forget that lawmakers are predominantly wealthy.

Why Do the Courts Convict Young, Poor Men of Color?

Taken together, data on courts show that the typical convict in the United States is a young male of color, as you'd expect given who is being stopped and arrested by police.

Table 6.5. Convictions in State Courts by Race (2006)

	White	Black	Other
Violent crime	58%	39%	3%
Property crime	65%	33%	2%
Drug crime	55%	44%	1%
Total	60%	38%	2%

Source: Sourcebook of Criminal Justice Statistics (2006). Table 5.45.2006. Percent distribution of characteristics of felony offenders convicted in State courts. Retrieved June 4, 2013 from: http://www.albany.edu/sourcebook/pdf/t5452006.pdf.

Table 6.6. Convictions in State Courts by Sex (2006)

	Male	Female
Violent crime	89%	11%
Property crime	75%	25%
Drug crime	82%	18%
Total	83%	17%

Source: Sourcebook of Criminal Justice Statistics (2006). Table 5.45.2006. Percent distribution of characteristics of felony offenders convicted in State courts. Retrieved June 4, 2013 from: http://www.albany.edu/sourcebook/pdf/t5452006.pdf.

Table 6.7. Convictions in Federal Courts by Age (2003)

	20 and under	21–30	31–40	40+
Violent crime	8.2%	36.1%	28.1%	27.5%
Property crime	3.9%	30%	29.1%	37%
Drug crime	5.5%	30%	29.1%	37%
All crime	4.9%	39.2%	31%	24.9%

Source: Sourcebook of Criminal Justice Statistics (2003). Table 5.18.2003. Federal defendants convicted in US District Courts by offense and characteristics, fiscal year 2003. Retrieved June 4, 2013 from: http://www.albany.edu/sourcebook/pdf/t5182003.pdf.

Table 6.8. Convictions in Federal Courts by Race (2003)

	White	Black	Other
Violent crime	53.2%	30.4%	16.4%
Property crime	66.9%	24.9%	8.2%
Drug crime	67.7%	29.6%	1.7%
All crime	71.2%	24.8%	2%

Source: Sourcebook of Criminal Justice Statistics (2003). Table 5.18.2003. Federal defendants convicted in US District Courts by offense and characteristics, fiscal year 2003. Retrieved June 4, 2013 from: http://www.albany.edu/sourcebook/pdf/t5182003.pdf.

Table 6.9. Convictions in Federal Courts by Sex (2003)

	Male	Female
Violent crime	92.4%	7.6%
Property crime	73.4%	26.6%
Drug crime	87.4%	12.6%
All crime	86.8%	13.2%

Source: Sourcebook of Criminal Justice Statistics (2003). Table 5.18.2003. Federal defendants convicted in US District Courts by offense and characteristics, fiscal year 2003. Retrieved June 4, 2013 from: http://www.albany.edu/sourcebook/pdf/t5182003.pdf.

Are the courts biased against young men of color simply because they are more likely to be processed through the courts? No, not unless by bias you mean "innocent bias." After all, the courts do not determine who their clients are (with the exception of prosecutors who decide which cases proceed to the courts after the point of arrest), they merely process people through the system sent to them by the police. So, given that young, poor men of color are disproportionately likely to be arrested, of course we'd expect them to comprise a large portion of defendants in the courts.

Contextual Bias in the Courts

Are there additional biases within the courts? The review of contextual bias in criminal justice processes presented in Chapter 1 also found evidence of bias in the courts (Walker, Spohn, & DeLone, 2013). Recall that in some places, race and ethnicity impact pre-trial decision-making including **bail**, **charging** by prosecutors, and **plea bargaining** in the courts. That is, studies find that, in some places, people of color are less likely to be offered bail or are given inflated bail amounts as compared to whites. African Americans and Hispanics are also, in some places and contexts (e.g., drug crimes), charged with more serious crimes than whites. And, in some places, they are less likely to be offered plea bargains when compared to whites. These findings are less common in the most serious of crimes and more common in borderline cases when prosecutors and judges actually have discretion (Walker, Spohn, & DeLone, 2013).

Further, people of color are, in many jurisdictions, denied the right to serve on trial juries through the use of **peremptory challenges** based solely on their race. While it is illegal for potential jurors to be stricken from jury pools based solely on their race, numerous cases exist where all African Americans have been struck from jury pools using peremptory challenges. In these cases, lawyers are required to give alternative explanations for striking these potential jurors, if they are challenged by attorneys on the other side or by judges. Incredibly, illogical and even absurd explanations have been found acceptable by judges, and so we still occasionally have people of color being tried and convicted by all-white or nearly all-white juries (Walker, Spohn, & DeLone, 2013).

Additionally, African Americans and Hispanics who are convicted of certain types of crimes (e.g., drug crimes and violent crimes against whites) are treated more harshly than whites for those crimes. Studies at the state and federal level have found evidence that African Americans and Hispanics tend to receive harsher sentences for drug crimes than do whites, at least at some times and places; legally relevant factors do not fully account for these tougher sentences. And when people of color commit violent crimes against white victims—especially when black men offend against white females—the toughest sanctions of all are often handed down (Walker, Spohn, & DeLone, 2013).

Finally, tougher sentences tend to be handed down to racial minorities than to whites in "borderline cases" where prosecutors and judges tend to have discretion about whether to pursue probation or a term of incarceration, as noted earlier. This makes sense because, for the most part, legal factors such as offense seriousness (determined by the law) and prior record (determined by interactions with police) highly predict the type and length of sentence a person receives. Thus, it is very hard to discriminate or treat differently one murderer versus another, or one rapist versus another, and so forth. Instead, when legal factors are not determinative and prosecutors have discretion to seek one charge that calls for a harsh punishment or another lesser charge that carries a relatively less severe punishment, it is there that prosecutors can and sometimes do abuse this discretion in the favor of whites (Walker, Spohn, & DeLone, 2013).

Thus, there is strong evidence, in some places at least, evidence of serious racial biases within the criminal courts. It is also clear that nearly everyone convicted for street crimes is poor or middle class (and certainly not wealthy). Studies find meaningful evidence that most court clients are poor, and that social class bias exists in numerous forms including the inability to pay for competent defense attorneys. A survey of capital punishment experts found this to be the primary source of bias against the poor in capital cases (Robinson, 2009). Experts responded that the major source of bias in capital cases is not being able to afford competent defense attorneys, but also they noted that many forms of culpable killings (i.e., elite deviance) are not even identified as murders.

Even though the poor were guaranteed access to defense attorneys in criminal cases in the US Supreme Court ruling, *Gideon v. Wainwright*, 372 U.S. 335 (1963), the fact remains that in many areas today, the ruling is largely ignored and the poor do not have access to quality defense attorneys (Nice, 2012). For example, according to Carrie Johnson (2013), 50 years after the decision, "many lawyers say the system for providing defense attorneys for the poor is in crisis." The reasons? First, at least 18 states leave funding for indigent defense to counties. Second, data are not collected in rural areas or on misdemeanor defendants, so no one knows for sure the degree to which clients there are receiving their constitutional protections (Nice, 2012).

Third, and probably most importantly because it applies to virtually every jurisdiction, there are too many felony cases and too few resources to handle them. As shown in Chapter 1, courts receive only about 22% of funds allocated to criminal justice. As police arrest more and more people, and correctional facilities are built to hold them, the courts face long backlogs in cases, delaying cases and mandating plea bargaining in order to continue to function. The likelihood that a typical defendant will receive an adequate defense in these conditions is slim to none. After all, courts don't collapse like buildings or bridges when they are overburdened, they continue to function. They do this by *not* having trials but instead by coercing defendants to plead guilty. Plea bargaining operates by coercion, where defendants are presumed guilty and thus not worthy of trials.

Other studies find meaningful disparities in court processing. For example, a study of state court sentences found that race and ethnicity, along with numerous other factors, had real and independent effects on sentencing outcomes (e.g., whether a person went to jail or prison). According to the authors,

> the effects of race and ethnicity on sentencing were significant in their own right, and—more important—were conditional on the size of the county black or Hispanic population ... individual Hispanics and blacks are punished more severely among counties with larger Hispanic or black populations, perhaps reflecting greater perceived threat ... the findings look the way one would expect them to if black and Hispanic offenders were perceived as more criminally threatening and dangerous in areas of higher minority concentration (Ulmer & Johnson, 2004: 166).

That severe punishment is more likely to follow in counties with large populations of people of color, is also consistent with the *minority threat* or *racial threat* or *social threat* hypothesis, introduced earlier. Here, it is suggestive that prosecutors, judges, and/or jurors are more likely to impose more severe sanctions against people convicted of crimes when they are afraid of crime based on living with or near larger populations of people of color.

Similar findings have been demonstrated in federal courts, as well. Certain classes of people (African American and Hispanics, males, and younger defendants) tend to receive the harshest sentences, even after controlling for legal factors that should explain sentencing variations. According to the authors of one study that found this: "When these effects are examined in combination, young Hispanic male defendants have the highest odds of incarceration and young black male defendants receive the longest sentences" (Doerner & Demuth, 2010: 1).

Again, contrast those who make the law — white, older, rich men (WORMs) — with those we convict — non-white, younger, poor men — and you see the only common demographic characteristic between those who make the law and those who suffer most from it is maleness. It is undeniable that males are generally more dangerous than females; the same cannot be said for young people, poor people, or people of color, unless one completely ignores acts of elite deviance.

So we have a criminal justice system that functions to catch and convict mostly young, poor men of color, even though they are not the greatest threat to our safety or property. This is what innocent bias looks like in American criminal justice. As a result, the most dangerous people in the country are walking free, while the nation's correctional facilities are filling up with young, poor minority men.

The End Result of Criminal Justice: Race, Class, and Gender in Corrections

Corrections is the end result of criminal justice practice. Thus, it is perhaps the best place to look for disparities in criminal justice practice, because the culmination of any biases that exist in the law, policing, and courts will be evident here. Unfortunately, an examination of correctional data reveals the stark reality of American criminal justice today — prisons and jails and virtually every other form of punishment are administered disproportionately to the young, the poor, the male, and the black and brown.

This should not be surprising given the data on police and courts above. After all, it is corrections that merely carry out the sentences of those convicted by the courts after being arrested by the police. Table 6.10 shows inmates by gender and race in **jails**. More than 85% of jail inmates are men, and more than 55% are people of color.

Table 6.11 shows a similar reality in **state prisons**. Specifically, more than 90% of inmates are men and about 58% are people of color.

Men also make up more than 93% of inmates in **federal prisons**, and people of color comprise about 75% of people in federal prisons. These data are illustrated in Table 6.12.

Table 6.10. Jail Inmates by Sex and Race (2011)

Male	87.3%
Female	12.7%
White	44.8%
Black	37.6%
Hispanic	15.5%
Other	2.2%

Source: Sourcebook of Criminal Justice Statistics (2011). Table 6.17.2011. Jail inmates by sex, race, Hispanic origin, and conviction status, United States, 1990–2011. Retrieved June 4, 2013 from: http://www.albany.edu/sourcebook/pdf/t6172011.pdf.

Table 6.11. State Prison Inmates by Sex and Race and Offense Type (2009)

	Male	Female	White	Black	Hispanic
Violent crime	96.4%	3.6%	36.6%	44%	16.2%
Property crime	89.4%	10.6%	50.4%	33.8%	13.2%
Drug crime	90%	10%	30.4%	50.5%	17.1%
All crime	93.1%	6.9%	38.9%	42.6%	15.5%

Source: Sourcebook of Criminal Justice Statistics (2009). Table 6.0001.2009. Estimated number and percent distribution of prisoners under jurisdiction of State correctional authorities. Retrieved June 4, 2013 from: http://www.albany.edu/sourcebook/pdf/t600012009.pdf.

Table 6.12. Federal Prison Inmates by Sex and Race and Offense Type (2011)

Male	93.5%
Female	6.5%
White	58.6%
Black	37.9%
Hispanic	34.2%
Other	3.5%

Source: Sourcebook of Criminal Justice Statistics (2011). Table 6.0022.2011. Prisoners under the jurisdiction of the Federal Bureau of Prisons by selected facility and demographic characteristics, 1990, 2000, 2009, and 2011. Retrieved June 4, 2013 from: http://www.albany.edu/sourcebook/pdf/t600222011.pdf.

Finally, the most extreme punishment available to those states where it is still legal (as well as in the federal government and military system) is **capital punishment** or the **death penalty**. Here, males and people of color are also overrepresented among death row inmates. Specifically, more than 98% are men, as shown in Table 6.13, and about 57% are non-white.

Table 6.13. Death Row Inmates by Sex and Race (2010 and 2012)

Sex (2010)
Male	98.2%
Female	1.8%

Race (2012)
White	43.2%
Black	41.8%
Hispanic	12.4%
Native American	1.1%
Asian	1.4%

Sources: Sourcebook of Criminal Justice Statistics (2010). Table 6.83.2010. Hispanic and female prisoners under sentence of death by state, 2009 and 2010. Retrieved June 4, 2013 from: http://www.albany.edu/sourcebook/pdf/t6832010.pdf; Table 6.80.2012. Sourcebook of Criminal Justice Statistics (2012). Prisoners under sentence of death by race, ethnicity, and jurisdiction, on April 1, 2012. Retrieved June 4, 2013 from: http://www.albany.edu/sourcebook/pdf/t6802012.pdf.

It must be reiterated that agencies of criminal justice do not release data with regard to the social class status of correctional populations. Yet, we know with no doubt that correctional populations tend to comprised of poor people — whether in jails, prisons, or even on death row.

As noted by Paul Butler (2013: 2178):

- In 1997, more than half of state prisoners earned less than $1,000 in the month before their arrest. This would result in an annual income of less than $12,000, well below the $25,654 median per capita income in 1997.
- The same year, 35% of state inmates were unemployed in the month before their arrest, compared to the national unemployment rate of 4.9%.
- Approximately 70% of state prisoners have not graduated from high school. Only 13% of incarcerated adults have any post-high school education, compared with almost 50% of the non-incarcerated population.
- College graduation ... serves to insulate Americans from incarceration. Only 0.1% of bachelor's degree holders are incarcerated, compared to 6.3% of high school dropouts ... high school dropouts are sixty-three times more likely to be locked up than college graduates.

From these data, we can be confident that correctional populations are comprised of mostly poor people.

Butler's argument about criminal justice is consistent with those offered by scholars whose work was reviewed in Chapter 1. The problem of bias in criminal justice is systemic, meaning all of criminal justice must be considered in order to understand why poor people (and people of color) are disproportionately under the supervision of corrections, not to mention make up the majority of people incarcerated. He explains that the processes involved in explaining the poor and often black or brown face of the typical inmate include:

- Lawmakers ignoring the social conditions that create crime (as noted in Chapter 1 by Reiman & Leighton, 2013).
- Overpolicing of poor and African American areas, leading to more stops and arrests, as noted earlier.
- Implicit and explicit biases by police, prosecutors, and judges against African Americans (i.e., where stereotypes and myths of crime impact behavior of criminal justice officials).
- A presumption of guilt at the point of arrest, allowing "prosecutors, using the legal apparatus of expansive criminal liability, recidivist statutes, and mandatory minimums (to) coerce guilty pleas by threatening defendants with vastly disproportionate punishment if they go to trial."
- Ineffective punishment so that "two-thirds of freed prisoners are rearrested, and half return to prison, within three years of their release."

Remember the argument of Jeffrey Reiman & Paul Leighton (2013) from Chapter 1 that nothing succeeds like failure when it comes to criminal justice? There is little doubt that correctional punishment generally fails to stop *recidivism* (repeat offending). Richard Frase (2009) blames this on the very way we go about trying to "fight crime" without even addressing the conditions which so often breed it, instead creating a cycle which virtually guarantees it will continue. He notes that

> poverty and lack of opportunity are associated with higher crime rates; crime leads to arrest, a criminal record, and usually a jail or prison sentence; past crimes lengthen those sentences; offenders released from prison or jail confront family and neighborhood dysfunction, increased risks of unemployment, [and other crime-producing disadvantages] this make them likelier to commit new crimes, and the cycle repeats itself (p. 263).

In the end, the United States has the largest and most expensive criminal justice apparatus in the world. Yet it fails to meaningfully reduce crime, especially acts of elite deviance, and is inherently unfair in its treatment of people of color, the poor, and especially young, poor men of color.

Out-of-Class Activity:
Find the website for the Department of Corrections for your state. Examine the racial makeup of people incarcerated in your state. Are people of color overrepresented among inmates? Why or why not?

A Safe Conclusion: What It All Means

A very safe conclusion from these data is that the people who end up being processed through the criminal justice system (i.e., getting arrested, convicted, and punished) are nothing like the people who make the law and own the media. It is thus an empirical fact that the criminal law is made by white, older, rich men (WORMs), and the media are owned by WORMs, while those who suffer most from the law and enhanced criminal justice because of intense media depictions of crime are people of color, poor people, and younger men. This certainly serves the interests of lawmakers and people like them, and it also serves the interests of the media who make so much money broadcasting street crime in the news and outlets of entertainment and infotainment.

But this does not mean the criminal justice system is intentionally biased against young, poor men of color. And it certainly does not implicate the police, courts, and corrections are the sources of bias in criminal justice. But a criminal justice system targets some crimes and some criminals while largely ignoring other crimes and criminals is a criminal justice system that fails to meet its ideal goals of reducing crime and doing justice. And it is a criminal justice system that, in practice, fails to live up to the American ideals found in the Declaration of Independence of allowing all people to pursue happiness and protecting their equal rights and liberty, and the American ideals found in the US Constitution of ensuring our domestic Tranquility, providing for the common defence, assuring our general Welfare, and protecting Justice and Liberty. That is, we live in a society where we are at serious risk of property loss, injury, and death—threats to our happiness, Tranquility, common defence, and Welfare—and we live in a nation that treats people unequally, thereby threatening the liberty of some and providing more or less justice for people based on their social class, skin color, and gender.

We fail to meet these goals and ideals because our criminal justice system fails to pursue the worst offenders—those white-collar and corporate criminals who cause more property damage and who kill and injure more people than all street crime combined, even as we pursue tougher and tougher policies to deal with the latter. All of this results in an unfair criminal justice system, one that most harms young, poor, people of color (and mostly young, poor men of color) while disproportionately benefiting older white males. The primary benefit to older white males is that their harmful behaviors are not pursued by criminal justice, allowing them to mostly get away with their deviant acts even as they impose enormous costs on society that dwarf all street crimes combined.

The argument of this book is that the failures of criminal justice are not intentional—that we do not operate a racial caste system or social class maintenance system, or a patriarchal system (as others scholars whose work was reviewed in Chapter 1 argue). Instead, the argument here is that criminal justice functions to control some segments of the population and to serve some interests more than others, even though it is not done so intentionally. The argument, stated differently, is that criminal justice functions to achieve these outcomes though not intentionally.

At the least, we can conclude that neither the police, courts, or corrections intend to produce biased outcomes based on race, class, or gender; after all, they are merely carrying out the law. It is the law that is the problem—because the law determines what is illegal and what is serious (and what is not). And, as argued in Chapter 3, the media share some of the blame because it is the media who determine what we fear and worry about (as well as what we don't). So, the major problems facing criminal justice today are institutional in nature.

Together, the law and media create and reinforce myths and stereotypes about crime, criminals, and criminal justice, those myths and stereotypes identified in Chapter 5. Because the law defines the acts of poor people of color as crimes and serious crimes, and because there is so much more coverage by the media of their crimes, Americans tend to be more afraid of and worried about young, poor minority men, because they see crime as a poor, minority male phenomenon, as discussed in Chapter 3. This owes itself to myths of crime created and reinforced by the law and media.

In the book, I argued that it is politics and ideology that explain why we have the criminal justice system we have. Politicians define acts of the young and the poor and the powerless (including people of color) as crimes and serious crimes while largely ignoring the acts of the wealthy and the white and the older folks who tend to commit them. Since lawmakers are overwhelmingly white and older and richer and male (WORMs), it is logical that they would ignore the kinds of acts that people like them tend to commit. Further, since funding for political races tends to come from the same group of people, logic would lead us to expect dangerous acts committed by WORMs to be largely ignored. Finally, since the media are owned by powerful organizations and individuals—also WORMs—it also makes sense that the media tend to ignore elite deviance while focusing heavily on street crime, especially violent street crime committed by certain types of people under certain circumstances.

As for ideology, the now dominant conservative political ideology surrounding issues of crime and criminal justice—which first emerged at the national level in the 1960s, started to take hold in the early 1980s, and is now embraced by most Republicans and Democrats—explains why we continue to pursue tougher and tougher and ever expansive criminal justice policies even as evidence mounts that the policies do not help us reduce crime, drugs, or terrorism and that they are discriminatory in their application. Specifically, it is young, poor, minority males and their families who have suffered the most from criminal justice policies, with little to no public safety benefit to the neighborhoods in which they reside.

There is little demand for change among lawmakers because neither they nor their supporters are directly impacted by it. Further, as shown in Chapter 2, as long as conservative arguments about crime are intertwined with race and class, it is people of color and the poor who will be most victimized by the policies of criminal justice politicians create. Finally, it should be obvious that mainstream media organizations also benefit from the current arrangement because they profit by covering issues of crime and criminal justice in the news as well as entertainment and infotainment outlets.

Given all this, can we conclude that the biases in and failures of American criminal justice are intentional? That is, do lawmakers intend to create laws that lead to bias in policing, courts, and corrections? Are they targeting poor people, people of color, and young men in order to harm them and their communities? Is criminal justice a racial caste system or a class maintenance system or about control of women?

I'd still say no—lawmakers do not intentionally pursue policies intended to harm young, poor men of color. I am appealing here to my sense of optimism that no one could be that evil, not in contemporary America. But we can be sure that something— or some things to be more precise—are intended by the actions of politicians. After all, lawmakers create laws and policies with intent; they are pursuing goals and outcomes in pursuit of their political ideology. It is likely accurate to conclude that lawmakers— at least those who embrace the conservative ideology—intend to:

• Focus our attention on street crime.

- "Get tough" or go after street criminals.
- Reduce street crime in order to protect people from it.
- Provide justice for victims of street crime and their families.
- Aim to reduce drugs and terrorism in the same ways they generally try to reduce crime—through conservative, get touch, war approaches.
- Protect the capitalist economy.
- Empower corporations and other elites to pursue wealth at nearly any cost.

Each of these goals is surely consistent with the conservative political ideology embraced now by both Republicans and Democrats. Even if pursuing these goals produces unequal outcomes—for people of color versus whites, for poor people versus rich people, for men versus women—that does not mean these differential outcomes are intended by lawmakers.

A similar argument can be made that, even though the media focus far more attention on street crime than white-collar and corporate crimes and on young, poor men of color than older, wealthier, whites, this does not mean the media are intentionally biased against some groups in society. Another possible explanation is that media organizations are merely pursuing, packaging, and presenting the stories, shows, episodes, and so forth that are found to produce the greatest profits. In other words, it is possible that biases resulting from lawmaking and media activities are not intentional.

Still, even if biases or differential outcomes in policing, courts, and corrections are not intended, they nevertheless exit. And they are certainly not unforeseeable or unknown to elites. America's criminal justice system does disproportionately harm poor people of color, and especially poor young men of color. Further, the criminal justice system does fail to bring to justice those offenders who commit the worst crime in the nation, even as it pursues the supposedly most "serious" crimes by law.

Given these realities, a sound conclusion is that the criminal justice system in the real world falls vastly short of its ideal goals of reducing crime and doing justice. Further, an argument can be made that the criminal justice system in the real world fails to live up to the ideals set out in the Declaration of Independence and US Constitution. That is, we live in a nation where people are not equally able to pursue happiness, and where all people do not have equal rights and liberty. Further, life is not equally tranquil for all, people do not equally enjoy well-being, people are not equally defended, and there is no equal justice in the United States. These are undeniable truths based on the data, studies, and arguments of scholars presented within this book.

So What Can Be Done?

Given the realities outlined in this book, what can be done to make things better? That is, what steps can be taken in order to make criminal justice practice in the real-world more consistent with its ideal goals of reducing crime to protect the people from the acts committed by others that are most likely to harm them (i.e., crime control) and doing justice in order to assure that people's rights are protected and that people are treated equally by the criminal justice system (i.e., due process)?

Since the most significant problems of criminal justice—the primary sources of the injustices identified in the book—are in the law and the media, the most significant reforms of criminal justice must be directed at these institutions. Below I conclude the book with recommendations to reform the law, the media, as well as criminal justice practice more generally.

Recommendations about Reforming the Law and Crime

1. As the criminal law currently is not made by people who are representative of the population, it should not be a surprise that the criminal law does not serve the interests of most Americans. Thus, we need to make the law more representative by increasing the representativeness of lawmakers.

It should be easier for normal people to run for office, and they should not have to rely on private parties to pay for their campaigns or to engage in near-endless fundraising in order to gain and maintain a seat at the legislative table. We should also subsidize elections by providing equal resource support to each candidate running for major political office in order to reduce the impact of special interests on the legislative process. Further, serious efforts must be made to recruit a more diverse body of representatives, so that African Americans, Latinos, and other groups have a regular seat at the table as laws are planned, written, and implemented.

2. Lawmakers should pledge an oath to the citizens of the jurisdictions they represent to represent them rather than special interests. And all their meetings should be free and open to the public.

Our legal system functions, even if not intended, to serve the interests of the few instead of the many. White, wealthy, older men have a near monopoly on access to policy-makers, and corporations and other large, powerful groups use their connections to enact laws and rules that benefit them and harm citizens, especially relatively powerless groups such as people of color, the poor, and young people. Citizens should be able to demand that their lawmakers sign an oath, publicly available to anyone who wants to view it, to pledge to serve the people in the districts to which they represent. Finally, the business of government is the business of the people; as such their meetings should be free and open to the public.

3. We must make it easier to vote, pledge to get people to register to vote and show up on election days.

Any and all laws that make it more difficult to register to vote or to exercise your right to vote should be immediately repealed, and no new such laws should be enacted. Voter ID bills and similar laws that make it harder for currently underrepresented groups to participate in democracy cannot stand. Yes, voter fraud also cannot stand, but in the absence of actual widespread fraud, such laws do nothing but make it harder for certain underprivileged and disadvantaged people from being able to exercise their right to vote. Not only should these laws be struck down but citizens ought to have a much easier time getting to register to vote, vote, get to the polls, and have time to cast their ballots without standing in long lines.

4. We should encourage people to participate in the political process at all times, not just on election days.

Civics classes should be offered at all levels of schools in the public education system. Students should learn the value of participating in democracy at all levels, from voting, to writing letters and emails to representatives, to attending town hall meetings, to asking tough questions of representatives, to forming and utilizing interest groups and political action committees—across the whole spectrum of political participation. Workshops should be organized across the country to teach people how to register to vote, to show them where the voting places are, and to educate them about their choices of candidates. Voting is an important part of democracy, but political participation must be ongoing or else legislators lose touch with their constituents, thereby increasing the odds they will come to serve special interests instead of the people.

5. Laws should be passed to specify that corporations are not people.

Corporations are not people. Yet, they are made up of people and operated by people, and those people already have the rights to register to vote, vote, and participate in the political process in numerous ways, including by donating to their political party and candidate of choice. By giving such rights to corporations, we've empowered corporations to have more rights than actual human beings. This is dangerous largely because corporations serve no nation or principle (other than profit). The law has been perverted by corporate power, and if we want the law to serve the people again, it must be informed by the people and the people alone.

6. We must shift our focus from criminalization to harm reduction.

Americans and their leaders apparently think that we can stop people from engaging in harmful behaviors by criminalizing them. In fact, the most effective controls of bad behaviors are informal in nature—that is, instilled by families, peers, schools, and religious institutions rather than by police, courts, and corrections. Instead of criminalizing behaviors to reduce harms, we ought to encourage policies of *harm reduction*, aimed at preventing harms associated with behaviors such as drug use and abuse. Rather than punishing drug users, for example, treatment options ought to be available for those who develop drug abuse problems or addiction.

7. "Victimless" crimes such as drug use and possession ought to be decriminalized.

American police spend a disproportionate amount of time and resources on some "victimless" street crimes, called this not because they are truly harmless but because they are engaged in by consenting adults so that no one involved feels victimized. The best example is the war on drugs. Law enforcement focus on drug crimes and mandatory sentencing laws that call for longer minimum sentences for drug offenders explain the United States' unprecedented overreliance on imprisonment. Many of those we are incarcerating are first-time, low-level drug dealers or people who simply were found in possession of marijuana. Meanwhile, victims of other forms of harms are virtually ignored. Drug use can be a normal behavior that occurs in various recreational contexts, and government can decriminalize or even legalize drug use while simultaneously discouraging people from using drugs. Criminalizing drug use will not deter our children from experimenting. In fact, the illegal status of drugs is precisely what leads to much drug use, as well as a lot of crime and violence in the United States. Ideally, illegal drugs will be legalized and regulated for access and safety. States are taking the lead on this now, as Colorado and Washington legalized marijuana in order to reduce the enormous costs associated with the failing policy of drug prohibition.

8. The government must define crimes based on degree of harm caused.

To the degree that the criminal law is necessary, acts ought to be as serious as the harms they cause. This entails careful study (much of which has already been done and is discussed in this book), about which behaviors are really most likely to kill, injure, and result in property loss for Americans. Those behaviors that are most harmful ought to be called the most "serious" and should be the focus of law enforcement, courts, and corrections. Those that do the least harm clearly should *not* be our focus, and any means to prevent them that do not involve policies such as mass incarceration will save the country enormous resources now and into the future.

9. Create and administer a national source of data on elite deviance.

To discover more accurately how much damage is caused by these types of acts, our government must create a measure to gather valid data on acts of elite deviance, much as it does on street crime. If we are to shift our focus toward the acts that cause the most harm in society, we must first commit ourselves to collecting data on the acts. Creating a national source of data on elite deviance will be a major impetus toward national recognition that such acts are in fact "serious" crimes.

Recommendations about the Media

10. End corporate ownership of the media.

The media are supposed to operate as the "Fourth Estate"—they are supposed to be a check on the powerful to make sure they don't lose their focus on serving the people. Yet as long as corporations own the mainstream media, the media will serve the profit motive more than anything else, including telling the truth and providing objective, reliable information to the people on which they can make informed judgments about the world and public policy. Governments should work to disentangle media organizations from the corporations that own them and help develop new models of media ownership that better serve the public interest. Not-for-profit media organizations exist and we should embrace this model for our news sources.

11. Utilize, advertise, and celebrate independent media outlets.

One thing we can all do, including criminologists and their students, is use independent media outlets that are not privately owned and that operate with the interests of the people in mind. We ought to tell our colleagues and students and everyday people to turn off the television unless they are watching public television, or to at least boycott television shows and networks that inaccurately depict crime and criminal justice and harm the nation in so doing. Furthermore, we should make a point to get our news from reliable sources that seek to provide accurate and reliable information to people rather than make money by selling false and inaccurate information.

12. Educate the media about crime and criminal justice through planned workshops.

The nation's crime experts can no longer afford to sit on the sidelines, watching the media continue to get it wrong. We seem to know how and why the media are misinforming citizens about the true nature of crime and criminal justice in the United States. It is our responsibility to ensure that this misinformation stops, especially given that most Americans get their crime information from media outlets. Part of the educational effort would be aimed at separating mainstream media from corporate ownership.

13. Develop a network of contacts between criminal justice scholars and the media.

Every criminologist and criminal justice expert owes it to the nation to insert himself or herself into the media when stories about crime and criminal justice are discussed. We cannot afford to allow politicians and the police to be the primary sources of information about crime and criminal justice in the United States, given their clear biases in favor of the status quo, and because we study crime and criminal justice for a living.

14. Demand that the media cover crimes of elites instead of merely street crime.

The mainstream news media are highly focused on street crime, especially violent street crime committed by certain people under certain circumstances. We must demand that—as part of the truth-telling function of the news and in order to fulfill its purpose of providing information to the people—the media tell the whole story about crime in the United States. Since our perceptions of crime and criminal justice largely come from media accounts and depictions, it is essential that those accounts and depictions be accurate, and this means they must focus on those acts most likely to impact and harm citizens—elite deviance.

15. Insist that the media get it right by reducing consumer demand for sleazy news.

We must encourage citizens to pursue alternative forms of education and news rather than crime shows and sensational news. Research shows that crime entertainment and news promote a "siege mentality" among some viewers, who become more likely to stay inside and to fear the poor and people of color rather than wanting to help them achieve legitimate success. The news media should develop and broadcast clear statements reflecting their intention to cease broadcasting sleazy, sensationalized crime stories.

Other Recommendations

16. Our government should write clear statements reflecting the goals of American criminal justice.

Given the importance of doing justice to Americans, due process values should be emphasized over crime control values. At every step of the criminal justice process, we must ensure that every individual's Constitutional rights are protected and that innocent people are not wrongfully subjected to criminal justice processes. In other words, we must act in ways consistent with the ideal of "innocent until proven guilty." Of course the government has a vested interest in reducing crime to achieve our crime control values; yet, the focus cannot remain universally on street crime.

17. Our government should develop clearly stated policies of government aimed at not discriminating on the basis of race, social class, and gender.

If justice is to be blind, and thus fair, we must first state clearly that we will not, under any circumstances, tolerate discrimination based on factors such as race, class, and gender. These values should be codified and exhibited by government for all to see. Police departments, courts, and correctional agencies must write and enforce these statements, but so too should legislators and other policy-makers since, as shown in this book, the most significant source of bias in the US comes from within institutions such as the law and media.

18. The government should also make a commitment to evaluate the performance of our criminal justice agencies at regular periods of time, in order to assess how well we are achieving our stated goals.

How can we know how well we are doing unless we assess our performance carefully? Evaluation can be relatively inexpensive. Given the importance of the goal of providing justice, an evaluation of the criminal justice system's performance on a regular basis is warranted. Criminologists and criminal justice experts should be involved in this regular evaluation and policy-makers must pledge to create and implement reforms as needed. Not only must we assess out goals of being fair and reducing street crime, we must also assess our performance toward reducing acts of elite deviance.

19. To be more effective at reducing crime, our government must encourage a fundamental shift away from punitiveness toward prevention, treatment, and restoration.

Conditions in communities and society that produce criminality must be eliminated, sick people who commit crimes must be treated, and both victims of crime and criminal offenders must work together toward restoration of each to noncriminal and nonvictim status. For this to happen, we must commit ourselves to forgiveness rather than vengeance. Forgiveness is the only mechanism proven to produce peace for victims of crime. Thinking outside the box allows us to imagine forms of community and restorative justice, staffed by normal people trained in conflict and dispute resolution and mediation of common problems. The conservative crime control policies of mass incarceration, capital punishment, and wars on drugs and terrorism have largely failed. It is time to do something different. Continuing to invest in policies that consistently fail and that disproportionately ham the least advantaged people in society is unjust.

20. Our government must shift its focus from criminal justice responses to violence toward medical, public-health models to treat violence as an epidemic in the United States.

Even though property crime is far more common than violent crime, many citizens see violence as the main problem in the United States when it comes to crime. Crime rates are not exceedingly high relative to other similar countries. Yet we suffer from alarmingly high rates of violent victimization, especially murder. And when you add on violent deaths and injuries produced by elite deviance, we have a true epidemic of deadly crime in the United States. We must shift our focus away from criminal justice approaches toward public-health approaches to reducing violence by treating violence as the epidemic that it is. This would entail identifying the causes of these acts and eliminating those causes.

21. Overall, Americans must insist that politics be taken out of crime and criminal justice issues.

Politicians have created cynicism in Americans by using partial facts and distorted truths about crime that have made developing sensible policy impossible. Recall the Willie Horton example discussed in the book. Horton had been out on furlough eight times in Massachusetts without committing any apparent criminal acts. On his ninth release, he committed a rape and aggravated assault. The 1988 presidential candidate, George H.W. Bush, used the image of Horton as evidence that his opponent, Michael Dukakis (who was then governor of Massachusetts), was soft on crime. This was, at the least, dishonest of the Bush campaign; at worst, it was deceitful and racist. Politicians promote criminal justice policies that they should know do not and cannot work, and Americans and our media should call them on it rather than giving politicians a free pass to say whatever they want.

22. A rational system of planned change should be used to reduce crime in the United States.

Currently, criminal justice policy seems to be made based on subjective decisions, characterized by unreliability and bias. Many, if not most American crime control policies simply do not work. The conservative crime control approach, which has traditionally involved more police, more prisons, and swifter, harsher punishment, has been a massive and expensive failure. This is because it is based on a flawed ideology that is uninformed by empirical evidence about what works to reduce crime. Criminologists have reached exciting conclusions about what works to reduce crime, and lawmakers must utilize this information as they create and implement policies. **Planned change** is aimed at carefully studying crime problems and responding to them with carefully planned efforts to address the root causes of criminality. This is a very promising alternative to quick-fix, feel-good, short-term approaches to reducing crime in the United States.

23. The nation's crime experts must strive to educate citizens about injustice in American criminal justice and about their true risks of victimization.

It is highly unlikely that many Americans are aware of how the criminal law is biased against particular groups of people in the United States. Given our devotion to justice, it is likely that when Americans become aware of injustice, they will revolt against it and demand change, as they did during the civil rights movement. Victims of other forms of culpable harmful acts, such as victims of elite deviance, often do not know they have been victimized or when they do, often do not know where to turn for help. If we truly want to stop victimization, we must make sure people know they are being victimized, and then increase and clarify their options for law enforcement assistance.

24. Police, courts, and corrections must be more focused on acts of elite deviance.

In order to prevent acts of white-collar and corporate crime, as well as to provide justice for victims of such acts, it is essential that those who commit these acts be apprehended, tried, and punished for their wrongdoing. Even to the degree we try *not* to rely so heavily in criminal justice for crime prevention, we also cannot continue to let people get away with the kinds of acts identified and discussed in the book, including those that nearly severely damaged and nearly wrecked the entire economy.

25. Organize the economy to serve the interests of American citizens.

The US capitalist economy does not operate in the interests of all American citizens equally. Yes, we benefit enormously from it, but it is designed first and foremost to help powerful individuals and corporations; this is largely due to the close connections between lawmakers and corporate interests. As the law is made by people more representative of the population and is voted for by people more representative of the population, the law will come to better represent the interests of all the people. Further, so too will the economy, because polices such as deregulation will be replaced with sensible regulation (to assure public, consumer, and worker safety). Further, policymakers can institute policies that will actually serve citizens, workers, and their families by providing wages that allow them to pay their bills and care for their families.

Out-of-Class Activity:
Identify groups working to promote the kinds of changes outlined in this chapter. What are they doing to help bring about change in the US? What can you do to help?

Conclusion

The criminal justice system is largely one characterized by failure. It does not meaningfully reduce crime (especially those crimes that most harm us), and it is unfair in many ways and therefore unjust. Further, it falls far short of the ideals laid out in the Declaration of Independence and US Constitution. Therefore, it is vital to adopt reforms like those laid out in this chapter in order to make criminal justice in the real-world match the ideal we expect of it.

The most needed and thus most important reforms address problems within the criminal law and the media, two institutions that create serious problems in criminal justice practice. In essence, the reforms offered aimed to make the law and the media better serve the interests of the people of the United States.

The reforms will not likely be rapidly accepted and implemented in the United States. Considering past efforts by criminologists and criminal justice scholars to make criminal justice processes more just, it may be unwise to expect many of these reforms to be adopted in the immediate future. Yet change is possible, and, on the basis of the evidence presented in this book, change is necessary.

Most change is gradual, but gradualism can lull us all to sleep. As Americans, we must insist that the criminal justice system effectively reduce crime and do justice. We must also work to assure the values we espoused in the Declaration of Independence and the US Constitution are enshrined and protected in the law for us all.

Bryan Vila (1997) has pointed out how ironic it is that as knowledge about what works to reduce crime becomes clearer, we live in a time when effective or promising efforts are less likely to be implemented. His research suggests that the media, politicians, and public impatience will be significant barriers to effective change. A team approach is required, based on consensus building between the media, politicians, and the public, to bring about effective change. And you, the reader of this book, have a tremendous opportunity to work from within agencies of criminal justice to bring about positive change. What ideas can you come up with help create the changes needed to make American criminal justice more just and more effective? Further, how can we assure that the changes that have been suggested are actually pursued?

Key Terms

- **Age-Crime Curve**: The age-crime curve depicts the relationship between age and crime, and shows that the risk of street crime tends to peak between the ages of 15 and 25 years of age.

- **Aging Out Phenomenon:** The aging out phenomenon is when people get older, mature, and desist from committing street crime.
- **Arrests:** An arrest is when a person suspected of a crime is taken into custody by police and is not free to go, pending charges.
- **Bail:** Bail is the sum of money paid by a defendant to the court upon release to assure his or her return to the court to resolve his or her case.
- **Capital Punishment or the Death Penalty:** Capital punishment or the death penalty is the ultimate sanction — the taking of a human life by the government — for the ultimate crime of murder.
- **Charging:** Charging is the decision made by prosecutors to either press charges or not and also which charges to press.
- **Discretion:** Discretion is the ability of an official to act or not act according to their own professional judgment, based on their own experience.
- **Federal Courts:** Federal courts have jurisdiction over criminal laws at the federal level of government, meaning they hear cases that are alleged to have violated the criminal laws of the US government.
- **Federal Prisons:** Federal prisons are run by the US government, and they hold people convicted of serious federal crimes that call for sentences of more than one year of incarceration.
- **Indigent:** Indigent means a person cannot afford a private attorney and thus he or she is appointed a public defender or contracted attorney.
- **Jails:** Jails are correctional facilities operated by county governments that hold people awaiting trails and those convicted of relatively minor crimes that lead to sentences of less than one year of incarceration.
- **Minority Threat or Racial Threat or Social Threat Hypothesis:** The minority threat or racial threat or social threat hypothesis refers to the idea that police officials devote more resources to areas inhabited by populations that are perceived to be dangerous or threatening to the social order.
- **Peremptory Challenges:** A peremptory challenge is when a potential juror is removed from a jury pool without a stated cause.
- **Planned Change:** Planned change is creating carefully considered programs and policies that aim to reduce a social problem, based on evidence by people qualified to create them.
- **Plea Bargaining:** Plea bargaining is an informal process whereby a prosecutor and defense attorney agree to charges and a sentence without a trial.
- **Stake in Conformity:** A stake in conformity is a reason to abide by the law, to not commit crime.
- **State Courts:** State courts have jurisdiction over criminal laws at the state level of government, meaning they hear cases that are alleged to have violated the criminal laws of states.
- **State Prisons:** State prisons are run by state governments, and they hold people convicted of serious state crimes that call for sentences of more than one year of incarceration.
- **Stop and Frisk:** A stop and frisk is a search by the police that seeks to ascertain if a person is carrying drugs and/or weapons and is meant to be conducted for public safety.

Discussion Questions

1) Illustrate how innocent bias is seen in criminal justice, including police, courts, and corrections.
2) What is an arrest?
3) Which groups are most and least likely to be arrested? Why?
4) What is the age-crime curve? What is the aging out phenomenon?
5) How does a stake in conformity stop people from committing crime?
6) How would the age-crime curve be different if we included corporate crime as well?
7) Identify and discuss contextual bias in policing.
8) What is a stop and frisk? What is the controversy in this policy in New York City?
9) What is discretion? How can it be abused?
10) What is the minority threat or racial threat or social threat hypothesis?
11) Compare and contrast state and federal courts.
12) Which groups are most and least likely to be convicted? Why?
13) What does the term indigent mean?
14) Define the terms bail, charging, and plea bargaining.
15) What is a peremptory challenge? How does race play a role in peremptory challenges?
16) Identify and discuss contextual bias in courts.
17) Compare jails with state and federal prisons.
18) Who is most likely to be in jail and in prison? Why?
19) What is capital punishment or the death penalty?
20) What role do race, class, and gender play in capital punishment? Why?
21) Summarize the main argument of the book.
22) What is planned change?
23) Which of the proposed reforms to make criminal justice more effective and fair do you agree with? Why?

References

Aaltonen, M., Kivivuori, J., & Martikainen, P. (2011). Social determinants of crime in a welfare state: Do they still matter? *Acta Sociologica, 54*(2), 161–181.

Acker, J., & Redlich, A. (2011). *Wrongful Conviction: Law, Science, and Policy*. Durham, NC: Carolina Academic Press.

Alexander, M. (2012). *The New Jim Crow: Mass Incarceration in the Age of Colorblindness*. New York: The New Press.

Almond, P. (2008). Public perceptions of work-related fatality cases. *The British Journal of Criminology, 48*(4), 448–467.

Angell, M.(2005). *The Truth About the Drug Companies: How They Deceive Us and What to Do About It*. New York: Random House.

Arnold, C. (2013). After five years, why so few charges in financial crisis? *NPR*, July 26. Retrieved July 30, 2013 from: http://www.npr.org/2013/07/26/205866019/few-on-wall-street-have-been-prosecuted-for-financial-crisis?sc=17&f=1001.

Associated Press (2013). Ex-Massey Energy CEO accused of warning miners. Retrieved May 15, 2013 from: http://www.timesdispatch.com/business/economy/ex-massey-energy-ceo-accused-of-warning-miners/article_d325fec9-e175-500e-9f55-0f9683cb6f80.html.

Bagdikian, B. (2004). *The New Media Monopoly*. Boston, MA: Beacon Press.

Bamford, J. (2005). *A Pretext for War: 9/11, Iraq, and the Abuse of America's Intelligence Agencies*. New York, NY: Anchor.

Barak, G., Leighton, P., & Flavin, J. (2010). *Class, Race, Gender, and Crime: The Social Realities of Justice in America*. Lanham, MA: Rowman & Littlefield.

Barboza, D. (2007). Why lead in toy paint? It's cheaper. Retrieved September 7, 2007 from: http://www.nytimes.com/2007/09/11/business/worldbusiness/11lead.html.

Barkan, S., & Bryjak, G. (2008). *Myths and Realities of Crime and Justice: What Every American Should Know*. New York, NY: Jones & Bartlett.

Barker, S. (2012). How nonprofits spend millions on elections and call it public welfare. August 18. Retrieved March 13, 2013 from: http://www.propublica.org/article/how-nonprofits-spend-millions-on-elections-and-call-it-public-welfare.

Beckett, K., Nyrop, K., & Pfingst, L. (2006). Race, drugs, and policing: Understanding disparities in drug delivery arrests. *Criminology, 44*(1), 105–137.

Beckett, K., Nyrop, K., Pfingst, L., & Bowen, M. (2005). Drug use, drug possession arrests, and the question of race: Lessons from Seattle. *Social Problems, 52*(3), 419–441.

Beckett, K., & Sasson, T. (2003). *The Politics of injustice: Crime and punishment in America* (2nd Ed.). Thousand Oaks, CA: Sage.

Beckett, K., & Sasson, T. (2000). *The Politics of Injustice: Crime and Punishment in America*. Belmont, CA: Sage.

Belknap, J. (2007). *The Invisible Woman: Gender, Crime, and Justice*. Belmont, CA: Wadsworth.

Berkes, H. (2013). Report: W.Va. fails to enforce new regs designed to prevent mine explosions. *NPR*, February 4. Retrieved May 15, 2013 from: http://www.npr.org/blogs/thetwo-way/2013/02/04/171085642/report-w-va-fails-to-enforce-new-regs-designed-to-prevent-mine-explosions.

Berkes, H. (2011). Union: W.Va. mine disaster was 'industrial homicide.' *NPR*, October 25. Retrieved May 15, 2013 from: http://www.npr.org/blogs/thetwo-way/2011/10/25/141681614/union-w-va-mine-disaster-was-industrial-homicide.

Bishop, D. (2006). The myth that harsh punishments reduce juvenile crime. In R. Bohm & J. Walker (Eds.), *Demystifying crime and criminal justice*. Los Angeles, CA: Roxbury.

Bjornstrom, E. E. S., Kaufman, R. L., Peterson, R. D., & Slater, M. D. (2010). Race and ethnic representations of lawbreakers and victims in crime news: A national study of television coverage. *Social Problems, 57*(2), 269–293.

Blake, J. (2012). Return of the welfare queen. *CNN*, January 23. Retrieved February 19, 2013 from: http://www.cnn.com/2012/01/23/politics/welfare-queen.

Bohm, R., & Walker, J. (2012). *Demystifying Crime and Criminal Justice*. New York, NY: Oxford University Press.

Britton, N. (2000). Race and policing. *The British Journal of Criminology, 40*(4), 639–658.

Brody, H. (2007). *Hooked: Ethics, the Medical Profession, and the Pharmaceutical Industry*. New York: Rowman & Littlefield.

Brody, R., & Kiehl, K. (2010). From white-collar crime to red-collar crime. *Journal of Financial Crime, 17*(3), 351–364.

Butler, P. (2013). Poor people lose: Gideon and the critique of rights. *Yale Law Journal*, June, 2176.

Calavita, K., & Pontell, H. (1990). "Heads I win, tails you lose": Deregulation, crime, and crisis in the savings and loan industry. *Crime and Delinquency* 36(3): 309–341.

Casey, L. (2012). The Role of Money & Incumbency in 2009–2010 State Elections. Retrieved January 28, 2013 from: http://www.followthemoney.org/press/ReportView.phtml?r=489.

Cavender, G., & Bond-Maupin, L. (1993). Fear and loathing on reality television: An analysis of *America's Most Wanted* and *Unsolved Mysteries*. *Sociological Inquiry, 63*(3): 20–30.

Center for American Progress (2013). ALEC: Aiding ALEC & spinning disinformation in the states. Retrieved April 5, 2013 from: http://www.sourcewatch.org/index.php/Center_for_American_Progress.

Center for Media and Public Affairs (2002). Scandalous business: TV news coverage of the corporate scandals. Retrieved September 21, 2009 from: http://www.cmpa.com/files/media_monitor/02sepoct.pdf.

Center for Public Integrity (2013). States of disclosure. Retrieved January 28, 2013 from: http://www.publicintegrity.org/accountability/waste-fraud-and-abuse/states-disclosure.

Center for Responsive Politics (2013). Influencing & lobbying. 527 organizations. Retrieved March 13, 2013 from: http://www.opensecrets.org/527s/index.php.

Center from Responsive Politics (2013). Influence & Lobbying. Lobbying database. Retrieved January 28, 2013 from: http://www.opensecrets.org/lobby/index.php.

Center from Responsive Politics (2013). Influence & Lobbying. What is a PAC?. Retrieved January 28, 2013 from: http://www.opensecrets.org/pacs/pacfaq.php.

Center from Responsive Politics (2013). Politicians & elections. Donor demographics. Retrieved January 28, 2013 from: http://www.opensecrets.org/overview/donordemographics.php.

Center from Responsive Politics (2013). Politicians & elections. Incumbent advantage. Retrieved January 28, 2013 from: http://www.opensecrets.org/overview/incumbs.php.

Center for Responsive Politics (2013). Influencing & Lobbying. Tobacco. Retrieved March 8, 2013 from: http://www.opensecrets.org/industries/indus.php?ind=A02.

Center for Responsive Politics (2013). Politicians & elections. Stats at a glance. Retrieved January 28, 2013 from: http://www.opensecrets.org/overview/index.php.

Center for Responsive Politics (2013). Influence & lobbying. Revolving door. Retrieved March 28, 2013 from: http://www.opensecrets.org/revolving/index.php.

Centers for Disease Control and Prevention (2013). Smoking & tobacco use. Fast facts. Retrieved March 8, 2013 from: http://www.cdc.gov/tobacco/data_statistics/fact_sheets/fast_facts/.

Chermak, S. (1995). *Victims in the News: Crime and the American Media.* Boulder, CO: Westview Press.

Chermak, S. (1994). Crime in the news media: A refined understanding of how crime becomes news. In G. Barak (Ed.), *Media, Process, and Social Construction of Crime: Studies in News Making Criminology.* New York: Garland.

Chermak, S., & Chapman, N. (2007). Predicting crime story salience: A replication. *Journal of Criminal Justice, 35*(4), 351.

Chesney-Lind, M. (2006). Patriarchy, crime, and justice: Feminist Criminology in an era of backlash. *Feminist Criminology, 1*(1), 6–26.

Chesney-Lind, M., & Pasko, L. (2004). *The Female Offender: Girls, Women, and Crime.* Thousand Oaks, CA: Sage.

CNN (2007). FDA panel: No cold medicines to children under 6. Retrieved January 31, 2008 from: http://www.cnn.com/2007/HEALTH/10/19/coldmed.fda/index.html.

Cole, D. (2009). *Torture Memos: Rationalizing the Unthinkable.* New York, NY: Free Press.

Cole, D. & Dempsey, J. (2006). *Terrorism and the Constitution: Sacrificing Civil Liberties in the Name of National Security.* New York, NY: New Press.

Common Cause (2013). Buying Influence: How the American Legislative Exchange Council 27 Uses Corporate-Funded "Scholarships" to Send Lawmakers on Trips with Corporate Lobbyists. Retrieved April 15, 2013 from: http://www.commoncause.org/atf/cf/%7Bfb3c17e2-cdd1-4df6-92be-bd4429893665%7D/BUYING%20INFLUENCE%20-%20ALEC%20SCHOLARSHIPS%20REPORT%20-%2026OCT2012%20-%20FINAL.PDF.

Common Cause (2013). Legislating Under the Influence: Money, Power, and the American Legislative Exchange Council. Retrieved April 15, 2013 from: http://www.common cause.org/atf/cf/%7BFB3C17E2-CDD1-4DF6-92BE-BD4429893665%7D/ MoneyPowerAndALEC.pdf.

Common Cause (2013). Money in politics. ALEC. Retrieved April 4, 2013 from: http:// www.commoncause.org/site/pp.asp?c=dkLNK1MQIwG&b=7743229.

Consumer Product Safety Commission (2013). CPSC Overview. Retrieved March 15, 2013from http://www.cpsc.gov/about/about.html.

Contreras, R. (2013). *The Stickup Kids: Race, Drugs, Violence, and the American Dream.* Berkley, CA: University of California Press.

Crista, G. (2007). *Generation Rx: How Prescription Drugs Are Altering American Lives, Minds, and Bodies.* New York: Mariner Books.

Critser, G. (2004) *Fat Land: How Americans Became the Fattest People in the World.* New York: Houghton Mifflin.

Cullen, F., Cavender, G., Maakestad, W., & Benson, M. (2006). *Corporate Crime Under Attack: The Fight to Criminalize Business Violence.* Cincinnati, OH: Anderson, p. 21.

Cullen, F., Hartman, J., & Jonson, C. (2009). Bad guys: Why the public supports punishing white-collar offenders. *Crime, Law and Social Change, 51*(1), 31–44.

Dansky, K. (2012). Did President Obama just open the window to smart criminal justice reform? *ACLU Blog of Rights,* December 21. Retrieved February 19, 2012 from: http://www.aclu.org/blog/criminal-law-reform-prisoners-rights/did-president-obama-just-open-window-smart-criminal.

Death Penalty Information Center (2013). National statistics on the death penalty and race. Retrieved November 19, 2013 from: http://deathpenaltyinfo.org/race-death-row-inmates-executed-1976#defend.

Democracy Now (2011). Massey Energy guilty: West Virginia probe finds coal giant systemically failed to comply with law. May 23. Retrieved May 14, 2013 from: http:// www.democracynow.org/2011/5/23/massey_energy_guilty_west_virginia_probe.

Desmond, M., & Valdez, N. (2013). Unpolicing the urban poor: Consequences of third-party policing for inner-city women. *American Sociological Review, 78*(1), 117.

Dixon, T. (2007). Black criminals and white officers: The effects of racially misrepresenting law breakers and law defenders on television news. *Media Psychology, 10,* 270–291.4

Dixon, T. (2008). Crime News and Racialized Beliefs: Understanding the Relationship Between Local News Viewing and Perceptions of African Americans and Crime. *Journal of Communication, 58*(1), 106–125.

Dixon, T., & Azocar, C. (2007). Priming crime and activating blackness: Understanding the psychological impact of the overrepresentation of blacks as lawbreakers on television news. *Journal of Communication, 57,* 229–253.5

Dixon, T., Azocar, C., & Casas, M. (2003). The portrayal of race and crime on television network news. *Journal of Broadcasting & Electronic Media, 47*(4), 498–523.

Doerner, J., & Demuth, S. (2010). The independent and joint effects of Race/Ethnicity, gender, and age on sentencing outcomes in U.S. federal courts. *Justice Quarterly, 27*(1), 1.

Donoghue, K. (2002). Casualties of war: Criminal drug law enforcement and its special costs for the poor. *New York University Law Review, December,* 1776–1804.

Dowler, K. (2004). Comparing American and Canadian local television crime stories: A content analysis. *Canadian Journal of Criminology and Criminal Justice, 46*(5), 573–596.

Duke, S., & Gross, A. (1993). *America's Longest War*. New York, NY: GP Putnam's Sons.

Easton, D. (1953). *The Political System*. New York: Knopf.

Eichenwald, C. (2005). *Conspiracy of Fools: A True Story*. Portland, OR: Broadway Books.

Einat, T., & Herzog, S. (2011). Understanding the relationship between perceptions of crime seriousness and recommended punishment: An exploratory comparison of adults and adolescents. *Criminal Justice Studies, 24*(1), 3.

Ellis, C., & Stimson, J. (2011). *Ideology in America*. New York, NY: Cambridge University Press.

Evans, S. & Lundman, R. (1983). Newspaper coverage of corporate price-fixing. *Criminology 21*, 529–541.

Evers, J. (2006). Computer crime costs $67 billion, FBI says. News.com. Retrieved July 30, 2007 from: http://news.com.com/Computer+crime+costs+67+billion,+FBI+says/2100-7349_3-6028946.html.

Federal Bureau of Investigation. Murder. Retrieved August 1, 2007 from: http://www.fbi.gov/ucr/05cius/offenses/violent_crime/murder_homicide.html.

Federal Trade Commission (2001). Facts for Business. Frequently Asked Advertising Questions: A Guide for Small Business. Retrieved November 8, 2007 from: http://www.ftc.gov/bcp/conline/pubs/buspubs/ad-faqs.shtm.

Federal Trade Commission (1983). FTC Policy Statement on Deception. Retrieved November 8, 2007 from: http://www.ftc.gov/bcp/policystmt/ad-decept.htm.

Federal Trade Commission (1980). FTC Policy Statement on Unfairness. Retrieved November 8, 2007 from: http://www.ftc.gov/bcp/policystmt/ad-unfair.htm.

Felson, M. (2002). *Crime and Everyday Life* (3rd Ed.). Beverly Hills, CA: Sage.

Flock, E. (2012). Pollster: Only 37 percent of Americans following election. *US News,* June 20. Retrieved December 20, 2012 from: http://www.usnews.com/news/blogs/washington-whispers/2012/06/20/pollster-only-37-percent-of-americans-following-election-closely.

Frase, R. (2009). What explains persistent racial disproportionality in Minnesota's prison and jail populations? *Crime and Justice, 38*, 201, 263.

Freeden, M. (2003). *Ideology: A Very Short Introduction*. New York, NY: Oxford University Press.

Friedman, L. (1993). *Crime and Punishment in American History*. New York, NY: Basic Books.

Friedrichs, D. (2006). *Trusted Criminals: White Collar Crime in Contemporary Society* (3rd Ed.). Belmont, CA: Wadsworth.

Friedrichs, D.(1995). *Trusted Criminals: White Collar Crime in Contemporary Society*. Belmont, CA: Wadsworth, p. 70.

Friedrichs, D. (2006). The myth that white-collar crime is only about financial loss. In R. Bohm & J. Walker (Eds.), *Demystifying crime and criminal justice*. Los Angeles, CA: Roxbury, p. 20.

Gest, T. (2001). *Crime & Politics: Big Government's Erratic Campaign for Law and Order*. New York: Oxford University Press.

Gillens, M. (2012). *Affluence and Influence: Economic Inequality and Political Power in America*. Princeton, NJ: Princeton University Press.

Gilliam, F., & Iyengar, S. (2000). Prime suspects: The influence of local television news on the viewing public. *American Journal of Political Science, 44*, 560–573.

Ginsberg, B., Lowi, T., Weir, M., & Tolbert, C. (2013). *We the People: An Introduction to American Politics*. New York: WW Norton.

Gioia, D. (1992). Pinto fires and personal Ethics: A script analysis of missed opportunities. *Journal of Business Ethics* 15(5/6): 379–389.

Glasberg, D. & Skidmore, D. (1998). The role of the state in the criminogenesis of corporate crime: A case study of the savings and loan crisis. *Social Science Quarterly* 79(1): 110–128.

Governor's Independent Investigation Panel (2011). Upper Big Branch: Report to the Governor. Retrieved May 13, 2013 from: http://www.nttc.edu/programs&projects/minesafety/disasterinvestigations/upperbigbranch/toc.asp.

Graedon, J., & Graedon, T. (2007). Cold-remedy ads fool parents. *The News & Observer*, December 23.

Green, E. G. T., Staerklé, C., & Sears, D. O. (2006). Symbolic racism and whites' attitudes towards punitive and preventive crime policies. *Law and Human Behavior, 30*(4), 435–54.

Hanson, J., & Jost, J. (2012). *Ideology, Psychology, and Law*. New York, NY: Oxford University Press.

Harrigan, J. (2000). *Empty Dreams, Empty Pockets: Class and Bias in American Politics*. New York: Addison-Wesley Longman.

Harrigan, J. (2000). *Empty Dreams, Empty Pockets: Class and Bias in American Politics*. New York: Addison-Wesley Longman, p. 120.

Healthytoys.org (2008). Findings. Retrieved January 31, 2008 from: http://www.healthytoys.org/about.findings.php.

Herman, E., & Chomsky, N. (2002). *Manufacturing Consent: The Political Economy of Mass Media*. New York: Pantheon Books.

Hess, S. (1981). *The Washington Reporters*. Washington, DC: Brookings Institution.

Holtfreter, K., Piquero, N., & Piquero, A. (2008). And justice for all? investigators' perceptions of punishment for fraud perpetrators. *Crime, Law and Social Change, 49*(5), 397–412.

Holyoke, T. (2011). *Competitive Interests: Competition and Compromise in American Interest Group Politics*. Washington, DC: Georgetown University Press.

HoSang, D., LaBennett, O., & Pulido, L. (2011). *Racial Formation in the Twenty-First Century*. Berkeley, CA: University of California Press.

Human Rights Watch (2004). *Blood, Sweat, and Fear: Workers' Rights in U.S. Meat and Poultry Plants*. Retrieved January 31, 2008 from: http://www.hrw.org/reports/2005/usa0105/usa0105.pdf.

Hurwitz, J., & Peffley, M. (2010). *Justice in America: The Separate Realities of Blacks and Whites*. Cambridge, MA: Cambridge University Press.

Ifill, G. (1992). The 1992 campaign: New York; Clinton admits experiment with marijuana in 1960's. *New York Times*, March 30. Retrieved February 12, 2013 from: http://

www.nytimes.com/1992/03/30/us/the-1992-campaign-new-york-clinton-admits-experiment-with-marijuana-in-1960-s.html.

Inside Politics (2013). Candidate ads: 1988 George Bush "Revolving Door." Retrieved February 12, 2013 from: http://www.insidepolitics.org/ps111/candidateads.html.

Jarrell, M., & Ozymy, J. (2012). Real crime, real victims: Environmental crime victims and the crime victims' rights act (CVRA). *Crime, Law and Social Change, 58*(4), 373–389.

Johnson, C. (2013). 50 years after key case, problems defending the poor persist. *NPR*, March 15. Retrieved August 1, 2013 from: http://www.npr.org/2013/03/15/174331300/50-years-after-key-case-problems-defending-the-poor-persist.

Johnson, J., Bushman, B., & Dovidio, J. (2008). Support for harmful treatment and reduction of empathy toward blacks: "Remnants" of stereotype activation involving Hurricane Katrina and "Lil' Kim." *Journal of Experimental Social Psychology, 44*(6), 1506–1513.

Johnson, K., & Dixon, T. (2008). Change and the Illusion of Change: Evolving Portrayals of Crime News and Blacks in a Major Market. *Howard Journal of Communications, 19*(2), 125–143.

Jones, C. (2012). Confronting race in the criminal justice system. *Criminal Justice, 27*(2), 10–15.

Justice Policy Institute (2008). Clinton crime agenda ignores proven methods for reducing crime. April 14. Retrieved February 11, 2013 from http://www.uslaw.com/library/Criminal_Law/Clinton_Crime_Agenda_Ignores_Proven_Methods_Reducing_Crime.php?item=113235.

Kappeler, V., & Potter, G. (2004). *The Mythology of Crime and Criminal Justice.* Long Grove, IL: Waveland.

Karmen, A. (2006). *Crime Victims: An Introduction to Victimology* (6th Ed.). Belmont, CA: Wadsworth.

Klaidman, D. (2012). *Kill or Capture: The War on Terror and the Soul of the Obama Presidency.* New York, NY: Houghton Mifflin Harcourt.

Kliff, D., Mathews, D., & Plumer, B. (2013). The 2012 election in charts. *Washington Post Wonk Blog.* November 7, 2012. Retrieved January 28, 2013 from: http://www.washingtonpost.com/blogs/wonkblog/wp/2012/11/07/the-2012-election-in-charts/.

Kochel, T., Wilson, D., & Mastrofski, S. (2011). Effect of suspect race on officers' arrest decisions. *Criminology, 49*(2), 473.

Krajicek, D. (1998). *Scooped! Media Miss Real Story on Crime While Chasing Sex, Sleaze, and Celebrities.* New York: Columbia University Press.

Lab, S. (2004). *Crime Prevention: Approaches, Practices, and Evaluations.* New York: Elsevier.

LaRussa, C. (2010). Tobacco: Background. Retrieved March 8, 2013 from: http://www.opensecrets.org/industries/background.php?cycle=2010&ind=A02.

Lasswell, H. (1936). *Politics: Who Gets What, When, How.* New York: McGraw-Hill.

Law, J. (2006). *Big Pharma: Exposing the Global Healthcare Agenda.* New York: Carroll & Graf.

Lemaitre, R. (2012). Obama Drug Policy: Reforming the Criminal Justice System, White House, December 5. Retrieved February 19, 2013 from: http://www.whitehouse.gov/blog/2011/12/05/obama-drug-policy-reforming-criminal-justice-system.

Lithwick, D. (2013). What's the matter with North Carolina? *Slate*, July 24. Retrieved July 27, 2013 from: http://www.slate.com/articles/news_and_politics/jurisprudence/2013/07/north_carolina_s_voter_id_law_is_the_worst_in_the_country.html.

Loewen, J. (2007). *Lies My Teacher Told Me: Everything Your American History Textbook Got Wrong.* New York, NY: Touchstone.

Lynch, M. J. (2000). J. Phillippe Rushton on crime: An examination and critique of the explanation of crime and race. *Social Pathology, 6*(3), 228–244.

Lynch, M., Stretesky, P., & Hammond, P. (2000). Media coverage of chemical crimes, Hillsborough County, Florida, 1987–97. *The British Journal of Criminology, 40*(1), 112–126.

Mallicoat, S. (2011). *Gender and Crime: A Text/Reader.* Belmont, CA: Sage.

Marion, N., & Oliver, W. (2011). *Public Policy of Crime and Criminal Justice.* Upper Saddler River, NJ: Prentice Hall.

Mastro, D., Lapinski, M., Kopacz, M., & Behm-Morawitz, E. (2009). The influence of exposure to depictions of race and crime in TV news on viewer's social judgments. *Journal of Broadcasting & Electronic Media, 53*(4), 615–635.

McChesney, R. (2004). *The Problem of the Media.* New York: Monthly Review Press.

McLean, B., & Elkind, P. (2003). *Smartest Guys in the Room: The Amazing Rise and Scandalous Fall of Enron.* Portfolio Publishers.

McLean, B., & Nocera, J. (2010). *All the Devils are Here: The Hidden History of the Financial Crisis.* New York, NY: Portfolio.

McMullan, J. (2006). News, truth, and the recognition of corporate crime. *Canadian Journal of Criminology and Criminal Justice, 48*(6), 905–939.

Merriam-Webster (2012). Entry for "politics." Retrieved December 10, 2012 from: http://www.merriam-webster.com/dictionary/policy?show=0&t=1355155172.

Merriam-Webster's Dictionary (2013). Entry for "myth." Retrieved January 13, 2013 from: http://www.merriam-webster.com/dictionary/myth.

Montross Jr., W., & Mulvaney, P. (2009). Virtue and vice: Who will report on the failings of the American criminal justice system? *Stanford Law Review, 61*(6), 1429–1461.

Mother Jones (1977). What's your life worth? Retrieved January 31, 2008 from: http://www.motherjones.com/news/feature/1977/09/worth.html.

Moynihan, R. & Cassels, A (2006). *Selling Sickness: How the World's Biggest Pharmaceutical Companies Are Turning Us All Into Patients.*New York: Nation Books.

Muraskin, R., & Domash, S. (2007). *Crime and the Media: Headlines vs. Reality.* Upper Saddle River, NJ: Prentice Hall.

National Association for the Advancement of Colored People (2013). Death Row USA, Spring 2013. NAACP Criminal Justice Project. Retrieved November 19, 2013 from: http://www.deathpenaltyinfo.org/documents/DRUSASpring2013.pdf.

National Institute on Money in State Politics (2012). Explore. Features. National overview map. Retrieved January 28, 2013 from: http://www.followthemoney.org/database/nationalview.phtml.

Nestle, M. (2007). *Food Politics: How the Food Industry Influences Nutrition and Health* (2nd Ed.). Berkeley, CA: University of California Press.

Nguyen, H., & Reuter, P. (2012). How risky is marijuana possession? considering the role of age, race, and gender. *Crime and Delinquency, 58*(6), 879.

Nice, J. (2012). Whither the canaries: On the exclusion of poor people from equal constitutional protection. *Drake Law Review, Summer*, 1023–1067.

Nigg, J., Knottnerus, G., Martel, M., Nikolas, M., Cavanagh, K., Karmaus, W., & Rappley, M. (2008). Low blood lead levels associated with clinically diagnosed Attention-Deficit/Hyperactivity Disorder and mediated by weak cognitive control. *Biological Psychiatry*, 325–331.

Nigg, J., Nikolas, M., Knotterus, G., Cavanagh, K., & Friderich, K. (2010). Confirmation and extension of association of blood lead with attention-deficit/hyperactivity disorder (ADHD) and ADHD symptom domains at population-typical exposure levels. *Journal of Child Psychology and Psychiatry, 51*(1), 58–65.

Obama, B. (2007). *Dreams From My Father: A Story of Race and Inheritance*. New York, NY: Crown.

Omi, M., & Winant, H. (1994). *Racial Formation in the United States: From the 1960s to the 1990s*. New York: Routledge.

Packer, S. (1968). *The Limits of the Criminal Sanction*. Stanford, CA: Stanford University Press.

Parker, K., & Maggard, S.(2005). Structural theories and race-specific drug arrests: What structural factors account for the rise in race-specific drug arrests over time? *Crime and Delinquency, 51*(4), 521–547.

Pavlo, W. (2012). Former Massey Energy security chief sentenced to 36 months in prison. *Forbes*, February 29. Retrieved May 15, 2013 from: http://www.forbes.com/sites/walterpavlo/2012/02/29/former-massey-energy-security-chief-sentenced-to-36-months-in-prison/.

Perry, B., & Sutton, M. (2006). Seeing red over black and white: Popular and media representations of inter-racial relationships as precursors to racial violence. *Canadian Journal of Criminology & Criminal Justice, 48*(6), 887–904.

Pew Research Center for the People and the Press (2005). Public sours on government and business. Retrieved April 23, 2009 from: http://people-press.org/report/261/public-sours-on-government-and-business.

Pew Research Center for the People and the Press (2002). News media's improved image proves short-lived. April 23, 2009 from: http://people-press.org/report/?pageid=629.

Piquero, N., Carmichael, S., & Piquero, A. (2008). Research note: Assessing the perceived seriousness of white-collar and street crimes. *Crime and Delinquency, 54*(2), 291.

Platt, A. (1994). Crime and justice in the Clinton era. *Social Justice, 21*(3), 1–2.

Potter, G., & Kappeler, V. (1998). *Constructing crime: Perspectives on making news and social problems*. Prospect Heights, IL: Waveland Press.

Public Broadcasting (2012). The rules that govern 501(c)(4)s. Retrieved March 13, 2013 from: http://www.pbs.org/wgbh/pages/frontline/government-elections-politics/big-sky-big-money/the-rules-that-govern-501c4s/.

Quinney, R. (2001). *The Social Reality of Crime*. Piscataway, NJ: Transaction.

Rawls, J. (2005). *A Theory of Justice*. Harvard, MA: Belknap Press.

Reiman, J., & Leighton, P. (2013). *The Rich Get Richer and the Poor Get Prison: Ideology, Class, and Criminal Justice.* Upper Saddle River, NJ: Prentice Hall.

Reiman, J., & Leighton, P. (2006). Getting tough on corporate crime? Enron and a year of corporate financial scandals. Retrieved April 30, 2013 from: http://paulsjusticepage.com/RichGetRicher/fraud.htm.

Reinarman, C., & Levine, H. (1997). *Crack in America: Demon Drugs and Social Justice.* Berkeley, CA: University of California Press.

Richardson, L., Kinisky, D., & Milyo, J. (2011). Public approval of state legislatures. Retrieved January 28, 2013 from: http://projects.iq.harvard.edu/files/cces/files/richardson_konisky_milyo-_legislative_approval_lsq_021111.pdf.

Robinson, M. (2013). *Crime Prevention: The Essentials.* San Diego, CA: Bridgepoint.

Robinson, M. (2007). Freedom in an era of terror: A critical analysis of the USA PATRIOT Act. *Justice Policy Journal 4*(1).

Robinson, M. (2006). Defective Products. *Encyclopedia of Corporate and White-Collar Crime.* Golson Books and Sage Publications.

Robinson, M., & Beaver, K. (2009). *Why Crime? An Interdisciplinary Approach to Explaining Criminal Behavior* (2nd Ed.). Durham, NC: Carolina Academic Press.

Robinson, M., & Murphy, D. (2009). *Greed is Good: Maximization and Elite Deviance in America.* Lanham, MA: Rowman & Littlefield.

Robinson, M., Scherlen, R. (2013). *Lies, Damned Lies, and Drug War Statistics: A Critical Analysis of Claims Made by the Office of National Drug Control Policy.* Albany, NY: SUNY Press.

Rosenmerkel, S. (2001). Wrongfulness and harmfulness as component of seriousness of white-collar offenses. *Journal of Contemporary Criminal Justice, 17*(4), 308–327.

Rosenthal, A. (2008). *Engines of Democracy: Politics and Policymaking in State Legislatures.* Washington, DC: CQ Press.

Rosoff, S., Pontell, H., & Tillman, R. (2002). *Profit Without Honor: White-Collar Crime and the Looting of America* (2nd Ed.). Upper Saddle River, NJ: Prentice Hall.

Russell-Brown, K. (2008). *The Color of Crime: Racial Hoaxes, White Fear, Black Protectionism, Police Harassment, and Other Macroaggressions.* New York, NY: NYU Press.

Russell-Brown, K. (2006). The myth of race and crime. In R. Bohm & J. Walker (Eds.), *Demystifying crime and criminal justice.* Los Angeles, CA: Roxbury, p. 29.

Samaha, J. (2013). *Criminal Law.* Belmont, CA: Wadsworth.

Sampson, R. & Laub, J. (2003). Life-course desisters? Trajectories of crime among delinquent boys followed to age 70. *Criminology, 41*(3), 555–592.

Sandel, M. (2010). *Justice: What's the Right Thing to Do?* New York, NY: Farrar, Straus and Giroux.

Schlosser, E. (2002). *Fast Food Nation: The Dark Side of the All-American Meal.* New York: Harper.

Schlosser, E. (2001). The chain never stops. *Mother Jones* (July/August). Retrieved January 31, 2008 from: http://www.motherjones.com/news/feature/2001/07/meatpacking.html.

Schwartz, M., & Watkins, S. (2004). *Power Failure: The Inside Story of the Collapse of Enron.* Strawberry Hills, Australia: Currency.

Shelden, R. (2007). *Controlling the Dangerous Classes: A History of Criminal Justice in America*. Boston, MA: Allyn and Bacon.

Shelley, T., Chiricos, T., & Gertz, M. (2011). What about the environment? assessing the perceived seriousness of environmental crime. *International Journal of Comparative and Applied Criminal Justice, 35*(4), 307–325.

Sides, J. (2013). White people believe the justice system is color blind. Black people really don't. *Washington Post, Wonkblog*, July 22. Retrieved July 29, 2013 from: http://www.washingtonpost.com/blogs/wonkblog/wp/2013/07/22/white-people-believe-the-justice-system-is-color-blind-black-people-really-dont/.

Simon, D. (2006). *Elite Deviance* (8th Ed.). Boston, MA: Allyn & Bacon.

Simon, J. (2007). *Governing Through Crime*. New York, NY: Oxford University Press.

Simon, M. (2006). *Appetite for Profit: How the Food Industry Undermines Our Health and How To Fight Back*. New York: Nation Books.

Smith, B., & Holmes, M. (2003). Community accountability, minority threat, and police brutality: An examination of civil rights criminal complaints. *Criminology, 41*(4), 1035–1063.

Sourcebook of Criminal Justice Statistics (2009). Table 2.0013. Attitudes toward approaches to lowering the crime rate in the United States. Retrieved March 31, 2009 from: http://www.albany.edu/sourcebook/pdf/t200132006.pdf.

SourceWatch (2013). Koch industries. Retrieved April 5, 2013 from: http://www.sourcewatch.org/index.php?title=Koch_Industries.

SourceWatch (2013). Massey Energy. Retrieved May 14, 2013 from: http://www.sourcewatch.org/index.php?title=Massey_Energy.

Squire, P., & Moncrief, G. (2009). *State Legislatures Today: Politics Under the Domes*. Upper Saddle River, NJ: Prentice Hall.

Stephens, J. (2013). Congress approval rating lower than cockroaches, Genghis Khan and Nickelback, poll finds. *Huffington Post*, January 9. Retrieved January 28, 2013 from: http://www.huffingtonpost.com/2013/01/08/congress-approval-rating-nickelback-cockroaches_n_2435601.html.

Stephey, M. (2013). Top 10 memorable debate moments. Dukakis' deadly response. *Time*. Retrieved February 12, 2013 from: http://www.time.com/time/specials/packages/article/0,28804,1844704_1844706_1844712,00.html.

Surette, R. (1992). *Media, crime, and criminal justice: Images and realities*. Pacific Grove: Brooks/Cole.

Sweeten, G., Piquero, A., & Steinberg, L. (2013). Age and the explanation of crime, revisited. *Journal of Youth and Adolescence, 42*(6), 921–38.

Taibbi, M. (2011). Why isn't Wall Street in jail? *Rolling Stone*, February 11. Retrieved July 30, 2013 from: http://www.rollingstone.com/politics/news/why-isnt-wall-street-in-jail-20110216.

Tillyer, R., Charles, F., & Robin, S. (2012). The discretion to search: A multilevel examination of driver demographics and officer characteristics. *Journal of Contemporary Criminal Justice, 28*(2), 184.

Tonry, M. (2012). *Punishing Race: A Continuing American Dilemma*. New York, NY: Oxford University Press.

Tonry, M. (2004). *Thinking About Crime: Sense and Sensibility in American Penal Culture.* New York, NY: Oxford University Press.

Ulmer, J., & Johnson, B. (2004). Sentencing in context: A multilevel analysis. *Criminology, 42*(1), 137–177.

Unnever, J., & Cullen, F. (2010). Racial-ethnic intolerance and support for capital punishment: A cross-national comparison. *Criminology, 48*(3), 831.

US Census (2013). Voting hot report. Retrieved January 28, 2013 from: http://smpbff1.dsd.census.gov/TheDataWeb_HotReport/servlet/HotReportEngineServlet?reportid=767b1387bea22b8d3e8486924a69adcd&emailname=essb@boc&filename=0328_nata.hrml.

US Department of Justice, Bureau of Justice Statistics (2012). Employment and Expenditure. Retrieved January 29, 2013 from: http://bjs.ojp.usdoj.gov/index.cfm?ty=tp&tid=5.

US Department of Justice, Bureau of Justice Statistics (2004). Felony Sentences in State Courts, 2002, Bulletin NCJ 206916. Washington, DC: US Department of Justice.

US Department of Labor (2012). Review of MSHA's Actions at the Upper Big Branch Mine-South Performance Coal Company Montcoal, Raleigh County, West Virginia. Executive Summary. Retrieved May 15, 2013 from: http://www.msha.gov/Fatals/2010/UBB/ExecutiveSummary.pdf.

Velez, N. (2013). NYPD releases stop-and-frisk data for first time. *New York Post*, February 5. Retrieved July 31, 2013 from: http://www.nypost.com/p/news/local/nypd_releases_stop_frisk_data_whf644ouNc8P7dP8u7NPcJ.

Vogel, B. L., & Meeker, J. W. (2001). Perceptions of crime seriousness in eight african-american communities: The influence of individual, environmental, and crime-based factors. *Justice Quarterly: JQ, 18*(2), 301–321.

Walker, S. (2011). *Sense and Nonsense About Crime, Drugs, and Communities.* Belmont, CA: Wadsworth.

Walker, S., Spohn, C., & DeLone, M. (2012). *The Color of Justice: Race, Ethnicity, and Crime in America.* Belmont, CA: Wadsworth.

Walsh, T. (2008). Policing disadvantage: Giving voice to those affected by the politics of law and order. *Alternative Law Journal, 33*(3), 160.

Warren, P. Y. (2010). Inequality by design: The connection between race, crime, victimization, and social policy. *Criminology & Public Policy, 9*(4), 715. Retrieved from http://0-search.proquest.com.wncln.wncln.org/docview/761419725?accountid=8337.

Weber, L. (2006). *Profits Before People? Ethical Standards And the Marketing of Prescription Drugs.* Bloomington, IN: Indiana University Press.

Weitzer, R. (2000). Racialized policing: Residents' perceptions in three neighborhoods. *Law & Society Review, 34*(1), 129–155.

Welsh, W., & Harris, P. (2012). *Criminal Justice Policy & Planning* (Fourth Ed.). Cincinnati, OH: Anderson.

Wilcox, P. (2005). Beauty and the beast: Gendered and raced discourse in the news. *Social & Legal Studies, 14*(4), 515–532.

Williams, J. (2008). The lessons of 'Enron': Media accounts, corporate crimes, and financial markets. *Theoretical Criminology, 12*(4), 471.

Withrow, B. (2010). *The Racial Profiling Controversy.* Flishing, NY: Looseleaf Law.

Wright, L. (2007). *The Looming Tower: Al-Qaeda and the Road to 9/11.* New York, NY: Vintage.

Wright, P., & Herivel, T. (2003). *Prison Nation: The Warehousing of America's Poor.* New York, NY: Routledge.

Wu, Y., Sun, I., & Triplett, A. (2009). Race, class or neighborhood context: Which matters more in measuring satisfaction with police? *Justice Quarterly, 26*(1), 125.

Zarrella, J. (2002). Wuornos' last words: "I'll be back." *CNN*, October 9. Retrieved February 25, 2013 from: http://articles.cnn.com/2002-10-09/justice/wuornos.execution_1_serial-killer-aileen-wuornos-wuornos-shot-richard-mallory?_s=PM:LAW.

Index

Note: *f* indicates figure; *n*, footnote; and *t*, table.